Race

Race

A Philosophical Introduction

Second edition

Paul C. Taylor

polity

Copyright © Paul C. Taylor 2013

The right of Paul C. Taylor to be identified as Author of this Work has been asserted in accordance with the UK Copyright, Designs and Patents Act 1988.

First published in 2013 by Polity Press

First edition published in 2003 by Polity Press

Polity Press
65 Bridge Street
Cambridge CB2 1UR, UK

Polity Press
350 Main Street
Malden, MA 02148, USA

ISBN-13: 978-0-7456-4965-8 (hardback)
ISBN-13: 978-0-7456-4966-5 (paperback)

A catalogue record for this book is available from the British Library.

Typeset in 10/11.5pt Utopia by Toppan Best-set Premedia Limited
Printed in Great Britain by
Clays Ltd, St Ives plc

The publisher has used its best endeavours to ensure that the URLs for external websites referred to in this book are correct and active at the time of going to press. However, the publisher has no responsibility for the websites and can make no guarantee that a site will remain live or that the content is or will remain appropriate.

Every effort has been made to trace all copyright holders, but if any have been inadvertently overlooked the publisher will be pleased to include any necessary credits in any subsequent reprint or edition.

For further information on Polity, visit our website: www.politybooks.com

Contents

Preface to the Second Edition

The world has changed a great deal since Polity generously consented to publish the first edition of this book in 2003. Barack Obama burst upon the world stage, ascended to the presidency of the United States, and established his African American wife and children as the nation's "first family"; the US economy nearly imploded and almost took the rest of the world with it; autocratic regimes in what we usually call "the Middle East" faced massive protest movements and in some cases fell to them; the US continued its "wars" on terror and on drugs; and a frightening series of natural disasters caused unimaginable losses and heartache around the world, from the Mississippi Delta region and the Caribbean to Australia and the coast of Japan.

These are of course not the only events worth noting from the last eight years. But one could plausibly claim that they count as among the most significant. And each has a racial dimension. The rise of the Obamas is racially significant in perfectly obvious ways that I'll say more about later on. The same is true, I hope, for the wars on terror and drugs, which depend heavily on racialized assumptions about Muslims, blacks, and Latinos and Latinas. The racial overtones of the other events may not be immediately obvious, but it shouldn't take much to make them clear.

The so-called "Arab Spring" took observers in places like the US by surprise, in part because of a racialized image of Arabs as inherently anti-democratic. Arabs are terrorists, after all, not non-violent protesters. The Great Recession still manages to evade a proper accounting in part because of political figures in the US who should and likely do know better, but who continue to blame "minority" homeowners who couldn't pay their mortgages.[1] This account derives what little plausibility it has in part from old racist myths about lazy Negroes, the most recent prior incarnation of which was the welfare mother.

The early depictions of Hurricane Katrina's aftermath read like a collaborative project of Thomas Hobbes and Joseph Conrad: the disaster, we heard, had broken the tenuous grip on civilization long unevenly maintained by places like New Orleans, and unleashed a wave of savage black barbarism – except that it hadn't, and the stories of baby rapes in the Superdome and the assumptions of criminality that led to lethal police vigilantism turned out to be uniformly false.

And, finally: the varying capacities of places like Japan, Indonesia, and Haiti to guard against and respond to natural disasters is a function of their relationship to the processes of development, which is built on profoundly racialized assumptions about the pace, markers, requirements, and human agents of civilization. Which is to say: There are reasons that Haiti didn't have uniform building codes while Japan had lavish safeguards against tsunamis, and some of those reasons have to do with choices that the mid-century US made about how it would help those nations structure their relationships to the global economy – choices that we made, I should add, while firmly in the grip of racist ideas about how far along the path to civilization the yellow and black races were, and how much they could be expected to advance.

I've used these events to introduce the second edition of *Race* in order to specify part of the burden that the book carries. I've prepared this new edition with the aim of trying to keep up with a world that, through all its transformations, is never *just* about race but is often *still* about race. This of course does not mean speaking directly to each and every important new development. That would require a much larger book of a very different kind (much of which would be devoted to explaining just what counts as important, and why). What it does mean is that the book's framework for thinking about race philosophically should help readers grapple productively with the world after Barack Obama, the "Arab Spring," and the rest. So I've tried to tweak and extend the framework a bit in order to suggest just how it does this work.

Just as the world as a whole has changed since 2003, the worlds of Anglophone philosophy and critical race theory have also undergone significant changes. Others are more qualified to speak to the respects in which these fields have developed along distinct pathways. I'm most qualified, and concerned, to discuss what has happened at their points of intersection.

There have been two crucial developments in the family of specifically philosophical approaches to critical race theory, what some people have begun to refer to as "critical philosophy of race," over the last decade or so. First, the field is now much nearer to the mainstream of professional philosophy than it was just a few years ago. A couple of gestures may make the point. As of this writing, the president-in-waiting of the American Philosophical Association's eastern division – the most important division of the most important US professional organization – will be a Latina who is known to many people primarily as a philosopher of race and identity (Linda Martín Alcoff); and a recent past president is a man of African descent who rose to prominence largely on the strength of his work in race theory (K. Anthony Appiah).

Appiah's early work is worth special mention here because there is a sense in which it helped make race theory safe for professional philosophy. A sub-field that had been established on a fairly radical politics (for the time) and devoted largely to issues in ethics and social philosophy suddenly opened its doors to people with interests in the traditional "core" sub-fields of analytic philosophy – language, metaphysics, and philosophy of mind – and to people whose political commitments scarcely went beyond the generic anti-racism that now sets the boundaries of most polite conversation. This mainstreaming of philosophical race theory strikes some who work in the field as politically and philosophically dangerous. The thought seems to be that it will lead, or has led, to the philosophical equivalent of what journalist Nelson George calls "the death of rhythm and blues." R&B became disco, lost its soul and its privileged access to a distinctive market, and died; similarly, philosophical race theory might lose touch with the issues and methods that called it into being and disappear into the milquetoast methods and politics of the mainstream academy. Whatever one's view on this question, there is no disputing that some kind of shift, however one values it, has taken place.

One way to think of this shift from margin to mainstream is to focus on the second key development in philosophical race theory since 2003: the shifting terms of debate. One might without too much distortion break the recent history of philosophical race theory into three broad periods. After segregation seemed vanquished in the US – call this, for obvious reasons, the post-segregation era – the most prominent debates focused on issues like affirmative action and the politics of nationalism (integration vs separatism, and so on). After Reagan left office – call this the post-civil rights era, to signify the retreat of traditional civil rights issues from the center of public discourse – the debates focused on racial metaphysics and the meaning of racism. And now, since we became aware of the Obamas – call this, if you're like many people, the post-racial era, and agree to disagree with me about the reasonableness of doing so – we've turned our attention to such issues as the philosophical psychology of race-thinking (as revealed by cognitive psychology and experimental investigation), the prospects for post-racialism, and the persistence of racism.

This is not the place to say much more about these developments, though of course there is much more that one could say. My point right now is that just as the wider world has changed in ways that the first edition of *Race* didn't clearly countenance, so too has the world of philosophy changed. And as before, while I cannot speak directly to all of these changes or comprehensively to any of them, I can point the way toward a responsible engagement with them.

Preparing the way for this responsible engagement has meant making at least these three changes.

1. *Reconsidering the debates over racial metaphysics*, principally to credit the fact that what some people think of as a consensus has emerged. (We might do better to think of this not as a consensus but as a modus vivendi or an unstable détente; but more of this anon.)
2. *Updating the discussion of racism* to include recent work in experimental philosophy and, on the other side of the metaphilosophical aisle, recent re-readings of Foucault.
3. *Broadening the discussions of ethics and politics* to accommodate both the declining significance of affirmative action in public discourse and the increasing prominence of issues like global justice, the corrections industry, and immigration. This change was far-reaching enough to require the addition of an entirely new chapter, which now closes the book.

Just how and how well I've made these changes you'll be able to see from the text itself. People I respect tell me that the first version of this book has served them well, both in their classes and in their own work. I'm grateful to them for this vote of confidence, and for entrusting their students to the care of my little book in the first place. I hope that these revisions will keep the book serving a new generation of readers in the same way.

Preface to the First Edition

This book started taking shape in the immediate wake of the events of September 11, 2001. Just after the hijacked jetliners did their terrible work, US public discourse resounded with demands for justice, security, and, sometimes, retaliation. These demands led not just to a national discussion about appropriate responses, but also to a rash of vigilante attacks on, as an Associated Press reporter puts it, "people who look Middle Eastern and South Asian, whatever their religion or nation of origin . . .". This book is about the kind of thinking – what I'll call race-thinking – that picks out the targets for these backlash attacks.

I will claim soon enough that race-thinking does not always lead to such unfortunate outcomes, that it can be of some use to us in the struggle for justice. But if we are to use it effectively and appropriately, we'll need to understand what it is, how it works, and how we've come to think of it as we do. Otherwise we'll use it ineffectively, and inappropriately, and offensively. We'll continue to question and imprison people who look like the people we count as enemies. And we'll continue to ignore moral tragedies affecting people who don't look right, or who fail to dress, talk, live, or worship in the ways we're used to – even when the tragedy is our doing, and when it kills more than 3,000 people.

Seeking understanding in the way I have in mind is a peculiarly philosophical endeavor. I don't mean that only philosophers have done it or can do it; I mean that it is the sort of activity that has mostly defined Western philosophy at its best. Philosophers have long been keen on pointing out that we don't know as much as we think we do – even to the point of showing that we often don't know, really, what we're talking about when we use perfectly familiar ideas and expressions. Plato shows Socrates taking people to task over the definitions of "piety" and "justice," for example; and the classical US pragmatists famously insisted that we tend to misuse notions like "truth" and "experience." What can be more obvious than race? And what can be more puzzling, as soon as one presses on it even a little? Oddly, or perhaps not so oddly, philosophers have been relatively uninterested in race. Sociologists, anthropologists, and others have been thinking about it for quite some time, but only in the last few years have people like K. Anthony Appiah, Linda Martín Alcoff, and David Theo Goldberg taken up the peculiarly philosophical questions that arise from thinking about race-thinking.

Let's divide these philosophical questions into two broad categories. The first, which we can somewhat misleadingly identify as the domain of theory, has to do with metaphysics and epistemology. It includes questions like these: Do races and racial identities exist? If so, and especially if we take the evidence of modern genetics seriously, what can they be? What is the appropriate method for studying racial phenomena? Can these phenomena be analyzed in terms of some concept other than race, like nation, ethnicity, class, or gender? And how does racial identity relate to the self and to that self's perception of the world?

The second category of philosophical questions about race, which we can somewhat misleadingly identify as the domain of practice, has to do, broadly, with value, It includes questions like these: When is it morally permissible to distinguish between people on racial grounds, say, for the purposes of distributing some social good? If it is ever permissible, on what grounds can it be justified? How should racial identity relate to one's sense of self? And how should it shape one's perception of the world?

Race: A Philosophical Introduction will survey the most promising answers to these theoretical and practical questions, and gently recommend the answers that I find most persuasive. Part I, comprising the first three chapters, discusses the theoretical questions outlined above. The first chapter sets the stage by indicating the scope of the discussion and the method of approach. Here I'll explain what race-thinking means, and what a philosophical examination of race involves (including, for example, why it can start out with race-thinking and race-talk, when our concern, to paraphrase John Dewey, is not with words but with things), and to what extent the argument here will be both local, or geared to the United States in the early twenty-first century, and global, or relevant to the phenomenon of race-thinking wherever and whenever it occurs.

The second chapter considers three preliminary challenges to race-thinking. I call them "preliminary" because one must meet these challenges, or show that they can be met, before one can even raise many of the interesting philosophical questions. The challenges assert that engaging in race-talk leads to racism, that advances in the biological sciences clearly reveal the silliness of the race concept, and that other concepts – like class and caste – fully capture whatever aspects of the world the race concept usefully points us to.

Chapter 3 closes the first part of the book by surveying the main answers to the questions of racial metaphysics. Here are some of the questions I have in mind: Do races exist? What are they like if they do exist? And if they don't, what is race-talk for, or up to? Various philosophers and philosophically inclined students of racial phenomena have proposed or presupposed answers to these questions; unfortunately, most of their answers are partial or otherwise problematic. I'll try to help out by offering my own view, which I'll refer to as radical constructionism. (If you've done race theory before, think of this as a metaphysical rendering of racialization theory. If you've done philosophy before, think of it as what John Dewey might have said about race if he'd been black. If you've done neither, or for some other reason those references don't mean anything to you, that's okay. That's what the rest of the book is for.)

On the way to doing the work of these first three chapters I will have several occasions to talk about how things stand in the world, empirically, and how they've gotten that way. I do not propose to offer novel analyses of these empirical matters. I propose simply to recruit respectable analyses into what will hopefully be a useful philosophical essay. I will rely on empirical details in the manner of historicist social philosophers, rather than in the manner of historians or sociologists. That means that I will use fairly bland but hopefully informative statistics when I need them, which will not be often. It also means that the historical accounts that show up here, mainly in chapters 2 and 3, will of necessity be impressionistic, for reasons of space and expertise. There is a steadily growing complement of writers who are interested in the history of race, many of whom I'll consult in the pages to come. For my part, I'll do what philosophers have always done, from John Locke's account of the birth of political society to Cornel West's account of the evolution of modern racism. I'll provide highly idealized narratives that use historical events and trends to paint a larger picture.

The second part of the book begins with chapter 4, which segues between abstract musings and applied ethics by raising some issues that will have been postponed or sidestepped by that point. After completing chapter 2's discussion of whether race-talk leads to racism, we'll consider some of the people and populations that standard US race-talk forgets, and we'll examine some of the existential and phenomenological implications of racial identification.

The fifth chapter discusses some prominent examples of race-related social problems. I will focus on affirmative action, racial profiling, and the burdens of what I'll call conjugal choice, not because these are the most compelling or important problems, but because they are familiar and, more important, illuminating. The basic issue in this chapter has to do with the scope and meaning of the increasingly widespread norm of colorblindness, and each of these issues high-lights an important feature of that norm.

Discussions like the ones I hope to have here unfold much more clearly, I think, when they can rely on illustrative parables. In speaking of parables I have in mind not just the stripped-down clarifying devices that contemporary analytic philosophers call thought experi-ments, but also the more or less fleshed out narrative modes of exposi-tion that figures like Plato, Nietzsche, Sartre, and Du Bois used, in different ways, to such remarkable effect. I'm thinking also, as will soon become apparent, of the brilliant little "simple Stories" that Langston Hughes used to dramatize certain essentially political but irreducibly philosophical questions about African American life. I have no illusions about matching the standards that any of these out-standing writers set; but I still want to try to show the role that argu-ment and deliberation and ideas play in the lives of concrete people. So I'll begin each chapter with a bit of conversation between two African-American men: Jesse B. Semple, Jr, who goes by the name "JJ," and his friend Boyd.

Acknowledgments

A number of people and institutions have made this book possible, some of whom I will have to implore to forgive me for forgetting to mention them. I developed the perspective worked out in the first edition of this book while teaching social philosophy and race theory courses at Le Moyne College, the University of Kentucky, and the University of Washington in Seattle. Accordingly, I owe a great deal to students at all three schools, and especially to Jennifer Pettit, Noah Purcell, Jasmin Weaver, and Stephanie McNees. I am grateful for the research support that each school provided, especially the fellowship that I received to participate in the 1999–2000 Society of Scholars at Washington's Walter Chapin Simpson Center for the Humanities.

Many people have guided and pushed me in conversation, including Nikhil Singh, Alys Weinbaum, and the other participants in our University of Washington colloquia on "Black Identity in Theory and Practice"; the participants in the Social Theory Committee's "Whiteness" symposium at Kentucky; the Affrilachian Poets, especially Kelly Ellis; and various other individuals, including Michele Birnbaum, Susan Bordo, Howard McGary, Ron Mallon, Michael Root, Ann Ryan, Lewis Gordon, Ron Sundstrom, Anne Eaton, and Cornel West. Linda Martín Alcoff and Charles Mills gave helpful comments on the original manuscript, and equally helpful encouragement.

Two anonymous reviewers gave helpful suggestions on revisions for the second edition, as did Chike Jeffers and Robert Gooding-Williams. The editorial staff at Polity was more supportive and patient than I could have expected, and Jean van Altena's careful copy-editing helped me in many cases to say what I really meant, or should have meant.

I owe special debts to Ken Clatterbaugh and Don Howard, my ever-supportive department chairs at Washington and Kentucky; to my sister, Mona Phillips, who keeps reminding me what it means to take thinking seriously; to Eddie Glaude, who has heard and seen and encouraged these ideas more than anyone else; and to my wife, Wilna Julmiste, who has been more supportive than I deserve.

Part I
Theory

1

What Race-Thinking Is

Prologue

I've just started drinking my root beer when JJ rushes into the bar. He shuts the door on the blast of wintry air that rushed in with him, deposits his coat on the old wooden coatrack, and hurries over.

"Sorry I'm late," he says. He settles on the next barstool and waves to get the bartender's attention. He points at my glass and then at the place in front of him where a glass will soon be, then looks expectantly at me. "I have finally, for good and all, called it quits with Zarita."

"So that's today's topic," I say. "Zarita again. What'd she do this time?"

"Not 'this time.' The last time. You're not hearing me. We are, as of this time yesterday, no longer kicking it. Our thing is over, finito, kaput. Do you want to know why?"

"Is that a serious question?"

"You're right. I'm gonna tell you anyway, no matter what you say. So listen. She was over at my place last night, parasiting off my wireless because she's too cheap to get her own and too lazy to go to Starbucks and parasite offa them. So she's watching mad videos on her ePhone, and –"

"I think you mean iPhone."

"No, I mean ePhone. Didn't I say the girl was cheap? You should see that thing. Looks like a tricorder from the old *Star Trek* show. Anyway, as I was saying: Soon she gets tired of her little screen and she's on my computer, surfing through Hoodoo –"

"Hulu."

"– and Netplex –"

"Net*flix*."

"– and eventually she comes and asks me to look at something with her."

"You weren't already watching?"

"Naw, bruh. I was transferring my old cassette tapes to mp3. I don't cotton to the web and email and all that. I just have the internet 'cuz Isabel had it and I never took it out when she left. And, of course, because Zarita always wants to use it. So she says 'come look' and I

go and see that she's pulled up a trailer for *Black Power Mixtape.*
You seen that movie?"

"Is that the one with all the old footage of the black power movement? With the Panthers and SNCC and so on?"

"If you are asking, then the answer to my question is no, you
haven't seen it. But at least you know what it is, which is more than
I can say for Zarita."

"Surely that's not why you broke up with her?"

JJ drained his glass, thoughtfully crunched a couple of ice cubes,
then motioned to the bartender for a refill. "There's more. Not only
does she not know what the movie is, she doesn't know what black
power is. So I try to tell her. I say, 'You know, black *power*, like after
Martin King and all them had done their best and things still weren't
right, some young brothers and sisters stepped up –'"

"Well, that's not quite right, historically," I say.

"Look man, you're talking calculus and I'm trying to teach this
woman to add. So I'm telling her about Stokely Carmichael and Fred
Hampton and I mention the NAACP and Zarita goes 'What's that?'
Meaning the NAACP. I say, 'The most important civil rights organiza-
tion in the USA.' She goes, 'Oh, *them.* I didn't hear you the first time.'
Then she says, 'What's that got to do with black power?'"

"I've about had it by now. I mean, I'm straight up seeing red. So I
say, 'Oh, I don't know: *black* power, *colored* people, race relations,
Negroes?' And she just looks at me, all puzzled-like, like she just
beamed down from Mars or just got off a boat from China, like in
one of those fairy stories we used to do in philosophy class.
Remember?"

"Thought experiments. Not fairy stories."

"Whatever. So since she's just looking at me, I make ready to go
back to my beloved cassettes. Just as I turn to leave she says, '*What
kind of relations?'*"

"Hm. She misheard you again?"

"That's what I'm thinking. So I say it again: '*Race* relations,' and I
lay into the 'race' so she'll know not to ask me anything else. But sure
enough, she won't be denied. She goes, 'Race . . . *race* . . . like, a foot
race?' I think she's messing with me so I ignore her and go on back
to Donnie Hathaway and Aretha and The Peculiar Fellow Once Again
Known As Prince. Sure enough, she follows me and keeps on. 'Say, JJ.
Say, JJ,' over and over, you know how she does. 'Say. What do you
mean, race?'"

JJ pauses to make sure that I'm as puzzled as he thinks I should be.
I roll my eyes and shake my head so that he can continue. "Now tell
me," he says. "How could a grown woman in the United States of
America not know what race means?"

"So that's why you broke it off with her?"

"Oh, no. I just just got tired of her always hogging my dang computer. Oh, em, gee."

1.1 The language of race

Let's stipulate what JJ leaves implicit: Zarita isn't pretending ignorance to make a point, a point concerning, as it might be, the essential unity of humankind. And she is a perfectly competent speaker of the English language (apart, I suppose, from this difficulty). It appears that she just doesn't know what the word "race" means.

Is this easy to imagine? Is it easy to imagine that someone could reach adulthood in the twenty-first-century United States without learning how to speak the language of race? I speak of "the language of race," of what I'll call race-talk or race-thinking, in part as a reminder that the complex of meanings that surrounds the concept of race is systematic, like a language. But I'll talk about race-talk also to show that this system resembles a language in other, more specific ways, ways that make it hard to imagine that someone like Zarita could fail to know a great deal about it.

Languages are, first of all, ambient phenomena: they are all around us. Language is the medium of human culture and cognition, and language use is the (beginning, or fruit, of the) distinctive capacity that, along with opposable thumbs, enables us to distinguish ourselves from the other animals. We think in language, we flirt and pray and plead in language; one might say that we live in our languages, and, fittingly, we usually learn our first ones almost in passing, as we grow up.

In a similar way, race-talk is all around us. It has been one of the principal media of modern Western society and culture, insinuating itself into our ideas of citizenship, family, education, crime, poverty, entertainment, and sex, and much more besides. It is both the condition and the consequence of the distinctive ways in which ideas like these get worked out on the soil of the United States. Could Zarita know anything about any of these things and not know something about race?

Languages are an ambient feature of our social environments in part because they are also interpretive devices: they shape our experiences of the world. To think is more or less to use concepts to categorize and make sense of the objects and events that populate the world. Languages facilitate this process by serving as reservoirs of concepts, and the contents of the reservoir directly influence the way we experience the world. Think of how often we describe foreign customs or unfamiliar objects – which is to say, customs or things we don't have our own names for – by self-consciously imprecise analogies: that item of clothing is like a skirt, only men wear it; that animal is like a deer, only it never sheds its horns; that rite of passage is like going to the prom, except that it explicitly involves, and ritualizes, with full social sanction, a great deal of what we'd call foreplay – and there's no dancing (not that anyone misses it). We survey the world through the lenses provided by our languages, and we tend to try as much as we can to reduce the unfamiliar – kilts, antelopes, rites of passage – to the familiar – skirts, deer, proms.

Race-talk is also interpretive, notoriously so. The most obvious and egregious evidence of this is the phenomenon of racial stereotyping, of relying on overly rigid generalizations about the behaviour of racially defined groups. This phenomenon has pushed its way to the forefront of recent public discussion in the form of debates about racial profiling, but it's become a part of our public sensibilities over the last forty years or so. If Zarita knows that nowadays we send people for diversity training, that we publicly proclaim the moral error of (what we all too often refer to just as) discrimination, and that we aren't sure how to handle hate speech, which reduces the complexity and uniqueness of human individuals to the simple interpretive frameworks provided by demeaning labels, then she almost has to know something about race.

In addition to shaping our experiences, languages are shaped by our experiences: they are not just interpretive but also expressive devices. Peoples who live in arctic regions may have more and more varied experiences with frozen precipitation than other peoples, and, as a result, their languages may have what strikes me as an unusually discriminating and varied vocabulary for describing all the stuff that I'd call snow. If I'd been born and raised in a community that has lived since time immemorial at the equator, at sea level, I might have no frozen precipitation words at all (in which case I'm left with it's like rain, but . . . and so on). My language is an expression of the conditions under which it's taken shape, and, in this sort of case, of the conditions under which I've taken shape too.

Like language, race-talk is also expressive – again, notoriously so. It is the expression of, for example, the conditions under which certain inhabitants of what became the United States were considered subhuman, and hence fit to be treated as property, while others were considered an archaic model of humanity (if not simply sub-human), and hence fit to be uprooted and pushed aside by the advance of civilization. It is an expression of the conditions under which newcomers to the nineteenth-century United States pressed their applications for citizenship by asserting their whiteness – the conditions under which a character in a 1940s Hollywood film could try to shrug off her mother's interest in her affairs by declaring *I'm free, white, and twenty-one* (*Mildred Pierce*, directed by Michael Curtiz). If Zarita knows anything about US history and culture, she almost certainly knows something about race.

Languages are also intuitive, or practical: using them involves knowing *how* more than knowing *that*. Most of us can use our native tongues quite competently, exploiting an intuitive grasp of rules and definitions to compose completely original yet intelligible sentences with impressive regularity, even at an early age. But few of us, especially at an early age, can clearly articulate the rules and definitions that we find in our grammar textbooks. Similarly, most people know what we mean when we talk about race, or what we take ourselves to mean, even if, like most of us, they're not quite sure why we talk that way, and even if they don't think we should talk that way. This common knowledge is overwhelmingly practical rather than theoretical: we know how to categorize people and, often enough, to react to them, or how race-thinking says we should react to them; but our grasp of the principles and definitions behind these practices, such as they are, is unclear at best. Even if Zarita doesn't quite know how to locate Sikhs on the US scheme of racial types, even if she isn't sure whether Jewish people or Lapps still count as distinct races, could she really not know what social phenomenon "race" refers to?

If Zarita's problem were just a lack of clarity concerning the grammar of race-talk, or the principles that govern what I'll call "the practices of racial identification," one could hardly blame her for that. For one thing, the practices are notoriously inconsistent. Different societies, separated by time, space, or both, may assign the same person to different races, if they assign racial identities at all. Also, history reveals that the principles variously appealed to in support of the practices tend to be either at variance with the facts, immoral, or both. The world just doesn't seem to work the way race-thinking requires it to, and those who try to make it work that way tend to behave badly, to say the least. And finally, the last two centuries or so have seen the development and refinement of a number of ideas about politically significant human groups, and these ideas often overlap or compete for attention. I'm thinking here of such notions as ethnicity, nationality, gender, caste, class, and sexual orientation, the notions that, along with race and other concepts, define what I'll call "social identities." We have become quite sophisticated in our understanding of social identities, largely because current social conditions demand greater sophistication. Still, we use these terms more sloppily than we have to, and this sloppiness often leaves it unclear what else we mean when we talk about race, and whether there is anything else to mean – whether talk of, say, ethnicity, is quite enough.

To talk about race, then, is usually to talk about events, conditions, and experiences that are familiar and ubiquitous. But it is also to talk about these things in somewhat muddled ways. This conceptual muddle is itself almost an invitation to philosophy, an invitation that one might be forgiven for accepting simply out of habit. But there is at least one other reason to approach this subject from the standpoint of philosophy: race-thinking has left an indelible mark on the contemporary world. Along with many other forces, of course, it has shaped and continues to shape the most private of personal interactions as well as the grandest of geopolitical policy choices. If anything remains of the Western philosophical tradition that takes the question of how to live as its subject, then this is certainly an invitation to philosophy.

1.2 What we mean by "race": what do you mean, "we"?

There's more to say about what it means to approach race philosophically. You should know, for example, how I propose to answer the question, "Philosophy as opposed to what?" But showing is usually better than saying, and this particular philosophical showing can't begin until I settle a couple of preliminary issues. First I have to explain how, why, and to what extent the discussion to come will be limited to a specific context. Then I have to explain why there's still something in this topic for a philosopher to write a book about, now that racism has fallen into public disrepute while race-thinking has virtually disappeared from the biological sciences.

So first, about context: In what follows, I'll frequently make reference to "what we mean" and to "our ideas" (or "our practices" or "our concepts" and so on). This is a way of making clear the deeply contextual nature of what I've called the practices of racial identification. People have become fond of noting that the practices of racial identification proceed differently in different times and places. Philosopher Michael Root has eloquently made the point by saying that race does not travel.[1] If this is right, if children in the USA who share both parents are thought to belong to the same race, while in Panama this need not be the case; if a person might be white in São Paulo but black in San Francisco, then it's inappropriate for a discussion of such matters to be too abstract, to pretend, as discussions like this did for centuries, that "race" points to the same thing everywhere and for everyone. And if one's perspective always reflects at least the influence of one's social environment, with the cultural resources that environment makes available for appropriation and revision, then it's inappropriate for me to proceed as if my thoughts on human difference come from nowhere, or from nowhere in particular.

So I'll say "we" as a reminder of what I'll now declare explicitly: I'm writing from the United States, from the perspective of what we often call an American but what I'll sometimes call an *estadounidense*.

(Because isn't Canada in the Americas? Isn't Bolivia?) And to say that is to say that I'm writing from and for a place fundamentally shaped by certain originally and distinctively English ideas of human diversity. ("English" rather than "British" because in certain ways the ideas that I'm thinking of, ideas of innate savagery and inferiority, got their start in English assaults, literal and symbolic, on the Welsh, Irish, and Scots. But there's no room for that story here.)[2] I'll focus in what follows on this Anglo-American model of race-thinking, not because it is the only or the most important one, but because it is one of the more important ones, because it's the one with which I'm most familiar, and because I can use it to make broader points about race-thinking in general.

In the same spirit of self-excavation, I have to say that in certain ways I will rely heavily on the sense of race that I've developed as a black *estadounidense* – or, as I will still say, in deference both to established practices and to the demands of expository convenience, as an African American. My version of "the black experience," and my ideas about how to access and use it, will shape my choices regarding how to populate the fiction world that my little framing narratives disclose, and regarding the historical examples that I'll sometimes use. But this book is specifically not another book that purports to be about race while really being about black folks and white folks. At least, I hope it isn't that sort of book. My aim is to tell a story about race by focusing on Anglo-American practices of racial identification, which I've come to see and understand, and which I'll sometimes describe, from a black perspective.

A declared focus on Anglo-American race-thinking might seem likely to frustrate, or at least to be in tension with, the aspiration toward a more general exploration of the subject of race. But the tension disappears when we introduce a distinction between race and races. Race doesn't travel in the sense that the same person might belong to different racial groups in different places and times, or in the sense that different cultures determine race membership in different ways. The terms in a racial vocabulary – "black" and "white" and so on – pick out people here that they wouldn't pick out there, which is to say that the races, with their specific constituents and conditions of entry, don't travel. But if a culture distinguishes and categorizes people using methods that appeal in part to such things as the way people look, then we might say of that culture that it has a concept of race. And exploring our uses of this concept might tell us something about what it means to think racially, whatever the categories and membership criteria happen to be. In this sense, race, as a principle of social differentiation, does travel.

If I'm right, focusing on the Anglo-American model of race-thinking doesn't have to get in the way of telling a more global story about race. Unfortunately, the narrower focus may have its own internal difficulties. I've already said that we use race-talk in unclear and inconsistent ways, so how do I propose to reduce that semantic diversity to a single model?

Semantic variety may be a problem less of race-talk than of talking, or of meaning things, period. The elements of language are tools, and like any other tools, they can play roles beyond the ones for which they were created. I know people who use irons not just to remove wrinkles from their clothes but also to make grilled cheese sandwiches, and we all know people – of a different generation, or from a different neighborhood or city – who use the same words we do but in strikingly different ways. (Try this out: go to a part of the USA you don't know well, and ask for a pop. Then wait to see if the person you're talking to hits you or gives you a soda.) The divergent evolution of linguistic tools is what brings slang into being, and it's the reason that a comprehensive sociological report of language habits is bound to turn up an array of uses for any particular word or phrase. Still, there will be core uses, uses encouraged by the long period of socialization during which we train people, both formally and informally, how and when to use their words, uses recorded, given the right social conditions, in dictionaries.

As it happens, perhaps the most obvious candidate for a core meaning of "race" is one that seems to defeat the purpose of this book. Some people would say that the meaning of "race" is fully specified in the official doctrine of, say, the Ku Klux Klan, or the Nazi Party, or, for that matter, in the original theology of the Nation of Islam. This might mean that all the interesting questions about race are scientific ones, concerning, for example, whether our best information about human physiology makes it plausible to think of the human race as naturally divided into the Klan's (and Nazis', and Nation's) small set of distinct, opposed, and hierarchically ranked natural groups. And since these questions seem to have been answered to the detriment of the Klansman, it's not clear that there's anything left to say about the philosophy of race – as opposed, say, to the philosophy of racism. I agree that the best testimony of the natural sciences refutes the kind of race-thinking one finds amongst Klansmen. The pages to follow will present some of the details of this scientific challenge (chapter 2) and survey various ways of responding to it (chapter 3), though anyone interested in sustained argument on the point should consult a physical anthropologist.

Many people take the success of the scientific challenge as sufficient reason to pronounce on the futility of all race-thinking, period. Sometimes these people express their quite reasonable doubts about the race concept's usefulness or applicability to human populations by surrounding the word "race" with quotation marks, what we sometimes call scare quotes. This blanket skepticism about race-thinking, some versions of which I'll soon call racial eliminativism (on account of its adherents' determination to eliminate the practices of racial identification), may turn out to be the right position to adopt. But even if it were, assuming this view from the beginning of the discussion would be inappropriate (not least because we're not all members of the Klan – but I'm getting ahead of myself).

The philosophy of race, as I understand it, involves studying the consequences of race-talk, the practices of racial identification for which race-talk provides the resources. And one of the scruples of philosophy as I understand it requires taking it seriously when people persist in using some idea or term – where "taking it seriously" means working to see how it might be useful to set the thing referred to apart from other things in just that way. I'll elevate this scruple to the level of a Law, and name it after the philosopher J. L. Austin, who puts the point this way: "If a distinction works well for practical purposes in ordinary life (no mean feat, for even ordinary life is full of hard cases), then there is sure to be something in it, it will not mark nothing."[3] Many people have committed themselves to the validity or utility or accuracy of race-talk, thereby becoming what I'll call *racialists*, while explicitly refusing to draw evaluative distinctions between members of different races. To say this is to say that there are many racialists who seem not to be Klan-style – or, as I'll say, classical – racialists or racists; and to say that is to start toward a distinction that, according to Austin's Law, a philosophy of race ought not to take as marking nothing.

As I say, the eliminativist may be right to identify all racialism with classical racialism. As Austin goes on to say, "ordinary language is not the last word: in principle it can everywhere be supplemented and superseded." But we'll need to work up to the arguments in support of this move. To assume the conclusions of these arguments from the outset would mean setting aside without motivation a distinction that many of us observe in our ordinary uses of race-talk. To quote Austin for the last time, from just after he concedes that ordinary language is not the last word: "Only remember, it [ordinary language] *is* the first word."

Of course, I'm not worried just about philosophical scruples. There are practical difficulties as well. My sense is that focusing from the outset on the dialect of race-talk spoken by Klansmen and others of that ilk will simply get in the way of understanding the workings of other dialects, for example, those spoken by advocates for specifically racial equality and diversity. Maybe an analogy will help: insisting on English as it's spoken in the USA may leave me, during my trips to London, unable to find a mass transit station or an alternative to the staircase (*I don't want a tube*, I say: *I want the subway*; and *No, I don't*

need a lift, just point me to the elevator). Similarly, focusing on a dialect
of race-talk that, as we'll see, was refined in the nineteenth century
and superseded shortly thereafter, may get in the way of studying the
diversity of contemporary practices that race-thinking underwrites
and motivates. In light of these considerations, and as you may have
noticed, I will use so-called "scare quotes" sparingly, mainly to indicate when I'm talking about the word, term, or concept, "race," rather
than about what the term denotes.

1.2.1 *"Race" and race, words and things*

Of course, to this point I've said little about anything apart from
words, terms, and concepts. You may be wondering: what happened
to the *things* we call races? When do we talk about them?

As I've said, in order to do the work of this book, which does, trust
me, involve examining the entities we call races, I'll need to find the
lowest common denominator for the various dialects of race-talk. I'll
need to find the conceptual role that "race" plays at various sites,
including at the opposed sites from which we receive the specific
dogmas of Klan-style racism and the critical reactions of anti-racist
racialists. Once we identify the core meanings that link these two
extremes, so that we can see the disagreement between them as a
disagreement about the same subject, we should be in a better position
to evaluate race-thinking as an instrument for organizing people and
thoughts about people.

All of this is to say: we can't talk about races until we get clear on
what it means to use the word. Once we do that, then we can ask
whether the things called races actually exist, and whether we'd be
better off not talking about them even if they do exist, and so on. But
we have to know what races are, what "race" means, what the core
instances of our talk about races commits us to, before we can take up
these questions.

The analogy between race and language with which this chapter
began points us toward another reason to focus on race-talk instead
of on the things that the talk points us to. Over the last couple of
centuries, philosophers, social theorists, and students of human cognition have done quite a good job of revealing the centrality of language,
or of linguistically structured systems of meaning called "discourses,"
to all of human activity. Culture is like a language, or discursive, and
participating in a culture turns most of what we do into a text, await-
ing its readers. When we dress a certain way – say, inappropriately
– that tells people something about us, or leads them to think that they
know something about us. The same holds true for when we eat
certain foods, or use certain gestures, or celebrate certain holidays. All
of these activities come from and shape the systems of meaning that

we call culture. And the way these activities become signs, creating opportunities for others to read us, to interpret our behaviour (or appearance, or whatever) and find significance in it, to make claims that aspire to truth (as opposed to expressing tastes), comes from the discursive character of culture.

Race-thinking has been an essential part of human culture, at least since the 1600s. And it has shifted along with those cultures. Different cultures, in different places and times, have different conceptions of race, which is to say that each may have its own complement of racial groups. Many people take this to show that races are socially constructed, that we create racial categories and sort ourselves into them the way we create clothing styles and fit ourselves into them. On this view race becomes an element in a discourse, a discourse, as it happens, of human social difference and biological variation. Social constructionism arose as a reaction to the view that races are natural kinds, that, like rocks and quasars, races are naturally occurring elements of a universe that is, in its arrangement and constitution, is utterly indifferent to our systems of meaning. Let's call this "racial naturalism."

I'll focus for a time on race-talk, but not to endorse the social constructionist view. I can't endorse it yet, since we haven't yet considered the scientific case against naturalism, and since, as I said a bit earlier, we aren't in a position to evaluate the arguments. But even if races are naturally occurring entities like rocks, even if nature sorts us into physically and culturally distinctive groups that we then try to reflect more or less accurately in our theories of human difference, our ideas about race have lived a life of their own. Racial discourse – whatever the underlying reality, biological or otherwise, that it may or may not represent – has shifted over time, woven itself into the politics and culture of societies the world over, and inspired all sorts of not-obviously natural practices and behaviours. So I'll focus on race-talk in much of what follows not necessarily to reject the naturalist approach, but to explore the relatively autonomous domain of racial discourse. In addition, I think we'll find that in living its own life, racial discourse has played a role in whatever the biology of race turns out to be. It can't be incidental to the racial composition of the United States, for example, that there were, for quite some time, laws against interracial marriage.

Before I start to work in earnest toward identifying the core instances of race-talk, there's a last word to say about *whose* talk I'm examining. It may seem, especially in the next section, that I'm telling you what *I* mean by race rather than what *we* mean by it: it may seem that I'm making it up as I go along. This is a professional hazard for philosophers, and hence another aspect, usually, of what it means to approach race as a philosopher.

I should say that this is an aspect of what it means to approach race as a philosopher of a particular kind – as someone working in the wake of figures like John Dewey and John Austin. Working in the traditions epitomized by those figures means taking terms in common usage and availing myself of their commonness. The philosopher working in this vein takes herself as a representative figure, empowered to think the thoughts that anyone with sufficient time and leisure might think, committed to using and refining the language that we all share. So in this spirit, what I say about what "race" means for "us" derives from my experience as one of us, as an observer of what we do, and as someone encouraged to tease out what we might call the logical structure of what we do.

I could, of course, approach all this very differently. I could in particular conduct surveys and polls, in the hope of producing empirical generalizations about what we think. Approaching race theory in that way might make me a social scientist of some sort: someone whose expertise comes in at the observation stage, or in working through that stage in a certain way, using certain tools (statistical analysis, experimental design, and so on). The expertise of the philosopher, such as it is, comes into play later, at the teasing-out stage, or perhaps earlier, in refining the language in which scientists pose their questions. This sort of work should be informed by the scientist's best hypotheses, but should consist principally in thinking through the implications of what we say.

Some philosophers have in recent years tried to use the tools of empirical inquiry – the polls and surveys and experiments mentioned above – precisely in order to think through the implications of what we say and mean. I am thinking here of what is now called "experimental philosophy," and of the way this work has been brought to bear on race theory by philosophers like Josh Glasgow and Edouard Machery.[4] The burden of this work is in part to improve upon the armchair reflection that defines so much of the philosophical tradition. Instead of debating about the ethical dimensions of human agency in a vacuum, experimental ethicists ask, in conversation with researchers in psychology and elsewhere, what conditions and considerations *in fact* lead us to behave in the ways that we think of as virtuous and vicious. (One of the findings: random strokes of good luck, like finding a dollar in the street, make people much more likely to act virtuously or beneficently. Taken to one logical conclusion, this might mean that several centuries of reflection on moral education has been misguided, and that the state of your soul at any particular moment, and the welfare of the people you might mistreat, depends to an uncomfortably high degree on how good a day you're having.) Similarly, experimentally inclined philosophers of race sometimes eschew the assumption of representativeness that I rely on above, and ask what people *in fact* mean when they use racial discourse.

There is considerable value in this experimental work. For one thing, it takes the real world seriously, thereby combatting another occupational hazard of philosophy. For another, it highlights the implications of our beliefs and commitments more clearly and directly than armchair reflection does. For example, if certain ways of thinking about race correlate more robustly with racial prejudice than others, this is something that people interested in fighting prejudice should know. And if the vast majority of people who use race-talk in fact understand themselves to be talking about pixies and goblins, this is something that theorists devoted to exploring "folk" concepts of race should know.

These virtues aside, though, experimental philosophy still leaves room for the sort of project I have in mind, and might require it. Like me, the experimental race theorist wants to know what we mean when we talk about race. Unlike me, he or she is willing to conduct the polls and surveys that will yield hard data in answer to this question. But just as with the social scientist, old-fashioned philosophical reflection will help in thinking through the limitations and the implications of these data. (I presume the thoughtful experimentalist will agree with this.) We still need to ask whether the survey questions import assumptions that need to be unpacked, and whether the experimental subject's assent means what it seems to. And it will be difficult to ask these questions responsibly without being informed by a body of critical reflections on the content, uses, history, and structure of racial discourse – without, in short, an old-fashioned philosophy of race.

Beyond these considerations of experimental design and interpretation, we need to ask specifically philosophical questions about the prospects for discursive innovation. Might a theoretical concept of race – a concept as distant from folk understandings as the physicist's account of light is from mine – do some useful work? Might an innovation in popular discourse be similarly useful, and in fact be on the horizon? These are not questions about whether people in fact assent to *P*, or whether their refusal to do so correlates with their assent to *R*. They are questions about whether assenting to some distinct but related proposition *Q* would be a worthwhile outcome if we could bring it into being, and whether some specific constellation of human practices is developing itself in ways that will incline people to think *Q* rather than *P* or *R*. If we answer these latter questions in the affirmative, we will have to work up the resources for finding, understanding, and deploying these new concepts. And we might have to unearth those resources from a painting or a play, rather than from a summary of survey responses. In short, and once again, we might have to do the work of old-fashioned philosophy.

This defense of (very) old-fashioned philosophy is in no way meant to provide a blanket defense of the stories I propose to tell in my capacity as a representative thinker. If my story about us – which is to say, about us by and large – fails to ring true, then take that as a provocation to compose a better story, one that does less violence to our intuitions about what we mean and do, or one that shows us how to reconstruct our practices until they serve us more effectively. I hasten to add that this provocation is also the work of philosophy.

1.2.2 What "race-thinking" means

So far we've gotten clearer, I hope, on the subject of this study, on the methods and limits of the discussion, some of them, and on why it's okay to talk about race-talk in advance of settling accounts with racial naturalism and with classical racialism. Now we can finally get down to the business of definition, which is after all what one expects from a philosophy book. What I've been calling "race-thinking" is a way of assigning generic meaning to human bodies and bloodlines. To make sense of that, and of how I mean for it to specify the conceptual role of "race," we'll need some more definitions.

By "bodies" I mean, well, bodies. To borrow, for now, an image from an old and problematic but familiar metaphysic, I mean the things our souls or minds travel around in, the things we try to alter with body-building or aesthetic surgery, the things we cover and call attention to with clothes and jewelry (and colored contact lenses, and hairstyles, and so on). I mean the human body as it figures into the world of, as philosophers sometimes say, medium-sized objects, which one can experience with the unaided human senses (without, say, a microscope).

Let's say a little more precisely that the body is the phenomenal aspect of human being: it is the way human being becomes known to the human senses. I put the point this generally because I mean to include here the sense of hearing, for reasons that may be obvious. We use language and speaking style as markers of racial identity, a fact that speaks to the close relationship between the physical and the cultural, and between the cultural and the ancestral. We'll say more about this later, in chapter 4, but for now let's take it as evidence for, or as a consequence of, two broader points. First, perception, the receipt of information through our senses, is always culturally mediated. Racial perceptions are no different, though they are more interesting and more significant than many others. And second, as feminist scholars and others have pointed out for over a hundred years, and as my references to bodybuilding and the like show, human bodies are always already bearers of meaning. They wait like paper to be inscribed with meaning (which isn't to say that they contribute nothing to the process; different kinds of paper, after all, have different properties). Race-thinking, even at the level of language, reflects an aspect of this broader fact of human association.

By "bloodlines" I mean ancestral lines, heritage, the causal antecedents of an organism that flow through the reproductive activities of other, sufficiently similar, organisms. I mean what used to be called the "stock," especially when it referred to some quality in a type of animals, or of humans, that breeders, or eugenicists, sought to cultivate by carefully monitoring reproduction. Ancestry is also already a repository of meaning, in a variety of ways. My family history tells me things: it provides me with information, for example, about my risks of developing certain diseases; and it can do this because the passage of traits from one generation to the next is a function of the flow of genetic information, of chemically encoded meanings. On a more distinctively human level, our family histories also tell us things, or so we often think, not just about how, or whether, or how long, our bodies will work but also about our identities, about who we are. That's why we go to the trouble of tracking down lost relatives and of plotting out family trees: family, the subset of the human population to which we are distinctly related, as we sometimes still say, by blood, is important to us. To think racially about ancestry is to assign meaning in a way that is loosely derived from analogies to breeding practices and to family relationships. In light of what we've learned from the biological sciences, this reliance on something like "blood" is the major weakness, or challenge, of racial thinking.

By "assigning meaning" I mean that we take the information, such as it is, provided to us by a human body and that body's ancestry as a license to draw inferences about more distant, often non-physical matters. I'll refer to the development, establishment, or application of this pattern of inference, and of the related assumption that certain bodies carry with them certain non-physical traits, as a process of racialization. It used to be conventional wisdom and accepted practice to say that people of certain races, which is to say people who have certain bodies or are descended from people with certain bodies, also have certain levels of intelligence, or that they are predisposed to like and produce certain kinds of music, or that they have a certain predilection to give themselves over to various passions, sexual and otherwise. Many people still say such things and many more still believe them, but we've mostly removed this kind of inference from overt public discourse. We've done so not just for reasons of what people insist on calling "political correctness," but because of the challenge I've already mentioned from the biological sciences. The transmission of traits across human generations just doesn't work the way this sort of thinking requires, for reasons and in ways we'll consider in the pages to come. Still, this running together of physiology, cognition, culture, and psychology isn't the only way to assign meaning. As we'll see later on, much thinner inferences are available. One might focus, for example, on the question of whether distinctions between racial groups correlate with, for example, income, or net worth, or access to credit, or proximity of domicile to industrial waste hazards.

One might draw an even thinner inference from bodily appearance and ancestry. One might conclude that people who look a certain way constitute a distinct type of human. This is in part what I had in mind in speaking of assigning generic meaning. If we look at John's face and decide that he looks smart, we probably haven't yet started thinking racially. If, on the other hand, we think he looks smart because his facial features mark him as a member of a type of smart people, then we're on the way to race-thinking. Race-thinking is about kinds, called races, and only derivatively about individuals, who thereby have racial identities.

1.3 Modern racialism: pre-history and background

We humans seem to have the habit – we'll soon consider how widespread a habit this is – of sorting ourselves into more or less distinct kinds based on a trio of factors: appearance, ancestry, and the deeper significance that is supposed to follow from the first two factors. Of course, we sort ourselves into lots of overlapping groups – neighborhoods, gangs, states, nations, families, unions, and fan clubs, to name only a few. And we do this while relying on many different principles of division. But specifically racial groups result from the particular method of sorting that begins, as I'll continue to say, with bodies and bloodlines.

To the extent that racial sorting involves comparing human bodies, it's worth noting that we can compare people with respect to a variety of traits. In principle, any of these – height, eye color, attached or detached earlobes, even – might provide the basis for drawing racial distinctions. But in practice, a particular regime of comparison has had a much wider impact on human social life around the world than any other. I'm thinking of course of the system that relies mainly on skin color, facial features, and hair texture to divide humankind into four or five color-coded groups – black, brown, red, white, yellow. Since this is the system that people in and in the wake of the modern West most often invoke when they think and talk about race, I'll call it "modern racialism." And I will refer to the groups that are the subject of this kind of race-thinking as "modern Races," or simply as "Races" with a capital "R." This typographic convention enables me to distinguish the specific and specifically located kind of race-thinking that we find in the modern West from just any process of assigning meaning to human bodies and bloodlines.

Distinguishing modern racialism from racialism per se immediately raises a couple of questions. First: what do words like "modern" and "Western" mean here? And second, it has become fashionable to claim, quite correctly, that modern Europe invented the concept of race. If that's the case, then how can I hold onto the distinction between racialism and modern racialism? Why aren't they the same thing?

About the first question, about what it means to talk about the modern West: I'm not using the word "modern" simply to connote novelty or recent origin. When it appears here, "modern" will be the adjective form of "modernity," which seems to name a period of history but actually names a cluster of intellectual and social conditions, all of which emerge in Europe during overlapping periods of history. We'll return to this in the next chapter, but for now let's just say that the modern condition involves capitalism, liberalism, and secularism; that Europe's path to modernity involved the establishment and spread of colonies, nation-states (as opposed, say, to feudal or ancient imperial states), scientific techniques, and the technological and economic fruits of applying these techniques; and that European modernization generated misleading narratives of cultural uniqueness, according to which only European nations, and not all of them, were enlightened enough to replace superstition with science. All of this is bound up in the idea of modernity, and much of it is bound up also in talk of "the West." In fact, this sort of talk usually refers less to a geographic location than to a kind of society; it is a way, usually, of talking about certain modern societies, typically the industrialized ones that had colonies – or, if they still have them, "possessions" – in the Americas, Asia, or Africa.

About the second question, concerning the difference between racialism and modern racialism: First, we might offer the conceptual or logical point that even if, as a matter of empirical, sociological fact, no one ever engaged in race-thinking outside of the parameters of the modern world, it is conceptually possible that they might. As I say above, we might in principle sort people by appeal to any number of traits. And in the sort of discussion we're trying to have here, it seems appropriate to start quite generally and abstractly and work back, in later chapters, toward the specific and concrete.

But a second, more substantive consideration encourages me to retain the distinction between racialism and modern racialism. As a simple empirical matter, it just seems to be the case that people outside the geographic borders and conceptual parameters of the modern West have assigned generic meanings to human appearance and ancestry. Race-thinking is a way of imagining the distinctness of human peoples, and societies everywhere and at all times have done that. It's just that after the seventeenth century or so, Europeans developed a vocabulary that highlights certain aspects of this process. And they didn't just develop this vocabulary. They refined it, exported it, tried to make it scientific, and built it into the foundation of world-shaping – world-historical, Marx would say – developments in political economy. But all of this was a variation on a deeper theme.

At this point, as a way of developing the idea that modern race-thinking is an instance of a broader phenomenon, I'd like to offer some general, historical remarks about race outside of the confines of modernity. But first I have to offer a couple of differently general remarks, first about how I'll make remarks like this, and then about the anthropological background to the development of race-thinking.

1.3.1 Philosophers on history

Whenever histories pop up in philosophical work, warnings are in order. Such popping up will occur with some regularity in the early bits of this book, so here are two warnings to the reader – *caveat lector* – to add to the one in the preface. First, I will quickly come to focus on what we misleadingly call "the West," and only a little less quickly, in the next chapter, on the English colonies in North America that became the United States. I adopt this increasingly narrow focus for reasons I keep repeating: the English, with some notable assistance from the Spanish, produced the distinctive form of race-thinking that laid the groundwork for contemporary US conceptions of race. And the USA is the context that I've chosen for this inquiry into a necessarily context-bound subject.

And second, I will make my way toward the idea that US racialism takes shape under conditions established by the European colonial project. I mention this because it is an idea that has to be developed, rhetorically and conceptually, with some care. The European colonial project was with great regularity and consistency imagined as a white supremacist project. The idea that white people, whoever they turned out to be, were superior to non-whites (and that some whites were superior to others) was crucial in establishing the social and political relations that shaped modern Race-thinking. So in what follows I'll sometimes refer to white supremacy in the manner recommended by philosopher Charles Mills, as a political system and system of thought on a par, conceptually, with other "isms," like liberalism and fascism.[5] In doing so I do not mean to suggest that all white people (again, whoever they turn out to be) are responsible for racism, that they were all of one mind on any subject, including that of race relations, or that white people are in some sense evil by nature. My aim is just to take a few steps toward explaining, among other things, how it is that we've come to think of races as we have. The ideas and the institutions of white supremacy have played a substantial role in that process.

1.3.2 *The anthropological background*

In all of its forms, race-thinking proceeds from the recognition of a basic truth about humankind. The human population has from time immemorial comprised smaller groups, each united, more or less, by a distinctive repertoire of cultural and physiological traits. As we'll soon see, the more problematic versions of race-thinking overestimate the distinctness and usually the size of these groups, and they misrepresent the likelihood that the traits that define these groups will occur together. But the core idea is right, and still appears in the accounts of physical anthropologists: the human population is made up of smaller groups, and the members of each group tend to be more like each other, physiologically and culturally, than they are like the members of other groups.

The members of these groups – call them peoples – become physiologically similar because peoples function as breeding populations: the members of each group mate with each other more often than they mate with representatives of other peoples. As a result, each group develops a more or less distinctive genetic repertoire. It is of course the case that humans are on the whole much more similar to each other than dissimilar. But there are some modestly systematic physiological differences, and some of these are readily perceptible. Some groups tend to be – *tend to be* – shorter than others, or more olive-skinned, or more heavy-set, or hairier. Notice that this is not yet an example of race-thinking: I haven't yet assigned any meaning to the physiological characteristics of these peoples. Nor is it an example of capital-R Race-thinking. On the basis of what I have said to this point, I have yet to distinguish the Twa people of the Congo, whom we still call "pygmies," and who average around five feet (152 cm) in height, from the Masai people of Kenya, who tend to be much taller.

For most of human history, geography did quite a good job of ensuring the distinctness of human breeding populations. Mountain ranges, oceans, rivers, deserts, and sheer distance divided humanity into its smaller groups. But when peoples overcame isolation to encounter each other – for example, under conditions of imperial domination or military alliance, or along trading routes – they found that they'd developed distinctive ways of life in their seclusion. In this way each people developed a distinctive culture, complete with narratives (often enough related in distinctive languages) about who they were and what made them distinct, about how people ought to behave and what they ought to believe. When geographical barriers weren't enough, these narratives of solidarity and identity often went a long way toward discouraging mating between groups.

1.3.3 The ancients

Ancient peoples realized that there are different kinds of humans, and that each kind is (somewhat) physiologically and culturally distinctive. They usually stated this realization in profoundly ethnocentric terms. The ancient Greeks, for example, are well known both for distinguishing themselves from the "barbarians" who inhabited other lands (as we see in Aristotle), and for the wealth of quasi-ethnographic description of the appearance and behaviour of these other peoples (as we see in Herodotus).

From the earliest times, these ethnocentric and ethnographic reflections involved a kind of race-thinking. It isn't biologically determinist race-thinking, according to which heredity is dispositive, overruling the influence of environment and culture. It couldn't be determinist in this way, since the ancients didn't have the right notions of heredity or of biology. But it does seem to involve race-thinking as we've defined it. The Chinese, for example, assigned meaning to ancestry and appearance from quite early on. In the third century BCE they complained about savage foreigners "who greatly resemble the monkeys from whom they are descended," and by the time of Europe's modernization they were well in the habit of taking the darker skin of the residents of Africa and South Asia, as well as the "ash-white" skin of Europeans, as a sign of inferior culture and debased humanity.[6] As another example, consider that the ancient Greeks were quite willing to assign deeper meaning to the shape of the human body. We find this willingness especially pronounced among the post-Aristotelian physiognomists, who practiced the "science" of deducing character from physical appearance. Often enough, they linked body and behaviour by deriving both from the work of the environment and climate; but they had a stable enough notion of heredity for Herodotus to trace Hellenic distinctiveness to language, religion, and "blood," in ways that Romans like Vitruvius and Tacitus would later refine.[7]

Of course, the Greeks and other ancient peoples weren't using the modern concept of Race. One of the distinctive things about modern racialism is that it is self-conscious: people explicitly appeal to race in organizing the social world and their perceptions of it. The ancients, by contrast, couldn't explicitly avail themselves of the concept of race, since it hadn't been invented yet – as we'll see, it wasn't available until the sixteenth century. Modern racialism is distinctive also in that it assigns great significance to the continents of Asia, Europe, Africa, and America, and, in some versions, to the Pacific islands of Oceania (which the UN takes to include Australia and New Zealand). For modern racialism, each of these places is supposed to be the aboriginal home of a distinctive type of human being. The ancients didn't know about the continents, and so couldn't think of human difference in this way.

The ancients lived in a world of multiple peoples, rather than a world of a few races; and while they were certainly aware of the visible traits that distinguish our colored races from each other, they didn't invest these traits with the same significance that we do. They did take appearance and ancestry as signs of deeper characteristics, but they didn't read those signs the way we do, and they didn't sort the world's peoples into our capital-R Races. In addition, they engaged in small-r race-thinking unevenly, usually paying less attention to the poorly understood process of what we now call genetic inheritance than to the influence of climate on culture, religion, psychology, and physiology.

1.3.4 Toward modernity

While the ancient world was for many of its inhabitants a world of multiple peoples, often enough these peoples were sorted into two sets: Us and Them, or Humans and Barbarians, or Our People and Everyone Else. This sort of division dominated pre-modern Europe, or what would come to be thought of as Europe. Modern racialism hadn't yet supplanted the pre-modern varieties just discussed, as the currents of thought that would become the biological sciences continued to travel the worn, speculative paths charted by Aristotle and Galen. So on the cusp of modernity, ideas about the relations between human types remained circumscribed by theocentric ethnographies: the important anthropological distinction was between Christians and heathens, rather than between peoples with different bodies and bloodlines. Near the end of the fifteenth century, this situation started to change rather rapidly.

After the fifteenth century, the central drama in the history of race-thinking is the history of modern, or Western, race-thinking. This is the perspective that gives us the four or five color-coded and geo-graphically based races – capital-R Races – that we're so used to today. As I've said, the bulk of this book will focus on the modern perspective, especially as it coalesced in the English colonies that became the United States.

1.4 Power, racial formation, and method

Western race-thinking didn't just happen to emerge as Europe became modern. Modernity and Race helped bring each other into being, and they sustained and spurred each other through different stages of development. We can note this by thinking just in terms of economic relations and institutions. Racialized labor systems produced the wealth that financed at least the latter stages of modernization and industrialization (and more than this in the USA), while providing commodities that affected European life-styles so deeply that packets of sugar in Spain still carry images of dark people in cane fields. And perhaps the most successful racializing institution in history prepared the way for today's global economy: the transnational exchange markets and financial frameworks of global capitalism cut their teeth on the transatlantic slave trade.[8]

The connection between modernity and Race allows us to add a final set of nuances to the idea of race-thinking, and a final bit of detail to the method I'll employ in approaching it. We've noted that modern ideas of race are deeply intertwined with the first truly global system of political economy, and that they helped establish that system on a profoundly exploitive and unjust basis. We might note further that the victims of modern racist injustices have often used race-thinking in their fight against oppression – think, for example, of the activist history of the National Association for the Advancement of Colored People. In light of all this we can insist on a connection between Race and power, or between the systems of meaning that define race and the distributions of social goods that define politics.

We can clarify and reinforce the connection between Race and power by using it to refine the idea of racialism. So far we've seen that "racialism" names a way of thinking, a commitment to the validity or accuracy of race-talk. But there are many names like this, especially in the realm of political and social philosophy, that play a dual role. "Capitalism," for example, like "liberalism" and "socialism," denotes a way of thinking while also pointing to certain modes of social arrangement. We speak not just of capitalists but also of capitalist societies. So far we've spoken of racialists; soon we will speak of racialist social formations. Because of the connection between Race and power, we should say that in the modern world "racialism" also denotes a system, or a broad family of systems, of social organization.

We can make the Race-power connection more precise by adopting the idea of *racial formation* from sociologists Michael Omi and Howard Winant. To speak of racial formation is to speak, as they say, of "the sociohistorical process by which racial categories are created, inhabited, transformed, and destroyed."[9] This process unfolds by means of *racial projects*, which are specific attempts to do two things: to assign meaning to human bodies and bloodlines, and to distribute social goods along the lines laid down by the resultant systems of meaning.

Racial projects, then, are binary constructions, with parallel semantic and structural aspects. When we decide on or debate which meanings to assign to human bodies and bloodlines – which, as Omi and Winant put it, is to interpret the concept of race – we occupy the semantic side of a racial project. And when we distribute social goods along racial lines – which is to say, when we offer a racialized proposal for organizing our practical affairs – we occupy the structural side of a racial project. Semantics and structure, meaning and social organization, are connected here like two sides of the same coin, and they work together to drive race-thinking and racial practices along their historical trajectories.

An example may help make clear how the two sides of racial formation are supposed to fit together. When nineteenth-century US slaveholders linked blackness to irrationality, emotionality, and incapacity for self-government, they were interpreting race to mean that blackness signified, to sum it all up, inferiority. But in offering this interpretation of race they were also justifying or explaining the enslavement of most black people and the economic and political marginalization of free blacks: they were explaining a white supremacist, radically anti-democratic, anti-egalitarian mode of social organization. Transatlantic slavery was, then, a racial project, one among many such projects – including more progressive ones, like the nobler forms of abolitionism – that suffused nineteenth-century European and American cultures.

The next chapter will approach modernity through the lens of racial formation theory, and I introduce Omi and Winant's racial project idea in part to prepare for that discussion. The main, reason, though, for introducing the racial formation approach is to ground the analysis to follow in some of the insights that the approach provides. I've started more abstractly than Omi and Winant do, since, on a conceptual level, I think it is right to define race-thinking as I do above, without reference to considerations of power and politics. It is true that race-thinking implicates quite ancient them-and-us mechanisms, mechanisms that we can trace to their evolutionary roots. But, as far as I can tell, there's nothing about racialism per se that necessarily rules out perfectly egalitarian, non-conflictual incarnations. Even if we are somehow deeply hard-wired to use race-thinking, or something like it, in our efforts either to thrive as individuals or to secure representation in the gene pools of future generations, that wouldn't mean that race has to remain limited by its original evolutionary role. After all, we've found all sorts of new ways of engaging in the activities demanded by our evolutionary imperatives – think of the social functions of eating (which, we might say, turn it into dining), or the social meanings of sex (which turn it, sometimes, into fornication), or of how these can get combined in the use of culinary aphrodisiacs. So it doesn't seem to be the case that race-thinking is necessarily bound up with social conflict.

But once we move from the conceptual level to the level of social theory, and once we locate our topic in the modern period and its aftermath, then it is clear that capital-R Race-thinking is invariably connected to politically charged racial projects. Even if I say that race means nothing, that we're all individuals whose bodies and blood-lines have no deeper meaning, I've interpreted race in a way that here and now, in the twenty-first-century United States, will have implica-tions for the distribution of social goods. Depending on what my other political commitments are, my interpretation might mean that we should correct for any historical deviation from colorblindness, perhaps to the tune of massive public investment in reparations pro-grams for the descendants of slaves and of displaced Native Ameri-cans. Then again, my interpretation might mean that we should proscribe all deviations from colorblindness for any purpose, so that we're forced to leave people with what they've gotten from the luck of the historical lottery, ruling out race-based reparations and restor-ative justice. In either case, on either reading, I am obliged to partici-pate in a racial project because of the degree to which race has saturated and shaped the society.

1.5 Conclusion

The first part of this book is building toward a discussion of the exis-tence and nature of the entities that we call races. Call this a question of racial metaphysics. So far I've tried to prepare the way for that discussion by introducing the contexts for the argument (the West and the USA), some definitions (of "race-thinking," "eliminativism," "racial formation," and "classical racialism"), and some methodo-logical considerations, both philosophical (encouraged by Dewey and Austin) and sociological (encouraged by Omi and Winant). I also introduced some distinctions, between modern Races and pre-modern Races, between talking about words and talking about things, between social constructionism and racial naturalism.

Much of the foregoing either argues for or adopts a typically philo-sophical way of proceeding – just think about what we all do, in ways that we might all think about it if we had sufficient leisure and were so inclined, and above all be abstract. Despite all my reassurances that this is a provisional approach, carefully tailored to certain ends, it may still seem too narrowly philosophical. So the next chapter will be more concrete, adding some historical and sociological detail to the philo-sophic analysis.

2

Three Challenges to Race-Thinking

Prologue

"Hey Boyd, do you think I'm a racist?"

"Do you really want me to answer that?"

"Quit messing around. You know black folk can't be racist."

"I'm sure you have your moments. We all do: black, white, whatever. It's in the air, and we're still breathing, knock on wood. Why do you ask?"

"I was at a community meeting last night, one of the ones they started after the last incident with the police. I said I was glad to see some Asian brothers and sisters. Too many times, you know, it's just blacks and whites, like that's all the people race relations has involved in this country. And this not-quite-white fellow – you'll see why I call him that in a second – this fellow stands up and calls me a racist. 'The people you're talking about are all individuals,' he says. 'And lumping them under those labels helps maintain the racist attitudes we're trying to defeat.' Then someone else chimes in: 'Racial categories are a precondition for racism,' this one says, 'so using them is racist.'"

"What did you do?"

"I wanted to say that cars are a precondition for grand theft auto, but using one don't make you a thief. But I didn't have a chance because the first guy started in again. About how racial categories are arbitrary anyway, and how he wouldn't have been white a hundred years ago, since he is Jewish, and how he takes this to mean that he is beige, if he is any color."

"That's an interesting argument. Or set of arguments. Biologists do tend to avoid race-talk nowadays, and anti-Semitism is on the rise. So what did you say to this beige fellow?"

"Nothing. The other ones jumped in again, talking about how it's better to talk about ethnicity or national origin instead of race. And then this old socialist starts talking about –"

"How do you know he was a socialist?"

"Cause he damn near said 'Workers of the world unite,' that's how. He starts going on about how everything we're saying is irrelevant to the real issue, which is the class struggle. Black folk are an oppressed class, he says. Capitalism invents the fiction of race to mask its divisive character. And on like that."

"Well, there's something in what he says."

"No doubt. But I ain't denied none of that. And that's what I told them. I stood up and said, 'There's a catch-hell situation out there for everyone. But different people catch hell differently under different circumstances. And race is about certain specific ways of catching hell." I mean, old 'dude can be beige if he wants, but here and now, on Main Street USA, that just means he's white. And as for class, there's a rainbow coalition of folks in line for food stamps, lily-white and beige included. But come in there speaking Spanish or with a Native American name and see what happens. And see what percentage of the people down there look like you.'"

"You said all that?"

"Well, in so many words. Then I said I was late for dinner with my black Senegalese buddy and his black Haitian girlfriend, who would be very interested to know that they share nothing with me or with each other as black people. I left, and here I am."

"Yes, here you are. At the bar. Shouldn't you be at dinner?"

"Aw, man, I was supposed to go, but I didn't feel like being around them French-speaking Negroes."

2.1 Introduction

The previous chapter explored the meaning of race-thinking and, along the way, defended my willingness to focus on ideas and discourse. In the next chapter we'll consider some philosophical arguments about whether to continue to use race-talk – or, as I've recently started to say, racial discourse – and about how its constituent ideas relate to the world of concrete things. But there are some threshold questions to answer before we can even raise the philosophical issues.

I'm thinking of the questions raised by Boyd's latest conversation with JJ, questions I'll give the following forms: Isn't race-thinking racist? Isn't racial biology false? And, as a way of thinking about social groups, shouldn't the race concept give way to notions like class? I refer to these as threshold questions because they present three challenges – one ethical, one empirical, and one conceptual – that threaten to prevent us from building onto the foundation established in chapter 1. If engaging in race-talk obviously leads to racism (the ethical challenge), or if advances in the biological sciences clearly reveal the bankruptcy of the race concept (the empirical challenge), or if other notions can adequately capture whatever aspects of the world the race concept might helpfully point us to (the conceptual challenge), then there may not be much point in going any further with the argument of this book. It might be better to stop talking about race altogether, and immediately, even in advance of asking the question of whether race-talk refers to anything. Let's refer to these challenges, respectively, as the challenges of anti-racism, of human variation, and of social differentiation. And let's take them up as a way of making the world safe for the rest of this book.

I'll address the challenges also as a way of continuing the hopefully clarifying work of the previous chapter. So what follows will include definitions of some key terms, like "racism" and "ethnicity," and it will provide a bit of historical background. This background is important to understanding the empirical and conceptual challenges that we'll consider, but it is also important in getting a clearer sense of what race-thinking means. Having used the previous chapter to specify the conceptual role that the notion of race plays, I want to use this chapter to explore some of the specific ways in which that role has been filled. So I'll frame the conceptual and empirical challenges with some glimpses of the past, to see how race-thinking has developed into the phenomenon we're so familiar with today. Here we'll work toward focusing on the bit of the contemporary world that this book will methodically zero in on, the late twentieth- and early twenty-first-century United States.

2.2 The anti-racist challenge, take 1: isn't race-thinking unethical?

One of the standing challenges to race-thinking is the connection between race and racism. Race-thinking makes racism possible, and the intertwined history of the two is, to say the least, sobering. One might claim, then, that race-thinking is unethical, or at least inappropriate, and hence ought to be proscribed, because it is an essential means to an unethical end.

Here's a version of the worry from the campaign for the "Racial Privacy Initiative" in California. This initiative, which its advocates in the American Civil Rights Coalition (ACRC) were trying to get on the California ballot for November 2002, would have banned the use of racial categories for any government purpose. Here's how they put the point on a web page that offered reasons for supporting the initiative:

> The history of race classifications is long, storied, and horrific. From the slave trade to the Holocaust, from the Japanese American internment to South African apartheid, race classifications have always divided people along artificial, hateful lines. The time has come to put an end to these terrible race classifications. . . .
>
> By re-emphasizing America's checkered racial history, race classifications focus our attention on what divides us, rather than what unites

us. If we are to solve the educational, social and economic problems of tomorrow, we must unite our hearts and minds pursuing common goals. As long as we keep counting by skin color, we can never become "one nation, under God, indivisible, with liberty and justice for all."[1]

Here we have two instrumental arguments for abolishing race-thinking. And, like any instrumental arguments, they are only as good as the cost-benefit analysis behind them. If race classifications have done nothing but wreak havoc, if they do nothing but divide us, then the conclusion of this argument – that we should abolish racial distinctions – almost surely follows.

It's not hard to envision what's troubling the advocates for racial privacy. Race-thinking is at the heart of Western doctrines of white supremacy, which led to the global tragedies of the transatlantic slave trade, the Nazi genocide targeting the Jewish and Roma peoples, and the colonial-era extermination of indigenous peoples in the Americas. On a more local scale, race classifications have led to civic unrest and political violence: think of the Tulsa Riot of 1921, in which white mobs attacked a prosperous African-American neighborhood, burned down over 1,100 African-American homes and businesses, and caused perhaps 300 deaths. Or think of the riots in the US city of Los Angeles in 1965 and 1992, or of the riots in Tottenham, UK in 1985 and 2011, or the 2005 uprisings in the French *banlieues*, all set off by concerns about racist police brutality. On an even more intimate level, we can see how "counting by skin color" divides us today if we think about all the interpersonal slights, insults, slurs, exclusions, and prejudices that racialism makes possible.

So the "racial privacy" crowd is right to say that the history of race classifications has many horrific moments. But many people claim that the most horrific moments are profoundly overdetermined – which is to say that race-thinking led to tragedy in these cases only with the addition of other factors, like a shaky commitment to democracy, or a failure to constrain the pursuit of profit, public order, or political power with norms of decency and justice. Many people claim also that racialism has important moments apart from the horrific ones, and that it is not seamlessly and entirely problematic. They say, for example, that it provides a basis for political mobilization and community building, or that it allows us to track the effects of racial discrimination, discrimination that has continued even in the absence of explicit appeals to racial categories. If that's right, or if there's even a plausible case to make for these claims, then the case for this "privacy" – a peculiar name for what the ACRC proposes – isn't so clear. (Some other people claim that even if race-thinking is seamlessly problematic, we're stuck with it, either because there's no plausible way to eradicate the socializing mechanisms that keep it alive, or because we are somehow cognitively hard-wired to assign generic meaning to bodies and bloodlines. If either of those claims is right, then it is profoundly unhelpful just to say that we should stop "counting by color.")

All of that is relevant here, as I've said, because this ethical challenge to race-thinking might seem to be a threshold question for this book. If the case for racial privacy is just obviously right, then there may be no reason to go on with this discussion. But the countervailing considerations mentioned above show that it isn't obviously right – which isn't to say that it isn't ultimately right; just that we need to discuss the point more thoroughly and carefully. And in any case, we'd still have some motivation for pressing on even if the case for "privacy" were a clear winner. For one thing, we'd need to know how to recognize race-thinking in order to proscribe it. And for another, we might want to study race historically, the way people study Aristotle's fascinating but quite incorrect theories about human reproduction and brain physiology. So, again, we'd need to be able to recognize the object of study.

The ethical challenge, then, won't derail our discussion before it leaves the station. But determining this doesn't yet enable us to resolve the overarching question: does race-thinking in fact do more harm than good? As I've suggested, we can't conduct the cost-benefit analysis that this question requires until we know quite a bit more about how race has worked, how it might work, and what it is. So, for the first of several times, I'll postpone consideration of this ethical argument for abolishing race-thinking until chapter 4.

As long as we're in the neighborhood, though, we may as well go on and say some more about just what racism is. For one thing, since I'll frequently refer to racism in what follows, it would be nice to have an idea of what the word means. And for another, anti-racist critics and activists have provided much of the impetus for the thoroughgoing reconsideration of racialism that we'll consider in the next two sections. Before we track the results of that reconsideration, we should consider the phenomenon that inspired it.

2.2.1 What racism is

I'm sorry to report that "racism" is one of those notions that seem much clearer than they really are. You know the ones I mean: "socialism" and "pornography," "philosophy" and "postmodernism." These words and others like them seem to denote unitary phenomena, but they stubbornly frustrate our attempts to find that unity in their definitions. And if you think any of the examples I just gave are clearer than I've made them out to be, just leaf through any book that aspires to introduce one of them. You won't go far without running into the obligatory gesture at how hard it is provide a satisfactory definition.

Defining "racism" is difficult in part because we use the word to describe many different things. Some of us speak of racist people, actions, attitudes, and beliefs; others speak of racist practices, ideologies, and institutions. Some of us refuse to complain of racism unless there is some intentional discrimination; others are willing to set aside intentions and focus on consequences. Some of us want to think of racism as a matter of prejudice in individual interactions; others insist that it is about social systems and structures of power.

To make matters worse, we offer many different explanations of the many different things that we identify as racist, and this also shapes how we apply the term. Some of us want to say that racism is irrational, involving either the mostly unmotivated fear of mostly unknown others, or the denial of obvious, or sufficiently obvious, facts, such as the falsity of nineteenth-century notions of natural difference and inequality. Others, by contrast, want to reserve the term for unjust discriminations that are perfectly rational, thereby showing that racism isn't a matter just of ignorance and fear, but also of rigging the processes by which social resources and goods get distributed. Still others want to say that it is rational but mistaken, based on drawing reasonable conclusions – about what people can and can't do, about whom to associate with and whom to avoid – from faulty racialist premises about human capacities and the distribution of human traits. And still others want to say that it is pre- or a-rational, the result of a natural predisposition toward xenophobia – involving, say, evolutionarily advantageous preferences for "kin."

My sense is that there's something to recommend most of these different approaches to racism, and that there's no particular need to try to reduce a diverse and complex phenomenon to a single model. Of course, some of the aforementioned views exclude the others. Fully committing to the idea that racism must be intentional effectively precludes the idea that it can be unintentional. But focusing on what's most fundamentally at stake for all of these views reveals a common theme, one that we can develop using ideas from philosopher Jorge Garcia.[2] (Garcia developed his view in a series of subsequent articles, in conversation with a number of thoughtful critics. The probity of what I mean to borrow from his view does not depend heavily on the outcome of those conversations.)

When we complain of racism in any of these senses, we seem to be complaining about an unethical disregard for people who belong to a particular race. "Disregard" in this context means the withholding of respect, concern, good-will, or care from the members of a race. We might do this because we dislike people with certain traits, and because we believe that membership in the race in question involves possessing these undesirable traits. This would make us what K. Anthony Appiah calls extrinsic racists. Then again, we might just dislike people who belong to that race, irrespective of the traits, if any, that come with race membership. This would make us intrinsic racists. Or, as I'll discuss below, we might not be thinking about races and their members at all. This would make us, as I'll soon say, indirect racists.

"Disregard" is an admittedly tame word for one of the central moral errors of the last few centuries. But its very tameness gives it several advantages. First, speaking of disregard (and of disrespect and the rest) allows us to cover a range of attitudes all at once, from outright hatred, to the simple failure to notice that someone is suffering, to the related failure to notice that there's a person in front of you, as opposed to the personification of a pre-existing stereotype. I disregard you when I assume that a racial stereotype accurately describes you. I disrespect you when I deny your application for a job, or a mortgage loan, or a place in an educational institution without regard for your individual qualifications. (This may sound as if I've already decided that affirmative action is racist. I haven't. We'll come to that in Part II.) I withhold concern from you when I ignore the social, political, and economic processes that produce your misery. And I withhold goodwill and care from you when I burn a cross on your lawn, when I yell insults at you, or when I drag you from your home, hang you or put you in an internment camp, and burn down or take over the business that you owned.

These instances of disregard become racist when they affect or target members of a race. I don't mean by this that some agent has to consciously have the welfare of the race in mind. Some of the examples I used above should make this clear. As I understand it, disregard can target the members of a race when it disproportionately or reliably affects the members of a race, quite apart from anyone's conscious intentions. This is what I mean by indirect racism. And the idea of indirect racism leads to the second advantage of linking racism to disregard: it makes room for us to focus on the consequences of acts, without losing sight of the individual motivations that many of us put at the center of ethical evaluation. I disregard you when I assume on the basis of how you look that you won't be able to speak English well. I disregard you when I, as your teacher, see your face and privately discount the possibility that your contribution to classroom discussion will be useful, and when my inner convictions affect my response to you. I may do either of these things without even noticing what I'm doing – if, for example, no one ever asks me to identify the people I've prejudged. But in either case there is a pattern to my behaviour that reliably picks out the members of (yes, what we think of as) a certain race. On my view, this would be a kind of racism, which isn't yet to say just how bad it is or what kind of sanctions, social or otherwise, it deserves.

We've seen that focusing on the idea of disregard allows us, through the idea of indirectness, to finesse the question of whether racism is a matter of consequences or intentions. This leads to a third advantage. The idea of disregard, construed in the way I've just explained, allows us to connect certain intuitions about what we call institutional racism to our strong biases in the direction of individual agency. People usually invoke the idea of institutional racism to talk about social systems that methodically work to the detriment of some racial group, even when no individual agent consciously manipulates the institutions to bring about that outcome. Treating this as a kind of racism makes many people uneasy. The accusation of racism, they think, should pick out individual malefactors, and where no one has racist intentions, the accusation is misplaced. But an institution reliably working to the detriment of certain people, people that we already think of as a unitary group, will leave evidence of its asymmetric operations. To the extent that this evidence becomes available – in statistics, say, about disparities in wealth, income, the frequency of disease, proximity to environmental health hazards, and criminal sentencing – refusing to respond to it constitutes a kind of disregard that targets the members of the injured race. (Of course, for those of us who aren't squeamish about ascribing agency to social institutions, we can just say that the institution withholds concern from certain people.) On this approach, the participants in the institution might become what I've called indirect racists.

The fourth advantage of focusing on disregard is that it makes clear just what's wrong with racism. Construing racism as the withholding of concern shows that it runs afoul of one of the central ethical ideas of modernity: that people should be treated the same unless there is a morally relevant difference between them. This principle proceeds from what we might call a presumption of abstract or moral equality, the presumption behind the claim that we're all equal in the eyes of God, or from the standpoint of being human.

The fifth advantage of focusing on disregard is that it helps settle questions about what sorts of entities can be racist. I said above that we ascribe racism to people, actions, beliefs, practices, institutions, and attitudes. Some people prefer to focus on one or another of these things, saying, for example, that beliefs alone aren't racist, because, unless supplemented by desires and action, beliefs don't have any consequences. I'll focus on this example for a moment, and then make a more general comment about this issue.

Beliefs are attitudes, of a sort; along with desires and hopes and the like, they are what philosophers call propositional attitudes: mental states involving orientations toward states of affairs. To believe that snow is white is to take a certain attitude – philosophers usually say, tepidly, a "pro-attitude" – toward the proposition that snow is white, and to commit myself to the truth of sentences that express the proposition (like "Snow is white"). I have some control over my attitudes, especially when I have reason to revise them. I might think, because of his music, that Wagner was a great man. But finding out that he was an anti-Semite gives me reason to revise this opinion, to alter my attitude. (How much I alter it, and whether that alteration should affect my estimation of his music, is quite a live philosophical question these days. Sadly, I can't say anything more about it here.) Similarly, finding out that not all Asian people are good at math gives me a reason to revise my attitude toward that stereotype. Failing to revise my attitude, failing to work to rid myself of that belief, constitutes a kind of disregard for the individuals who defy the stereotype.

More generally, the question of which entities can count as racist is probably a good place to return to the stance with which I nearly began this section: it's not clear that there's any particular need to try to reduce the diverse and complex phenomenon of racism to a single model. So consider how advocates for the "prejudice plus power" (PPP) model of racism insist that only white people can be racist. Non-whites, they say, collectively lack the power to make their prejudices operative. This is in some ways a useful thing to say, because it highlights the degree to which white supremacy has systematically and disproportionately shaped the development of Western societies. But offering this as a general account of racism obscures other ethically questionable phenomena that seem pre-theoretically to count as instances of racism. Imagine a non-white person who decides to beat up every white person he sees, and who does so just because he doesn't like white people. Such a person would be a racist, it seems to me. I agree with the PPP theorist that this racism doesn't amount to much in the grand scheme of things, especially if we're interested in combating the social ills that follow from centuries of white supremacist exclusionary practices. But why not just say that? Why not just say that this sort of individual racist assault pales in significance beside the systemic racism we find in, say, the transatlantic slave trade, or in the West's military adventures in mid-twentieth-century Asia? What do we gain by refusing to call it racism?

The pluralistic approach seems to be the best response to another of the obstacles to defining racism, the last obstacle I'll discuss here. I mentioned above a range of positions on the etiology of racism – on, that is, the question of what causes it. These differences are important, because they lead to different ideas about how to fix the problem. Some say that racism involves rational choices in the context of unequal power relations. For them the solution is political organization and mobilization. Some say it involves irrational prejudices in the context of segregation and social distance. For them the solution is integration and education, to overcome fear and ignorance. Some say it involves pre- or non-rational impulses, in the context of the workings of certain psychological and cognitive mechanisms. For them the solution, if there is one, might involve consciousness-raising or therapy, helping us to recognize the force of primal urges or subconscious drives and to integrate those forces into the overall economy of our psychosocial functioning.

Again, I'll say: Thinking of racism in terms of disregard allows us to treat these questions in the pluralist spirit they deserve. People are complex creatures, and we prepare ourselves to disregard people, as we do to love people, in a variety of ways. Sometimes we're irrational, driven by unexcavated fears, desires, and assumptions; but sometimes we're quite rational, driven to prepare strategies to advance our interests. Sometimes we behave in ways that are narrowly rational – if we consider our prospects in isolation or in the short term – while also being broadly irrational – if we consider our prospects as social creatures with long-range interests. Sometimes we're simply ill informed about the facts, including facts concerning the impact that certain behaviours and policies have on other people. At other times we're simply callous or invidiously self-centered. We might be racists at any of these times.

I've tried to accommodate all of the causal accounts I mentioned except one. I have quite little sympathy with the idea that racism derives from the operation of innate, race-specific mechanisms. This is an evidence-driven claim, so the cognitive psychologists have to hash this one out. But explanations are ways of answering why-questions, such as why do people act that way? We have plenty of ways of answering why-questions about racism, especially when it comes to modern racism, from which I've drawn all of my examples in this section. If we can appeal to centuries of cultural and social transformation during which we built up and forcefully promulgated comprehensive conceptions of human racial difference; if these conceptions shaped our socioeconomic arrangements, our educational processes, and our mechanisms for producing knowledge and culture; if we ensured that these conceptions would invoke passion by weaving them together with the deeply affecting human realities of sex and reproduction; and if all of this worked so clearly to the benefit of certain people that it was overwhelmingly in their interest to maintain it, and to avoid even noticing its peculiarity – if all of that is the case, *since* all of that is the case, it's not clear to me why we need to appeal to some hard-wired mechanism that routinely cranks out organisms that indulge in racist exclusions. We'd still have to explain the peculiar forms of exclusion that the mechanism produces under specific cultural conditions, which seems to me to leave all of the interesting questions unanswered.

2.3 Classical racialism: history and background

If the first challenge to race-thinking is its connection to racism, then the next challenge is the utter inability of the most visible, ambitious, and influential version of racialism to accomplish its own objectives. Classical racialism – the view that the previous chapter associated with the Klan – tries to reduce social and cultural differences between peoples to the biological and morphological differences between them, and it tries to explain these morphological differences with scientific precision, by appeal to the concept of race. But the dominant view among those who study human biological variation now is that this race concept is of little use to them, for a variety of reasons. Before we explore these reasons in the next section of this chapter, we have to see more clearly what this classical view involves, first historically, against the broader backdrop of modern racialism, then conceptually. Along the way we'll consider a perhaps larger number of historical details than is typical for a book of this sort. There are two reasons for this. First, I think philosophy – any humanistic theoretical work, really – unfolds much more productively when it declines to stray too far from the facts that give it its subject matter. And second, some of the details to follow will be of some use later on.

Modern racialism is the cultural formation – with its characteristic sensibilities, commitments, institutions, and practices – that emerges in the West as race-thinking refines and replaces the pre-modern anthropologies that we considered in chapter 1. This new formation develops in three stages,[3] two of which we'll consider here. Each stage begins with important temporal signposts, moves through significant watershed moments, and generates a distinctive racial project (see table 2.1.) You'll remember from chapter 1 that our understandings of and dealings with race emerge from the work of racial projects, each of which interprets the race concept while also providing a framework for distributing social goods along racial lines. The expression "black is beautiful" entered US culture as part of a racial project, one that reinterpreted race so that blackness would no longer automatically connote ugliness, and that proposed to redistribute, say, the social bases for self-esteem. Similarly, the participants in each period of modern racialism established new racialized structures for distributing social goods, while also offering new guides to the interpretation of racial difference. I'll demarcate these periods by appeal to specific dates, but these are of course no more than rough chronological

Table 2.1 The stages of modern racialism, 1492–1923

	Signpost	Additional watershed moments	Structural content (racialized distributive framework)	Semantic content (interpretation of race concept)	Ideological work
Early modern	Columbus, *Reconquista*, and expulsion (1492)	Bernier's 'A New Division of the Earth' (1684) Virginia assembly links race to condition of servitude (1660)	Colonies and slavery	Race as variety (monogenist synthesis)	Naturalizes difference
High modern (classical)	Jefferson's suspicions, Kant's convictions (1775/86)	Publication of S. G. Morton's *Crania Americana* (1839) US annexes Hawai'i (1899)	Comprehensive racist domination	Race as type (typological synthesis)	Rationalizes difference

coordinates. Selecting precise dates for the onset or conclusion of large-scale historic trends is an unavoidably impressionistic enterprise, but, often enough, a useful one.

2.3.1 Early modern racialism

Our first stage begins in 1492, with a couple of events on the Iberian Peninsula. First of all, Ferdinand and Isabella, rulers of what would thereafter be Spain, conquered the last Moorish stronghold on the peninsula, and ordered the expulsion of all Jews who did not convert to Christianity. They would soon present the conversion ultimatum to the conquered Moors, and even though many Jews and Muslims did become Christian, the Spaniards worried that there was still something deeply different about the *conversos* and *moriscos*, something carried, as it were, in the blood. This idea of heritable and essential human difference, deeper than culture and belief, soon made its way into the language. Southern Europeans had already used Latin or Arabic linguistic resources (the etymological evidence isn't clear) to develop a way of talking about breeds or strains of animals. By the time of the first Spanish dictionary, the 1611 *Tesoro de la Lengua Castellano o Espanola*, a single term – "*raza*" – refers both to breeds of horses and, derisively, to Moorish or Jewish human ancestry.[3]

Turning social and cultural difference into a physiological and heritable difference in "breed" – moving from culturally distinct peoples to essentially distinct *razas* – is the important semantic shift of the early modern racial project. This is less a new interpretation of race than the founding interpretation, introducing the *raza*-idea to examine social difference, and to depict difference and subordination as natural conditions. This naturalization of social status is, among other things, one of the key moments in the shift from anti-Judaism, a theological posture, to anti-Semitism, a race-based prejudice. We'll return to this subject a bit later.

In addition to paving the way to anti-Semitism, the naturalization of social status also facilitated the structural shift of the early modern period. This brings us to the other, obvious reason to focus on Spain in 1492. Ferdinand and Isabella backed Columbus's trip to "the Indies," which begins the era of European colonialism. Vastly different peoples and cultures came together during this era, with some of those peoples appropriating the land and labor of some of the others on an unprecedented scale. The transformation of theology into anthropology was an important ideological element in this process. Unbelievers can learn new ways and join the community of faith; but naturally backward peoples have little hope of becoming full persons with claimable rights – rights, for example, to the bodies they use for labor and the land that sustains them. Some people decried this innovation and its results – Bartolomé de las Casas, for example, the Spanish missionary who in the sixteenth century wrote stinging denunciations of Spanish practices of forced labor and human bondage. But by 1660, we find North American colonial charters explicitly linking race to, as they'd soon say, condition of servitude.[4]

According to one influential account of the etymology of "race," the southern European idea of a human *raza* spread quickly, first finding its way into the English language and then into French, where it arrived in the early sixteenth century. Here it was available to François Bernier, who was perhaps the first to use the notion of race in a recognizably modern sense. In a 1684 essay the French physician declares, "there are four or five species or races of men . . . whose difference is so remarkable that it may be made the basis for a new division of the Earth." This "new division" of humanity, into Europeans, Africans, Asians, Lapps, and Americans, rejects earlier classifications that were based solely on, as Bernier says, "country or region," and introduces a scheme based on such visible features as nose and face shape, skin color, and hair texture.[5]

Bernier's conceptual innovation developed into what we can call "the monogenist synthesis," the basic commitments of which provided the distinctive ideological content of early modern racialism. The first commitment is to monogenism, the view that human races are varieties of a single species, all, in the typical theological version of the argument, descended from Adam. A frequent corollary of this argument was that, far from being rigidly distinct and separable into a few discrete groups, the varieties "run into one another," as German naturalist Johann Blumenbach put it, "by insensible degrees."[6] The second commitment is to environmentalism. This is the view that the differences between the varieties of humanity, such differences as there are, reflect the operations of climate and other influences over time. On this view, the different human "breeds" mark degrees of divergence, typically of decline, from the original and basic human form, usually taken to be that of the white European. The last commitment of the monogenist synthesis, easily derived from the first two, was to a kind of abstract humanism. The differences between human varieties were, after all, differences between *human* varieties, caused by the influence of external forces over time. This humanism remained abstract, though, because it was compatible with claims about the obvious superiority of the white variety: many saw whites as the basic human form, and the other races as degenerate variations.

Monogenist humanism didn't always remain abstract. The Religious Society of Friends, or Quakers, for example, moved from the belief that all people were equal in the eyes of God to the conviction that the slave trade was immoral and should be stopped. The Quakers joined others to form the Society for the Abolition of the Slave Trade, which helped end British participation in the slave trade (in 1807). Unfortunately, these egalitarian sentiments hardly slowed the colonial enterprise, and they couldn't even bring slavery to an end in the United States.

2.3.2 High modern, or classical, racialism

The first stage of modern racialism sought to naturalize social difference. On the theoretical level this meant dividing humankind into deeply distinct but still related varieties, and on the practical level it meant turning social and cultural differences into elaborate and far-reaching relations of privilege and domination. The second stage of modern racialism – call this classical or high modern racialism – sought to *rationalize* social difference. It theorized, and thereby widened, the gaps between races, treating them not as provisionally differentiated varieties but as essentially distinct types. And it refined and expanded the techniques of racial domination and the mechanisms for disseminating the new racial "knowledge." Since this stage represents in many ways the high point of white supremacy, we should begin by noting that many people, of all colors, resisted the *zeitgeist*. This is also the era of abolitionism, of Nat Turner and John Brown, of the founding of the NAACP, of Ida B. Wells and her crusades against segregation and lynching, and of interracial coalitions. But our burden here is to explore the dominant trends; and during this period liberation and social justice movements were clearly playing catch-up.

We might begin the second stage of modern racialism with Immanuel Kant, whose 1775 essay, entitled "Of the Different Human Races," encapsulates what one writer refers to as "the first *theory* of race which really merits that name."[7] But Kant's work here, as elsewhere, is complex and detailed, more so than we have space to work through. So let's find our signpost in 1786, in Thomas Jefferson's *Notes on the State of Virginia*. Jefferson says:

> I advance it as a suspicion only, that the blacks whether originally a distinct race, or made distinct by time and circumstance, are inferior to the whites in the endowments of both body and mind. . . . The unfortunate difference of color, and perhaps of faculty, is a powerful obstacle to the emancipation of these people.[8]

Many theorists developed the key ideas here: that the colored populations of the modernizing West were "originally distinct races," and that this original, natural distinctness may be the source of, or justification for, racial inequality. In the nineteenth century Jefferson's

"suspicion" spawned a research program, an attempt to make racialism scientific by replacing monogenism with a *typological synthesis*.

Three changes shaped what I'm calling the typological synthesis.
First, the human races became rigidly distinct types rather than mere
varieties; the idea of "insensible shading" gave way to a belief in
clearly discernible differences. Second, this distinctness was taken to
be the result of processes that were not external but internal, involving
the heritability of essential traits across generations. At first this idea
of innate difference seemed to require a commitment to polygenism,
or the view that the different races had separate origins. But after
Darwin's *Origin of Species* (1859), it was enough for essential differences to emerge during eons of evolutionary development from
common ancestors. And third: on this typological view, human types
could be confidently ranked on scales of innate "talent," worth, and
value.

Adherents to this new reading of race as type assumed that the
deep differences between humans were intimately related to measur-
able differences in human bodies. Early modes of anthropometry, or
the study of human body measurements, developed from this assumption, and sought to quantify the evidence of differential human worth.
This scientific program really got underway in the 1830s, with Samuel
George Morton's attempts to specify and account for racial differences
by appeal to cranial measurements. By the second half of the century,
in the USA, in Latin America, in Japan, and elsewhere, Social
Darwinists were reducing social hierarchies to the outcome of compe-
tition between differently endowed biological groups. And by the
twentieth century, eugenicists were using public policy to manage the
hereditary fitness of national populations, perhaps most prominently
in Nazi Germany.

The influence of eugenics over public policy points to the structural
shift that marks the high modern era: the emergence of newly comprehensive forms of racist political domination. State-sanctioned
slavery and Europe's early acquisition of overseas colonies certainly
presupposed and encouraged forms of racist domination. But during
the high modern era, and especially after about 1870, states became
more ambitious in their global reach, and more actively engaged in
managing the lives of their subjects. After the emergence of mass
politics and the attendant need for managing public opinion, after the
fermenting of nationalist aspirations to self-determination, and after
industrialization and capitalist expansion began occasioning labor
migrations and other social upheavals, states needed ways to unify,
mobilize, and mollify their increasingly literate and politically active
populations, especially in the face of economic distress, cultural dis-
ruption, and potential class conflict. At the same time, individuals and
communities needed ways of understanding and coping with the

changes going on around them. Newly hardened forms of racism spoke to these needs, often using new or newly proliferating media, like journals, newspapers, scientific societies, film, and public exhibitions, to do so.

We can see the intertwining of these structural and semantic changes in many different parts of the world. In Europe, for example, anti-Semitism developed into a coherent ideology, turning Jews into scapegoats for the ills and challenges of modern society, and soon into the targets of violent pogroms. Racial nationalism also became a growth industry, using arguments about natural ties of solidarity and loyalty to replace class conflict with national unity. There was also a hardening of anti-black racism, which among Europeans targeted southern Asians and indigenous Australians as well as Africans. This happened in part because late nineteenth-century economic downturns led to renewed imperial ambitions. Colonial powers went overseas in search of markets, resources, and places to send their ne'er-do-wells, and this led to a feedback loop of racist reasoning. States won support for colonial adventures by emphasizing the need to civilize the backward races or to cultivate lands – under the doctrine of *terra nullius*, or empty land – that the natives had allowed to lie fallow. Meanwhile the colonial administrators and functionaries, trained above all to keep the inferior natives in check, brought invidious "knowledge" about their "savage" charges back to the European homelands.

The United States also traversed this racialized road to high modernity, perhaps most strikingly in the wake of the Civil War. Anti-black racism re-established itself after Reconstruction, as elites headed off class and regional conflict by appealing to racial loyalties; as concerned citizens complained that the ex-slaves were not fit to govern themselves, much less to rule over white people in democratic assemblies; and as demagogues warned of the indiscriminate rape of white women by black men. Meanwhile, as whites united to secure black deference, disenfranchisement, and subjection in the Jim Crow regime, the federal government decided that the Indians were wards of the United States rather than members of sovereign nations, and that their affairs were to be "managed" – which meant either shunting them onto reservations or assimilating them into modern society. During this time the USA also entered the scramble for overseas colonies, leading to the annexation of Hawai'i and the Philippines, as well as to the articulation of the Monroe Doctrine (with its Roosevelt Corollary), which effectively established the US right to intervene at will in Latin American affairs. (We had effectively claimed this right at mid-century by annexing Texas and claiming half of a defeated Mexico.) This is also the era of the Chinese Exclusion Act, the first volley in a barrage of race-based legislation that effectively barred Asian immigration until 1965 while also severely curtailing immigration from southern and eastern Europe.

The tight regulation of European immigration points to two last pieces of important historical detail. The first detail has to do with the link between race-thinking and new approaches to politics and state-craft. Following a line of argument that we find in the work of Michel Foucault, we can say that a recognizably contemporary conception of race – what I've referred to as high modern racialism, and will soon connect to late-modern racialism – emerges just as modern states begin to take seriously the thought that power has to do with promoting life as much as with threatening death. Instead of just of bringing potentially lethal force to bear on wayward subjects, states in the high modern period begin to develop and refine ways of promoting the health and life chances of citizens. Race-thinking, in short, emerges along with what Foucault calls "bio-power," which philosopher Eduardo Mendieta describes this way:

> Biopolitics . . . is a form of power that rules over a population, a people thought of as a living body, by attending, ensuring, securing and promoting its health. . . . The novelty of biopolitics is that it reverses the relationship between power, on one side, and life and death, on the other. Classical sovereignty ruled by taking life and letting live. Its control over death was absolute. The power of the monarch was a power to put to death, while life itself was beyond its purvey. Biopolitics, in contrast, is deployed over the living, attending to it as a pastor tends to a flock. . . .[9]

The idea of biopolitics gives us a way of thinking more generally about the schemes for managing human populations that we introduced above. We now accept, most of us, that the state can permissibly and effectively promote the health of its citizens by regulating the practice of medicine, or filling in malarial swamps, or providing "safety nets" for citizens too destitute to provide for their own needs. In the transition from high-modern to late-modern racialism, though, many thought that the state could much more directly manage the health of its constituent populations. This meant, among other things, managing reproduction, to make sure that only the best stock could renew itself in future generations; and managing problem peoples – populations whose very presence was a threat to public health. Here we have the context for and content of racial eugenics. If blacks (or Asians, or Indians, or whomever) are inferior, then mating with blacks would produce inferior offspring. The state, then, on account of its interest in promoting a healthy population, must criminalize "race-mixing." In fact, since it might be better if these inferior populations did not reproduce at all, perhaps the state should sterilize them.

There is much more to say about race-thinking as a form of or resource for biopolitics. We might mention the idea of "racial hygiene" in colonial contexts, or the use of blacks and "natives" as, in essence, lab animals, as in the famous Tuskegee Experiment (in which black men with syphilis were offered free medical care but denied relevant treatment so that researchers could study the progress of their disease).[10] Or we might follow out other ideas developed by readers of Foucault on race, such as that modern ideas about race and sex are very similar and emerge under similar conditions, or that racism is a way for the old power to kill – the purview of the Hobbesian sovereign – to keep itself relevant in a changed social context. There is unfortunately no room to follow out those thoughts in any detail, so I'll just say that some story like this, about the state's increased interest in directly managing human bodies and populations, must have a place in a responsible history of modern racialism. It must, in particular, play some role in an account that takes power seriously, as I pledged to in section 1.4 above.

The last piece of historical detail to consider pertains to the fragmentation and consolidation of white identity. As the nineteenth century progressed, growing nationalistic fervor in Europe contributed to the sense that there were different *white* peoples, and the high modern rationalization of human difference contributed to the sense that these intra-white differences were racial in nature. In the USA and UK these developments became manifest in the doctrine of Anglo-Saxon supremacy. Anglo-Saxonism divided the white race into multiple subdivisions, all sharing space at the top of the racial rankings, but with Anglo-Saxons at the very top – above, for example, the Celts and Slavs. US Anglo-Saxonism became an important political force after European immigration spiked in the middle of the nineteenth century. "Native" residents of the formerly English colonies felt overwhelmed by the culturally distinct, often impoverished, and therefore inferior white peoples from Italy, Ireland, Armenia, and elsewhere. And they responded with restrictive legislation and discriminatory practices, all expressing the sense that the inferior whites, like blacks, Indians, and Asians, lacked the prerequisites for democratic citizenship.

Unfortunately for the Anglo-Saxonists, as well as for those who worried about increased Asian immigration during the Gold Rush and the transcontinental railroad project, US racial policy originally comprehended only three racial groups: whites, blacks, and Indians. Accordingly, under the first US naturalization statute (1790), the key to becoming a naturalized citizen was to belong to the category of, as the act says, "free white persons." So after the mass migrations began, many travelers from Europe and Asia fought racial restrictions by bringing suit in Federal courts to establish their whiteness. The

Europeans generally succeeded, and this, along with their support for anti-black, anti-Asian, and anti-Indian policies and activities, eventually enhanced their claim to full-fledged whiteness.

By contrast, the Asians who petitioned to establish their whiteness generally failed, thereby driving a wedge between classical racialist practice and its scientific expression, and heralding the end of the high modern period. Around the turn of the twentieth century, the still-new sciences of human biological difference began to buck conventional wisdom: they decided that Asian Indians were, in the pseudo-scientific terminology of the time, not Mongoloid but Caucasian. This prompted the Supreme Court to declare in *U.S. v. Thind* (1923) that "the average well informed white American would learn with some degree of astonishment that the race to which he belongs is made up of such heterogeneous elements." The Court went on to detach the state's official race-thinking from scientific categories. "What we now hold," the majority said, "is that the words 'free white persons' are words of common knowledge, to be interpreted in accordance with the understanding of the common man. . . ."[11] Asians, as a matter of law, were not white, and whiteness, for the purposes of the state, was a condition to be decided not by appeal to science but by appeal to common sense.

2.3.3 *The concept of classical racialism*

Of course, science and common knowledge these days seem to agree on the deficiencies of classical racialism, even rejecting the shored-up version used by the scientists at odds with *Thind*. In light of this, we should detail the case against the theoretical content of high modern racialism. Of course, we should clearly lay out the conceptual structure of the position before we criticize it.

Classical racialism begins, like all racialism, with the standard strategy of assigning generic meaning to the appearance, makeup, and heritage of human bodies. And as a form of modern racialism, it focuses on the five or so geographically defined and color-coded populations that constitute the main categories on US census forms. If we add these basic commitments to the three aspects of the typological synthesis, we can identify five distinctive claims.

1 The human race can be exhaustively divided into a few discrete subgroups. To say this is to say that all humans fit into one race or another, that race-thinking offers us globally valid classifications, that race is a world-historical affair. (Which is to say, Races are discrete and global.)
2 Each of these smaller groups possesses a unique set of heritable and physiologically specifiable traits, the most striking of which are the

morphological differences in complexion and body shape. (Call this "somatic clustering," or "thin covariation.")

3 These distinctive sets of physiological traits vary with equally distinctive sets of moral, cognitive, and cultural characteristics, which can be inferred from the clusters of physiological traits. (Call this "extra-somatic clustering," or "thick covariation.")

4 The groups defined by these clusters of traits can be ranked along graduated scales of worth and capacity. The values represented on these scales typically include intelligence, beauty, sexual continence, bravery, creativity, individual initiative, degree of civilization, and the like, on the assumption that each race had these qualities to a greater or lesser degree than others. (Call this, well, "ranking.")

5 The features that distinguish these races are passed down as part of a racial essence that shapes the character, conduct, potential, and value of each individual member of each race. (Call this "essentialism," and don't worry if it seems less like a distinct claim and more like a summation of all the others.)

The view from which I've drawn these claims is an ideal type. Different people bought into different aspects of it, and many people, many prominent race theorists, declined to accept one or some of these claims. I nevertheless insist on thinking of the view as a single view because something like it served as a kind of anthropological common sense for the modern West. This version of race-thinking has been central to the institutions that have in turn been central to the formation of the contemporary world. That's what makes it *classical* racialism.

2.4 The challenge of human variation: isn't racial biology false?

What I'm calling "the challenge of human variation" arises from the inadequacies of the classical racialist view. I've borrowed the expression "human variation" from physical anthropologists, who use it to refer to what one studies when one asks "how and why humans differ from each other in their biological makeup."[12] Participants in this area of inquiry have developed new, non-racialist approaches to human biological difference, and have been persuaded to do so by three sorts of problems with classical race-thinking. The problems result from thinking in terms of discrete human types, from insisting on reliably clustered traits, and from relying on pre-modern theories of inheritance.

2.4.1 What's wrong with race

The first problem with classical racialism is its typological bias: it lumps people into putatively distinct categories on the basis of physiological traits that vary continuously. Think of skin color: the modern Races come in four or five hues. But so-called white people range from what we used to call "swarthy" to bronze to alabaster, while so-called black people can range from alabaster to what we used to call "high-yellow" to coal-black. We might plot the range of human complexional variation along a continuum, but race-thinking encourages us to cleave this continuum into a handful of supposedly distinct types. We do this with other aspects of human variation, like height and weight; but we don't pretend that rough categories like "short" and "tall" can do the work – in anatomy, for example, or in scouting for professional basketball teams – that we can get out of more fine-grained measures, like meters and centimeters, inches and feet. Biological race-thinking, with its impressionistic categories, tries to conduct scientific inquiry on the basis of this sort of pretense. (Would you rely on a pediatrician who reported on the growth of your child by saying only *She's pretty tall* or *No, still kind of short*? Or a boss who would tell you only that you've got a fair amount of money coming in your next paycheck? If not, then you understand the physical anthropologist's skepticism.)

Typological race-thinking has at least two more noteworthy, and troubling, consequences for the study of human variation. First, it requires highly tendentious efforts to mark off supposedly distinct segments along the continuum of human diversity. If people range in color from milk-white to coal-black, with all sorts of reds and browns and yellows in between, then someone has to decide where on this subtly variegated scale one human type ends and another begins. And people in different places and times have decided this differently – hardly a firm basis for scientific progress in the study of human variation.

The second troubling consequence of typological race-thinking follows directly from its almost arbitrary classification schemes: it inspires a mode of inquiry that ignores most of the variation in the human species. We're encouraged to disregard the subtle physiological differences that distinguish, say, "swarthy" whites from bronze ones, ebony blacks from "yellow" ones – to say nothing, yet, of all the other traits that these people possess – and we're urged to focus instead on whatever the local scheme of categorization anoints as the important differences between people. It turns out that human beings are more alike than not, and that the relatively few systematic differences there are develop between human groups that are much smaller than our Races. This opens the door to renewed talk of small-r-races, but scientists, to their credit, have mostly abandoned this language as needlessly confusing and emotionally loaded. Instead they prefer to speak simply of populations.[13]

So the first problem is one of arbitrary demarcation: none of the traits that are supposed to distinguish the races allow us to draw bright lines between groups. The second problem is one of illusory consistency: the traits that are supposed to define the races fail to present themselves in reliable clusters. The idea is that this skin color goes with that hair texture and with those facial features, consistently. But racial traits just don't hang together this way. Many dark-skinned people have straight hair, aquiline noses, eyes with pronounced epicanthic folds (that is, "slanted" eyes), or thin lips; and many light-skinned people have full lips, tightly curled hair, and wide noses. And, as is well known, the trait-clusters that are supposed to define the modern Races don't work at all well beyond the context of the North American colonial encounter. Which Race do the indigenous peoples of Australia belong to? Or the darker-skinned residents of South Asia? While the politics of race-thinking required that US policy-makers come up with answers to questions like these, the answers have more to do with the politics of diversity (or of colonial expansion) than with the science of human variation.

A further variation on the unreliable cluster problem has to do with the idea that non-physical traits vary with physical traits. This is the classical principle of "extra-somatic clustering": *this* skin color goes not just with *those* facial features, but also with *that* degree of intelligence, or cultural sophistication, or moral sensibility. The problem, of course, is that there doesn't seem to be any biologically specifiable connection between traits like these and high-profile physiognomic traits like skin color. Each mature human organism turns out the way it does thanks to the complex interplay of innate and environmental factors. This is true even of physical traits like height, and it is especially true of such characteristics as intelligence and cultural taste. Add in the fact that there are live scientific questions about how, and whether, we can define and measure such things as intelligence, and you'll have a clear indication of why the cluster problem almost completely disqualifies classical racialism from the field of scientific inquiry. (Why do I say "almost" completely? Because enough dissent remains to generate controversies like the furor over *The Bell Curve* some years ago and, more recently, over faux-evolutionary psychologist Satoshi Kanazawa's claims – his roundly and swiftly debunked claims – that black women are "objectively the least attractive females of all the races."[14] We will return to both of these.)

The problem of typological thinking and the cluster problem are both problems of description, and they derive, in a way, from an inability to explain how people and human populations come to be as they are. This incapacity reveals the third difficulty with biological race-thinking: it presupposes an archaic conception of inheritance. We still sometimes speak – as I have, self-consciously, in this book – of Native American "blood" or Asian "blood," as if there were some racial essence that we pass on to our children, complete with blueprints for all our race-defining traits. We recognize that these essences can mix, as when people of different races have children (who then become "mixed-bloods"), but the process is still supposed to be pretty straightforward, like diluting a potion. The attempt to turn classical racialism into biological science took this way of speaking seriously, to its detriment. Humans do have blueprints like this, of course, and their blueprints, or genotypes, do mingle in the process of sexual reproduction. But human heredity is much more complicated than the transmission of racial essences. It involves a myriad of genes that work in various combinations, under the influence of environmental factors, to produce the traits that distinguish humans from each other. Biological race-thinking is incapable of providing an adequate scientific account of this complexity.

I'll give a physical anthropologist the last word on the challenge of human variation. Here's what John H. Relethford says in his introduction to biological anthropology:

> Until the 1950s, much of biological anthropology was devoted to racial description and classification. Most sciences go through a descriptive phase, followed later by an explanatory phase. . . . Today biological anthropologists rarely treat race as a [scientifically useful] concept. It has no utility for explanation, and its value for description is limited.[15]

There you have it: race-thinking doesn't explain much, biologically, and it doesn't even describe the world of human variation clearly or well enough to get us asking the right questions. There are still holdouts, as there always are with science. Just as there are still Flat-Earthers, there are still people who insist that the modern West discovered its racial distinctions instead of inventing them, that the human population can be productively divided into racial groups in the way that classical racialism envisioned. But the weight of informed opinion has come down against this conception of race.

So why go on with the argument of this book? If classical racialism is as bad as all that, what else is there to say? The basic reason to go on is that the scientific repudiation of classical racialism didn't lead directly to the abandonment of its social and political uses. The history of race-thinking in the West doesn't end with the development of population genetics, as any student of the Holocaust, urban uprisings, or criminal justice will tell you. There's still a great deal to say about race-thinking as a social and political phenomenon, and I propose to say some of it in the pages to come.

Some of what remains to be said has to do with the development of an anti-racist racialism, driven by the ethical and political struggle against white supremacy. But some of what remains has to do with attempts to create new theories of the social phenomena that classical racialism purported to explain. These alternative theories lead us to the third threshold question that I promised to take up in this chapter.

2.5 The challenge of social differentiation: isn't the race concept just in the way?

I suggested above that classical racialism came to a close in the 1920s, when "common knowledge" about race diverged from the scientific approaches with which it once strove to be in harmony. There's more to say about the stage that begins here and that stretches into the present, but I'll save that for chapter 3. For now it's enough to say that the scientific approach would soon diverge even more sharply from common sense.

Common sense remained largely in lockstep with white supremacist social practice, while "race science" got stretched across two domains and, essentially, fell apart. Physical scientists, aided by the new twentieth-century field of genetics, sought to understand human physical variation without appeal to the race concept. And social scientists increasingly sought to understand human social differentiation without appeal to "natural" predispositions or tendencies. They continued to study race, but under the rubric of race *relations*, focused less on how nature shapes social life than on how certain social groups interact. From this perspective social forces caused the non-physical characteristics, including the differences in social condition, that were supposed to distinguish the races from each other.

Classical race-thinking didn't immediately die out, of course, even when it changed to accommodate the new views. Many theorists, for example, simply transposed the idea of natural inferiority into the idiom of cultural pathology, translating the claim that blacks are naturally inferior into the claim that blacks are culturally retarded, burdened by the slavery experience with inferior ways of life. Despite these atavisms, though, the new sociology and anthropology expanded the conceptual vocabulary available for analyzing "the race problem." Notions like "caste," "class," "nation," "minority," "ethnic group," "prejudice," and "assimilation" became the preferred resources for describing the differences in culture and social condition that earlier theorists had wanted to explain in terms of physiology.

We are the heirs of this social scientific revolution. But now that we've detached the problem of social differentiation, the problem of how we humans sort ourselves into groups and hierarchies, from the question of human biological variation, it may seem that people interested in the conditions of and relations between the groups that we call races ought to avail themselves of alternative notions like caste, ethnicity, and class. More to the point, it may seem that race-thinking points us to the wrong causal factors, thereby frustrating attempts to analyze the social forces that really shape our life chances and experiences. One might think that what's interesting about the black poor is that they're poor, and that it's better to think of the people we call Asians as an assortment of ethnic groups, since they really have quite little in common with each other. In light of considerations like this, what's left for the race concept to do? Does talking about race point us to any domain of social interaction or human experience that these other concepts don't? (Whether there is such a domain and whether we'd find anything if we went there are separate questions. Right now we'll just take up the first one.)

2.5.1 Ethnicity

The notion of ethnicity is a natural enough place to start considering whether the race concept is superfluous, not least because we often act as if "ethnicity" were synonymous with "race." Consider the *Oxford English Dictionary* (*OED*), for example, reporting the most common contemporary definition, such as it is, with all the confusion that it promotes. What does "ethnic" mean? "Pertaining to race," the *OED* says, unhelpfully. Also: "peculiar to a race or nation." And: "pertaining to or having common racial, cultural, religious, or linguistic characteristics, esp. designating a racial or other group within a larger system; hence (US colloq.), foreign, exotic." If ethnicity and race are as close as all that, then this threshold inquiry will be short-lived.

But attending a bit more carefully to the history of ethnicity-talk, and to our current practices, may shed some more light on the distinction in question. US social scientists started talking about ethnic groups in the twenties and thirties, in a couple of ways and for a couple of reasons. First, they started talking about white ethnic groups instead of about white races, to demonstrate their growing sense that intra-white social differences were the result not of biological forces but of social and cultural ones. And second, they continued to use "race" to talk about black–white relations and differences to express the lingering and quite correct sense that 'the Negro Problem' was qualitatively different from the problem of assimilating European ethnics.[16] The difference was in part supposed to be that blacks were still subject to discrimination based on physical difference, while the threat of such discrimination had diminished considerably for Irish, Italian, and Jewish "ethnics" (and others), who remained distinct, if they did, because of cultural differences like language.

So, to start, we can say that "race" points to the body while "ethnicity" points to culture. We can see this pattern affirmed in our common practice, three examples of which I offer below.

Example 1: During the height of the most recent Balkan crisis, we – newscasters, commentators, interested observers – said and heard a great deal about ethnic Albanians. These are people who have cultural and genealogical ties to Albania, but who reside elsewhere.

We don't talk about "racial Albanians," because with the way we use "race," talking that way wouldn't make any sense. Albanians for us are white people, albeit, when they come here, complicated ones – complicated, like they were during the nineteenth-century European migrations, by cultural difference and nationality and class.

Example 2: On February 4th, 1999, four New York City police officers shot an unarmed African immigrant named Amadou Diallo. The officers claimed that they mistook a wallet in Diallo's hand for a gun. Critics charged that, if the officers weren't simply lying, they saw, or "saw," the non-existent gun because Diallo was black, a fact which encouraged them to see him as a threat. This, the critics usually went on to say, was a case of (many things, including) racism.

The tragic Diallo story has the same moral as example 1: the way we use "ethnic," it would be beside the point to focus on Amadou Diallo's ethnic background. He didn't die, on the critics' analysis, because he was Guinean (his country) or Fulani (his culture group).[17] He died because of his race, because people assigned meaning – "dangerous" or "criminal" – to his body. He died, if the critics are right, because he was black. That's why the public outcry focused on racism rather than ethnocentrism. And that's why West African immigrants in the wake of the shooting sometimes said that they were learning what it meant to be black.

Example 3: On the questionnaire for the 2000 US Census tally, there are six racial categories: American Indian or Alaska Native; Asian; Black or African American; Native Hawaiian or Other Pacific Islander; White; and Some Other Race. There are also two ethnic categories: "Hispanic or Latino" and, cleverly, "Not Hispanic or Latino." The federal Office of Management and Budget, which is responsible for explaining how these things work, tells us, "Hispanics and Latinos may be of any race." The questionnaire for the 2010 census, which preserves its predecessor's way of distinguishing race from ethnicity (though it diverges in other ways, about which more anon), makes the point even more explicitly, and more clearly with an eye to the contingencies of history and government practice. "For this census," it explains, "Hispanic origins are not races."[18]

I appeal to the government here not as a final authority but in its sometime role as a codifier of common-sense attitudes (remember the *Thind* case). We think of Latino and Latina people as being united by a common culture, whatever their racial background. The culture in question is quite broad, encompassing Puerto Ricans and Mexicans, Nicaraguans and Dominicans, and more. But we – including many Latinos and Latinas themselves – think of the peoples and nations who remain in the wake of the Iberian colonial excursions into the Americas as united by such things as a common language and religion, by a common relationship to the USA as hemispheric hegemon, and a common experience of blending African, indigenous, and Iberian cultural influences. (I know: they don't all speak Spanish or Portuguese, and they're not all Catholic, especially these days. Hold on.) My sense is that rendering the complexity of Latino/a identity in terms of a bi-racial ethnic group is utterly unsatisfactory, and a symptom of our refusal to countenance the different approach to race-thinking that emerged from the Spanish and Portuguese colonies. But the point just now is, again, Austin's point, enshrined in the Law from chapter 1: we talk about race and ethnicity in ways that presuppose their distinctness, even as we define them, rather half-heartedly, in ways that run them together. I propose to take this distinction seriously.

The idea of ethnicity is of course quite close to the race concept. They share a focus on descent, descent in the case of ethnicity from a member of group that is united by shared cultural characteristics. (This starts us toward an understanding of why someone who doesn't speak Spanish and who isn't terribly invested in the religious customs that her Dominican grandparents brought to the USA can still be a Latina.) And ethnicity easily dovetails with race: it is readily available for racialization. I mean by this that ethnically distinct groups can think of their distinctness from each other in morphological terms. Serbians may insist that Albanians look different, Turks may insist that Kurds look different, Tutsis may insist that Hutus look different, and so on. And if that visible difference is supposed to mean something, such as that the people who look different are worth less and therefore deserving of death, then those ethnic differences and conflicts have been racialized, transformed into racial differences and conflicts – though they do not thereby become Racial differences, appealing to the five or so modern Races.

Just as we can racialize ethnicity, we can, forgive the expression, ethnicize race. People who find themselves in similar social locations on account of appearance and ancestry can come to see themselves as united, and they can create common ways of doing things – that is, a culture. This is what happened to the enslaved Africans who became African Americans, which is one reason that I tend not to use "African

American" and "black" interchangeably, the Office of Management and Budget – the census people – notwithstanding.

Despite these areas of similarity and overlap, the in some ways slender distinction between race and ethnicity is still an important one. As people have often pointed out, it simply isn't the case that all black people, for example, share a common culture. The countries of Africa, to say nothing of the Caribbean and Americas, are full of black people who participate in and are descended from vastly different cultures. The interesting thing about race is that when those people come to the USA, they are all black people, which is to say, we assign a certain meaning to how they look and treat them accordingly. In light of this, and as the first post-classical sociologists saw, there is some value in having a vocabulary for talking about predominantly cultural groupings, bound together by self-consciously shared traditions. And there is value in having a separate vocabulary for talking about populations that are bound together by what their bodies mean, in ways that have little to do with the cultures to which they belong. We tend to talk about race and ethnicity in ways that already suggest this distinction; I'm just urging that we be explicit about it.

Ethnicity, then, is principally about shared culture, and derivatively about "blood" ties. Race, by contrast, is less about culture than, as we've seen, about appearance and ancestry. More precisely, it has to do with how appearance and ancestry, in the right setting, provide entry conditions for certain social locations and certain modes of treatment. We might join certain contemporary theorists in speaking of ethno-racial groupings, as a way of expressing either the substantial empirical overlap between the extensions of "race" and "ethnicity" or the role of culture in shaping racial distinctions. But we should do this while remembering that there is a useful conceptual distinction to draw here: ethnic groups needn't be racialized, and the members of racial populations needn't have ethnic ties to each other. In both cases, they may; but they don't have to.

2.5.2 Nation

Perhaps the easiest notion to take up next is that of nationality. We've already encountered it in the *OED* definition of "ethnicity," as part of the haze of notions that obscures our thinking about social differentiation. Like those other concepts, the nation idea has had its share of confused and imprecise usage. A straightforward way to extricate the idea from those conceptual train wrecks is to think of nations as what communities become when they aspire to self-actualization or autonomy in the political sphere.

The nation idea is a way of thinking about – or, as historian Benedict Anderson puts it, imagining – political community, a way that begins by prizing and often overestimating a kind of basic com-monality.[19] Whether this commonality is "found" in the shared culture of an ethnic group, the shared essence that classical racialists imputed to their races, or somewhere else, the nationalist takes this commonal-ity as the ground for a shared form of life, one that is usually depicted as at least potentially unique and comprehensive, with distinctive and characteristic aspects in every important arena of human endeavor. The nationalist then demands for the participants in her shared form of life some degree of political self-determination – at the upper limit, a state; less ambitiously, representation in the affairs of government. The imperative of self-determination then serves to structure the ethical and social relations of the community. The result is that the nation figures prominently in the individual's ethical deliberations, and the nation's demands at least approximate the authoritative edicts of a sovereign. This is why ethnic Albanians who chafe under Serbian rule in Kosovo become – come to be called, and call themselves – Albanian nationalists, and demand unification with Albania proper.

It may appear that racial distinctions are a function of nationalist politics. For example, people in the United States organize race-based political groups to represent their interests, and this self-organization is a large part of what defines them as groups, to the extent that they are groups. And they've done this largely in response to the white racial nationalism that shaped the USA for so long.

But if nations are communities turned political, then the nation idea stands in much the same relation to race as ethnicity does – overlap-ping but distinguishable. What unites Amadou Diallo to the African-American New Yorkers who protested the acquittal of his killers is not that he saw himself as part of a political unit seeking self-determination. To be sure, the assembled protesters may have had this view, or may have said things that seem to express this view. But the Diallo protesters, most of them, didn't really act much like partici-pants in a nation. They acted more like they believed, to put it crudely, that what happened to Diallo could happen to them, and that they key to preventing it was to get the state – the state more or less as it stood, not a new black state – to do its job. They acted as if convinced that the conditions under which Diallo's physiognomy led to the end of his life are conditions that impact them and their loved ones daily. This complaint about injustice and insecurity doesn't require the ideo-logical or political apparatus of nationalism for its expression.

Since collective responses to perceived assaults almost inevitably take on nationalist contours, let's turn to easier examples than the Diallo case. The realtor who steers white clients away from neighbor-hoods that seem "unsafe" because of their diversity seems not to be engaged in a nationalist project. She doesn't have to be acting from a sense of solidarity to her clients, not least because she can do this, in ways that reinforce informal residential segregation, without being white herself. (Did you assume that she was? This sort of assumption will be of some importance later.) Similarly, think of the gynecologist who unconsciously thinks of endometriosis as a professional woman's disease, and who unconsciously associates professional status, and endometriosis, with whiteness. If she misdiagnoses a black patient's endometriosis as pelvic inflammatory disease, and therefore recommends treatments that are unwarranted and inappropriate, is there any reason to think of this as part of a nationalist project?[20] The nation idea doesn't illuminate these phenomena, but the race concept does. As we saw in the case of Amadou Diallo, here a person's appearance and what her appearance is supposed to say about her mediate her access to social goods like life, competent medical care, and a diverse neighborhood.

2.5.3 Class

Thankfully, the idea of social classes is more straightforward than either ethnicity or nationality. In the sense in which it has meaning for social theorists, class has to do with social and economic status. Following Marx, we might define it in terms of one's relationship to the mode of production: owners of capital belong to one class, while sellers of labor belong to another. In a more casual way, we might define it in terms of income, so that people above a certain benchmark are upper-class, while those farther down are lower class, those in the middle are, of course, middle class, and those at the very bottom, with little hope of rising for reasons that we'd have to argue about, are in the underclass. In any case, class seems to involve one's place in the economic life of society, and the social standing or life-style that attends people in that place.

Many people have become convinced that racial distinctions are, as Immanuel Wallerstein says, "blurred representations" of class distinctions.[21] On this view, "white" and "non-white" represent different collective niches in a global economic order, as evidenced by correlation between race and condition of servitude for enslaved Africans, Asian "coolie" or contract laborers, and Mexican *bracero* workers. Classical racialism then becomes a way of ensuring that certain economic roles get filled, and of justifying particularly exploitative economic relations, and Jim Crow becomes a way of enticing poor whites to throw their lot in with rich whites, to accept an egalitarian distribution of the right to Negro deference in exchange for an inegalitarian distribution of material goods like wealth and land.

There is a great deal to recommend an argument like this. It is, as far as I can tell, quite right. But it doesn't show that we can do away with the notion of race. (Luckily, this isn't Wallerstein's agenda.)

For one thing, every racial group has class stratifications: each one has its rich people, its poor people, its capitalists, laborers, and underemployed. It seems that some class-stratifying mechanism is at work within and across these groups, dividing them internally instead of separating them from each other. Racist practices can certainly result in the concentration of one race or another in particular economic niches. But the people who escape this kind of sorting have become increasingly numerous in recent years, with the growth, for example, of the black and Asian middle and upper classes. And being exempt from economic sorting hasn't exempted these people from racism.

The degree to which the economically privileged remain vulnerable to racist exclusions leads to the second consideration that allows us to distinguish race from class. There are race-stratifying mechanisms at work within classes. This is why black celebrities like Danny Glover used to complain about how difficult it was to get cabs to stop for them in Manhattan, while white celebrities – say, Glover's sometime co-star Mel Gibson – seemed to have no trouble (though Gibson has since had other difficulties, some of them related to his own approach to race-thinking). These complaints are no longer as prominent as they once were, which is surely a sign of progress. But tests for discrimination in housing and employment still produce the same old distressing results. I'm thinking of the sociological experiments that send "applicants" of different races but with identical class profiles – credit rating, education, profession, and so on – to lenders, rental agencies, and potential employers. These people tend to get treated differently: some are received warmly and eagerly, others not so much, and in patterned ways that reflect the same old forms of prejudice. This fact may result in the disproportionate representation of a race in a particular class, but it doesn't obviously follow from any class mechanism. To be simplistic about it: for some anti-black racists, it doesn't matter how much money Jay-Z makes; nor would it matter if, as is pretty likely, he makes more than they do. He will remain inferior and, if he tries to move into the neighborhood, unwelcome.

Someone truly committed to the class approach could press the issue here, of course. The racial phenomena I've been discussing might be instruments that the economic order uses to perpetuate itself, or inessential side effects, cast off by the orderly operation of the system the way cars expel exhaust. For our purposes here, there's no need to pursue the point any farther. Conceding that much autonomy, that large a sphere of independent operation, to the notion of race is enough to do the clarifying work I have in mind for this section. Race-thinking isn't class-thinking, essentially, because the two categories can get out of phase with each other: a race may be divided into many classes, a class may be divided into many races. Class, like ethnicity, can be racialized, as when the callused hands and sun-darkened skin of the worker come to signify rudeness or inferiority. And as the rhetoric and mythology of the black underclass shows, race can be intimately connected to class. But the first point just indicates the importance of detaching the notion of race from its modern manifestations (our Races), and the second just indicates that race and class, and other principles of social differentiation, interpenetrate and intersect. In deference to this fact, and at the urging of sociologist Stuart Hall, scholars now say things like "race is the modality in which class is lived."[22] Even if this is right, as it surely is, it doesn't mean that we can reduce either category to the other. We'll return to this point.

2.5.4 Caste

Caste is another principle of social differentiation that often seems poised to take the place of race. It was especially popular in the middle of the twentieth century, as sociologists of race relations groped for their new theoretical vocabulary. The definitions I've been working with so far have been drawn from other scholars or from my intuitions about common language use, as supplemented by, for example, governmental pronouncements and the *OED*. As social differentiation raises issues of considerable ethical and political importance, it's high time that we bring practitioners into the discussion.

In a report submitted to the UN's 2001 World Conference Against Racism, Racial Discrimination, Xenophobia, and Related Intolerance, researchers for the respected NGO Human Rights Watch (HRW) define caste in ways that clearly connect it to race. They explain that caste is "a system of rigid social stratification into ranked groups defined by descent and occupation." Descent, occupation, stratification: so far, this sounds quite a bit like race. They go on to say that distinctions between castes are often drawn using the rhetoric of "pollution and purity, and filth and cleanliness." This might put one even more in mind of some consequences of race-thinking, especially in the Jim Crow US South. What's behind the determination to prevent people from using the same water fountains, bathrooms, and hospitals, from living in the same neighborhoods and riding in the same vehicles, from sharing the same beds, if not a fear of contamination? The report eventually makes the connection to race perfectly explicit: "Casteism pre-dates racism and is a distinct form of racism." The idea that casteism just is racism seems to have become the standard view in the relevant policy and activist circles. The Durban conference yielded a plan of action that did not refer to caste, but it defined racism broadly enough for a variety of UN bodies – including the committee that monitors compliance with the UN's International Convention on the Elimination of Racial Discrimination (ICERD) – to find that caste does fall under the ICERD's guidelines.[23]

All of these connections aside, though, the HRW report provides the resources for distinguishing caste from race. Drawing from a range of examples, including the Dalits or untouchables of South Asia, the Buraku people of Japan, and the Osu of Nigeria, the report points out that "[l]ower-caste communities are almost invariably indistinguishable in physical appearance from higher-caste communities. . . . [T]he visual cues that otherwise accompany race or ethnicity are often completely lacking." Since I've been insisting that race-thinking has essentially to do with the assignment of meaning to the appearance of the human body, this is enough to mark out the distinctive place of the race concept in the universe of discourse that's defined by the problematic of social differentiation. HRW seems to support this conclusion. The same report that links casteism to racism ends by citing several UN authorities in support of the proposition that caste discrimination is *not* racial discrimination. And a later report co-sponsored by a number of other NGOs accepts this conclusion while trying to reconcile it with the moral authority that an anti-racist stance would confer: "Caste may not be race, but it does not mean that there is no discrimination on this ground."[24] So why, you may ask, all the effort to blur a conceptual line that the UN seems willing to keep distinct? The NGO and social justice communities seems to be locked in a frustrating diplomatic dance with countries like India, whose elites tend to use loopholes in the UN convention to justify their lack of urgency in fighting caste discrimination. *The agreement was about race*, they seem to say, *and we're not racists!* Hence the determination to insist that the ICERD – which was, after all, about racism *and related forms of discrimination* – does cover caste. Had the 2001 Durban conference simply included language on caste, there would be less pressure to subsume this egregious moral evil under a "recognized" form of injustice.

Of course, I've insisted that race-thinking is about appearance *and ancestry*, which may seem to push back in the direction of caste-thinking. The reliance on ancestry makes possible the phenomenon of passing, or of pretending that one doesn't belong to the race that one's background qualifies one for. (I've spoken here of pretending, which presupposes that one really belongs to the race that, as I say, one qualifies for. This is a delicate matter that I'll take up in the next chapter, but for now I request the same courtesy you've been extending to me at various points throughout: allow me to talk, for now, as if races are real, and once we see what's at stake and what the words mean, we can take up the metaphysical question in earnest.) People who pass would be (seen as), say, black, if the world knew what the people themselves know about their ancestry. That's why the voluminous literature on passing, crowned perhaps by Nella Larsen's *Passing* or James Weldon Johnson's *Autobiography of an Ex-Colored Man*, relies so heavily on the trope of a visibly black but long-disclaimed family member or friend returning to threaten the protagonist's secret.

I bring up passing because it presupposes a deeper reality that points back in the direction of caste-thinking. The person who passes is by definition perceptually indistinguishable from the race into which he passes. There are, as far as we know (!), many more people like this who do not pass, who, like the heroine of Mark Twain's *Pudd'nhead Wilson*, remain in their allotted social station and live their lives more or less as society requires. If these people are really indiscernible from the more favored group, then why not think of them as members of a caste?

You should be able to anticipate the shape of my answer by now. It is useful to have distinct vocabularies available to us to serve different purposes, to indicate the different realities that the core uses of these terms denote. Race is principally about appearance, and derivatively about the bloodlines that produce people who, in the general run of things, look a certain way. Caste is principally about hereditary, often occupational hierarchies that are not indexed to the morphology of the body. There are problem cases for both ways of thinking. The race-thinker has to deal with passing, while the caste-thinker has to deal with the distressing, but defensible, overlap between Dalit identity and dark skin. But there's no reason to say that castes can't get racialized, like ethnic groups or classes. And it's easier to say that sort of thing meaningfully after we get clear on the core cases.

2.5.5 Intersecting principles: gender

We've seen that caste, class, nation, and ethnicity can overlap with race. If I'm right, these principles of social differentiation don't occupy the same conceptual space as the race concept. They do, however, interact with it to provide social life with its distinctive textures and formations, its distinctive institutions and practices, beliefs and sensibilities, myths and fears. This fact points us to the field of what people now call intersectionality theory, some versions of which (there are, as you might expect, many approaches) inform much of what follows.[25]

Other principles of social differentiation also interact with the race concept, but without even making any claim to the same conceptual space. For example, no one would conflate the modern Races with gender groups, or insist that mechanisms of gender stratification can explain racial distinctions. But no one should dispute that US ideas about gender and race have developed and still work in close proximity to each other. Before I make more of this point, I'll have to say more about gender.

In speaking of gender I'll have in mind what happens when sex gets assigned a certain meaning. Sex is a matter of physiology, having

to do, for example, with the role that one's body suits one for in reproductive processes, or, alternatively, with having the "right" complement of the relevant chromosomes. (For simplicity's sake, I'll assume
something that some people would demand an argument for, that
there are only two reproductive roles, male and female.) Gender, by
contrast, is a matter of having, or of being supposed or predicted to
have, the social and psychological features – the impulses, the social
role and location – that are appropriate for people of a certain sex.
Maleness means having a certain set of reproductive organs or complement of chromosomes, while masculinity, depending on who's
defining it, means being the breadwinner and not the homemaker,
knowing about cars but not about fashion, preferring the movies that
make you cover your ears (since explosions and gunfire can be loud)
to the ones that make you wipe your eyes.

Ideas about gender, like any ideas, come in varying forms; that's
why I say discussions about gender will proceed differently depending on who's doing the discussing. The description of masculinity that
I gave above, for example, would be acceptable only in a certain
context, in the right period in time, among people in the right class,
belonging to the right race. People who study masculinity and gender
tell me that upper class white men in the nineteenth century, and
working-class black men in the 1940s, and others, aspired to know a
great deal about fashion; some teenage African-American males of my
acquaintance, with their detailed and passionate commitments to
Sean John, Enyce, and other designer labels that have probably superseded the ones I know about, show me that the same is true of them.
And if the statistics about "stay-at-home dads" are reliable, then the
injunction against being the homemaker has become increasingly flexible among middle and upper-middle-class men in recent years.

In light of all this diversity, people who study gender ideals tend
to distinguish between dominant or hegemonic conceptions and
oppositional or marginal conceptions. The dominant conceptions correspond to what we call the mainstream: they flow from our major
media outlets and characterize our culture in the eyes of observers.
Some would argue that the culture industries have developed to a
point at which the mainstream has disappeared, leaving a myriad of
boutique tributaries in its place. I know what might move someone
to argue this point: specialty cable channels, for example, and websites
for every conceivable interest. My sense is that the mainstream is a
little more resilient than that, especially since it's taken to shoring
itself up by congealing into ever larger media empires, synergistic
corporate behemoths that link content providers to multiple distribution outlets. But in any case, the mainstream seems to be alive and
kicking in the area of gender ideals. If you've any doubts about this,
think of the divergent career trajectories that aging actors and actresses

face. Men can still be action heroes and romantic leads well into their sixties – Harrison Ford and Al Pacino come to mind – but until recently only the most exceptional women escaped the oblivion of (the entertainment industry equivalents of) unemployment and underemployment. And often the women who do escape manage it using the same strategy that "personalities" like Paris Hilton and Kim Kardashian ride to fame: by insisting on their sexual allure. Kardashian and Hilton make the point even more clearly, having become famous principally for appearing in "leaked" sex tapes. It would be hard to make up a scenario that proved more clearly that women are still, to some degree, valued largely as sex objects. (Quick: who was the man in the sex tape with Paris Hilton? Why isn't he famous?)

Our mainstream conceptions of masculinity and femininity include ideas and oppositions that ought to be familiar. The elements of this way of thinking have long histories in Western culture, but of varying lengths. Some reach back to antiquity, some just to the nineteenth century. In any case, our social lives and arrangements bear traces, and more than traces, of their influence today. This of course doesn't mean that the perspective they constitute is fair or accurate or that everyone agrees with it. It may not even be consistent or plausible. But here it is: Men are active; women are passive. Men are rational; women are emotional. Women are nurturing; men are competitive. Men protect; women need protection. Men provide; women maintain the provisions. Men have sex; women have sex done to them. And: Women are for show; men are for action.

If you don't think these elements are still at work in the USA (though, of course, not without criticism and resistance), then consider these questions. In the most prominent sports, who are typically the athletes and who are the cheerleaders? How are the cheerleaders dressed? How many women have been elected to the presidency? Or, for that matter, to the Senate? Why is "the nude" in Western visual art almost always female? Why does women's formal wear leave large stretches of flesh exposed, while the masculine analogue provides layer after layer of cover?

Don't get me wrong: I don't mean to suggest that all of these things are necessarily bad, or that there aren't countervailing cultural trends. I'm just trying to provide some cultural background and conceptual detail. I take myself to be describing a sensibility that has encouraged us to create a social world in which women have been systematically subordinated to men. That we've done this should be uncontroversial; the statistics on violence against women and on relative income levels, women to men, attest to that. We'd have to argue about whether that systematic subordination is bad, and whether it should be contested in the ways we've seen over the last century or so. But such arguments would be out of place here. My aim just now is to say enough about gender ideas and relations in the USA to motivate what I plan to say about how gender intersects race.

Focusing on some broad patterns in our mainstream conceptions of gender makes it easy to see the first main point about the intersections of gender and race: Race and gender impact the social world in concert. To borrow and transform the line that we borrowed from Stuart Hall in the discussion of class: race is a mode in which gender is lived, and vice versa. Some examples of cultural trends may make this clearer.

First of all, races have been depicted in gendered terms. The nineteenth-century contests over immigration and imperialism that I mentioned earlier were frequently discussed explicitly in terms of masculine and feminine races. Anglo-Saxons were masculine, assertive but rational, while other races were feminine, either passive like Asians were supposed to be or irrational like blacks.

Secondly, gender ideals have been cast in racialized terms. True femininity, which is to say beauty, delicacy, and desirability to men, became a trait that only white women could possess. This led to several interlocking (quasi-)feminine myths, like those of the hot-blooded Latina, the Asian dragon lady, and the sexually voracious and hyper-fertile black woman. But it also fueled the mythology of the black male rapist, lusting after white women. This led in turn to white men using violence and terror to control the black community and protect "their" white women. In a similar way, true manhood involved access to the woman of one's choice (more or less) and the ability to protect and provide for one's family. On this view, black men in slavery and long after simply couldn't be real men. (The mythology of hypermasculine sexual prowess and appetites might seem to help here, but it didn't; combined with ideas about blacks being like animals, this didn't make black men any better than stud horses.)

Finally, we might build on the point about racialized gender ideals by saying that non-white femininity has been made doubly problematic, as women of color (as we say, as if white isn't a color) find themselves at the bottom of interlocking systems of oppression. The simultaneous operations of white supremacy and of male supremacy leave non-white women in what some refer to as a double bind. For activists this bind takes on a particular form. Nineteenth-century black feminists, for example, watched as their white feminist and male anti-racist colleagues debated whether white women or black men should receive the franchise first. An important anthology of black feminist thought brilliantly summed up this situation in its title: All the women are white, it said, and all the blacks are men.[26]

If the first point is that race and gender (and, by extension, other social categories) impact the social world and our experiences in concert, the second point must be that the impact of race has the potential to overshadow our interest in these other categories. We can see this in the example of non-white women being marginalized in not one but two campaigns for justice. As I've said, the worry with intersecting principles is not that race-thinking points us to irrelevant conditions, or that it's empty. The worry is that unduly focusing on race, or focusing on it in the wrong ways, can induce us to overlook or downplay social conditions that we should attend to. The African-American feminist's concern arises in analogous forms under the other intersecting principles. African-American gay rights activists complain, rightly, that the mainstream civil rights struggle makes heterosexuality compulsory, and that it ignores rampant and virulent homophobia, even in its own ranks. People concerned in a certain way with economic injustice – Marxists, perhaps, proponents of class analysis, in any case – complain that identity politics distracts people from seeking out general solutions to such problems as poverty, homelessness, and inadequate medical coverage, all of which know no race (though they do know some races better than others). And so on, through disability, age, national origin, and other potential grounds for unjust discrimination, mistreatment, or oppression.

The second main point, then, is that race-thinking carries with it the danger of, to borrow and slightly misuse a phrase from K. Anthony Appiah, "going imperial."[27] The idea of race seems inclined to crowd other ideas about social life from the conceptual field. It encourages us to neglect most of the many respects in which people are different or alike, most of the many grounds we've given ourselves for treating them less well than we otherwise might. And this neglect leads to shortsighted analysis, which fails to see or explain important realities, and to irresolute activism, which fails to respond to important injustices.

These are important issues, but ones that we should handle with some care. About the intersections between principles: it is true that race never enters our experience or our thoughts alone; it always works with other principles. Call this "the merger thesis." One traverses the social world as a person of a certain race, gender, age, sexual orientation, disability status, and class (and more), not just as a person of a certain race. And the race concept takes up its characteristic places in our thoughts and our intellectual cultures by triangulation, as it were: by establishing oppositional, parasitic, or symbiotic relationships to other notions. Similarly, about the danger of "going imperial": it is also true that people in the grip of race-thinking have all too often allowed themselves to forget how complex social differentiation is, and how complex people are.

Some people take the merger thesis to entail that we can never separate race from these other principles, which is to say that you always have to talk about all of them together. If that were the right

way to read the normative content of the thesis, then this book would
be colossally misguided. (If you think that, thanks for reading at least
this far.) But this is surely too strong a conclusion to draw. Like race,
solidity never enters our experiences alone. We interact with solid
things. But if I wanted to study the conditions under which solidity
exists, the conditions under which something ceases or starts to be
solid, you'd let me provisionally set aside the dependence of solidity
on solid things. You wouldn't, necessarily, make me examine, say,
chairs and custard (okay, cold custard). You'd let me ascend to the
abstract world of physics, a world denuded of furniture and food-
stuffs and populated only by the particles and forces that arrange
themselves into solids of every sort, as long as I promise to come back
down in due time. If intersectionality in the world of physical properties doesn't entail a version of the merger thesis, then why should it
do so in social theory?

In any case, the problems of ignoring complexity and of disregard-
ing the needs of others are problems that transcend race-thinking. One
of the principal mechanisms of cognition involves the diminution of
complexity: that's what all concepts do. The concept "rock" encourages you to forget, provisionally, about all the respects in which rocks
differ, and to focus on their common, well, rockiness. Keeping this
simplifying mechanism in check is a perennial burden, but one that
we can learn to bear well enough. Still, Race-thinking does present a
somewhat heavier version of the burden, what with its time-honored
stereotypes and socially sanctioned oversights. So we can start to
interpret the merger thesis correctly by thinking of it as a reminder to
be careful, to keep watch over our simplifying impulses in a particularly problematic sphere.

In addition to reminding us of the complexity of social life and
history, and of the hazards of unchecked abstraction, the merger thesis
also reminds us to take care in balancing our needs, desires, and
dearly held causes against those of others. Having to find this balance
is another perennial burden of human experience and social life. And
it's one we bear with the help of notions like justice, fairness, and
equity, along with the social and moral sanctions that we deploy in
support of them. The normative side of the thesis, I think, is a reminder
that we have to remain particularly alert to the possibilities of giving
short shrift to perpetually disfavored groups, and of forgetting the
degree to which social categories are bound up with each other. Just
as feminists working in or in the wake of a white supremacist culture
have to be reminded that some women are not white, anti-racist activists in or in the wake of a male supremacist culture have to be reminded
that not all victims of racism are men. These systems of oppression,
like others, operate in part by breeding myopia; so think of the merger
thesis as a corrective lens.

2.6 Conclusion

With that we can conclude our study of the three threshold challenges to the philosophy of race. We saw first that the danger of racism needn't lead to a moratorium on race theory. Then we saw that the failure of racial biology doesn't end the history of race-thinking, and so shouldn't end the theory of race-thinking. Then we saw that "race" still occupies a distinctive conceptual role among social theoretic concepts like caste, class, gender, and nation. While exploring this last challenge we saw further that we can specify the role that "race" plays in only the most abstract and provisional ways, or in quite misleading and inadequate ones, if we do not connect it to the other categories – or as I've sometimes said, the other principles of social differentiation – with which it conspires to produce our social world. Much of this book aims for just such an abstract and provisional discussion of race, but much of it also aims to ground this abstraction in some more concrete considerations. In deference to this aspiration to concreteness, I'll begin the next chapter by reviving the historical narrative that I've woven into the argument of this chapter.

The historical narrative provided a quick chronicle of modern race-thinking, one that focused on the West and on the English colonies that became the United States. The story unfolded in two stages, and each stage had its own temporal (and heuristic) signposts: the early modern era begins in 1492, and the classical or high modern period begins in 1786. Telling this story highlighted a number of historical, cultural, and conceptual details, and prepared us to consider the five basic claims of classical racialism. We touched on the mutability of racial categories, especially as this impacted the history of whiteness. We considered the etymologies of "race" and "ethnicity," and the connection between race, immigration, and US law. And, while discussing the threshold questions, we encountered phenomena like passing, the racialization of gender, and racial profiling by the police. Many of these phenomena and details will return in later chapters; that was, in fact, the main reason for introducing them early on. But first, in the next chapter, we have to take up the metaphysical questions that race-thinking generates.

3

What Races Are: The Metaphysics of Critical Race Theory

Prologue

"You may be interested to know that we don't exist," JJ says.

"Speak for yourself."

"No, I speak for both of us, and for everyone who thinks of himself or herself as a race person."

"A race person?"

"You know, a race man or a race woman, like they used to say back in the day. Someone who tries to work for the good of their race. Like my friend Lisa, who's got me thinking about all this. Earlier today she helped put on a memorial rally for the victims of violent hate crimes. She read this beautiful poem about Vincent Chin. You shoulda been there."

"Vincent Chin?"

"You know. The Chinese-American brother who got killed in 1980, beaten to death by some unemployed autoworkers. They blamed the Japanese for their troubles – you know how it was then: 'Toyota and Suzuki are taking over,' 'the Japanese are gonna own the whole country soon,' and like that – and Brother Chin was in the wrong place at the wrong time."

"I thought you said he was Chinese."

"I did. He was. Chinese American. But he looked Asian, and that was close enough. You know how people do: all black folk look alike, all Asians look alike. Anyway, so after Lisa reads her poem, she comes back to where I'm standing and I tell her it's a wonderful thing, this race work she's doing – she's Japanese, by the way. Of course, she doesn't see it this way. She says, 'It's not race work. It's justice work. There aren't any races, and people thinking there are is what got Vincent Chin killed. No good can come from that kind of thinking.'"

"She's not alone in thinking that way," I say.

"All them people that killed themselves at Jonestown weren't alone either. You can be wrong, and crazy as hell, with all kinds of company. So to impress upon her the magnitude of her wrongness, I say, 'What are you talking about? Thinking about race has been indispensable to me. Knowing I'm a black man keeps me sane. I don't expect cabs to pick me up, and I don't expect good service in restaurants. On the other hand, I do expect salespeople to follow me around in stores, and I do expect the police to bother me for no reason. So you see, I am always prepared. Emotionally and practically.'"

"Sounds like a pretty bleak way to live, if you ask me. Always expecting the worst."

"Who asked you? And I'd rather live bleakly than foolishly. What did that comedian say after Amadou Diallo got shot? If he ever dropped his wallet in front of a New York police officer, he wouldn't even pick it up. He'd just keep his hands up and kick the wallet in front of him till he got home."

"You shouldn't joke about that."

"Aw, lighten up. That's the only way black folks have gotten by: laughing when we ought to cry. Not just black folks, either. Everyone, from black to brown, red, white, and yellow. Read some Chekhov sometime. *The Cherry Orchard*."

"You're changing the subject, and you're forgetting Lisa's point. You're not really black, was her point. And she isn't yellow, and so on. There aren't any races, biologically."

"So I'm brown, not black. And a rubber chicken consists of exactly 100 percent rubber, and 0 percent chicken. Should we call it something else? Don't take things so literally. And who's talking about biology? I'm talking about how we live, and how we talk about how we live. You know very well who and what I mean when I talk about black folk."

"I know what you mean, but I don't think the words you use are the best vehicles for that meaning."

"I ain't talking about vehicles, either. I'm talking about what everyone means – everyone I know, anyway – when they talk about race. Maybe you don't know what we mean. Or maybe you know a better way to put it. But previous to today you and I have talked about it plenty without you gumming up the works like this. I think you're just being difficult."

"One of us is, surely."

3.1 Introduction

The previous chapter argued that there is still some work for race-thinking to do, still a conceptual role for the race concept to play, even in the face of various threshold questions. The principal burden of this chapter is to consider three additional questions. First: does the race concept's distinctive notional space correspond to anything in the real

– that is, the not-merely notional – world? Second: does it relate to its real counterparts in a way that makes it worthwhile for us to keep using it? And third: if it doesn't correspond to anything, what are we doing when we talk about it?

Answering these questions will mean leaving the domain of racial discourse, where we've spent the bulk of the preceding pages, and entering the domain of racial metaphysics and ontology. (I'll act for now as if "ontology" and "metaphysics" are synonyms. They're not, but that fact doesn't have to concern us.) We've seen what "race" denotes: a cohort of human individuals whose bodies and bloodlines are meaningful in ways that mark these individuals off as a set. And we've seen how the race concept is distinct from but connected to other principles of social differentiation, like gender, ethnicity, and class. Those were conclusions about kinds of discourse, principally about the kind that we've been calling race-thinking. Now we'll need to draw conclusions about the nature of things; we'll need to explore the puzzles not of race-related words or concepts but of the things that these words and concepts point us to.

If we're to talk about what, if anything, "race" points to in the real world, or about what we're doing when we act as if it does, it's important to see what sorts of things are out there for it to point to, and what the real world is like in the respects that we think of as racial. So let's begin by considering the contemporary racial situation. We can do this in two steps. First we'll pick up the brief history of Western racial projects where we left off in chapter 2, tracking the semantic and the structural developments in race-thinking as it adjusts to the collapse of classical racialism. Then we'll quickly explore some indicators of racial stratification in the USA. At that point we'll be in a position to ask what race can be, and whether the successor subjects to classical race theory, call these critical race theories, have any need of metaphysics.

3.2 After classical racialism: late-modern racialism

So far we've tracked the development of Western race-thinking through its early and high modern stages, in addition to the pre-history that we covered in chapter 1. During these periods a white supremacist social order established itself, which is to say that numerous political communities organized themselves in accordance with principles and assumptions that were widely shared throughout the modern world, in light of which these communities constitute the single, transnational social formation that some refer to as white supremacy. After its establishment, white supremacy refined its methods and spread its influence, despite various voices and traditions of dissent. The dissenters, like Bishop Las Casas, Ida B. Wells, and the Quaker abolitionists, grew louder and more numerous over the years; and the contradictions of political racism helped bring on large-scale crises like the US Civil War. But white supremacy didn't go on the defensive until the onset of late-modern racialism, when anti-racism started to carry the day.

Like the other stages, late-modern racialism has its distinctive sign-post and watershed moments, each of which helps to illuminate a distinctive interpretation of "race" and a particular social structure (see table 3.1). Treating this period as a unitary racial project, we can say that its social structure – its framework for distributing social goods along racial lines – involved a partial and ambivalent repudiation of race-thinking. Its semantic content – its way of interpreting the race concept – came from insisting that race was a sociopolitical product rather than a biological type or a natural-historical "variety." And we can sum up its ideological work by saying that by politicizing difference, instead of naturalizing or rationalizing it in the manner of earlier periods, it widened the conceptual space for rejecting the thought that racial difference and social inequality must necessarily and automatically be linked.

We've already encountered the temporal signpost for this era. In 1923, with the *Thind* case, the US Supreme Court distanced itself from scientific racialism and anchored white supremacy to the common understanding of the "average white American." This rift would only widen at first, as the new science of genetics and the newly independent social sciences continued to question classical race theory, and as "common understandings" remained bound by colonial and Jim Crow sensibilities. But mid-century developments reconciled science and common sense – and helped bring about the decline of classical racialism.

First the horrific results of Nazi racism in World War II became clear. In the minds of many, the Holocaust provided a tragically clear *reductio ad absurdum* of common understandings about race. (The principal immediate result was the acceptance of formerly problematic whites like Eastern European Jews, as we can see from the glacial pace at which the USA repudiated its internment camps and Jim Crow institutions. But even so.) Then, in 1951, mainstream science spoke with one authoritative, anti-racist voice. The United Nations Educational, Scientific, and Cultural Organization (UNESCO) published the *Statement by Experts on Race Problems*. This was the first high-profile, international statement of the view that classical racialism is false – and false as a matter of science, as determined by a gathering of recognized authorities.[1] The experts agreed that studying racial physiology fails to illuminate much of anything, including culture and psychology, which, along with political and economic relations, were

Table 3.1 The stages of modern racialism, continued, 1923–2011

	Signpost	Additional watershed moments	Structural content (racialized distributive framework)	Semantic content (interpretation of race concept)	Ideological work
Early modern	Columbus, *Reconquista*, and expulsion (1492)	Bernier (1684) VA assembly (1660)	Colonies and slavery	Race as variety (monogenist synthesis)	Naturalizes difference
High modern (Classical)	Jefferson's suspicions, (1786)	*Crania Americana* (1839) US annexes Hawai'i (1899)	Comprehensive racist domination	Race as type (typological synthesis)	Rationalizes difference
Late modern	*US v. Thind* (1923)	UNESCO report (1951) Civil Rights legislation (mid-1960s) Moynihan Report (1965)	Partial repudiation of racial stratification	Race as social product (social science revolution)	Politicizes difference
Post-modern	Reagan in Mississippi (1980)	9/11 aftermath Obama's election (2008)	Hegemony replaces domination	Race as aesthetic–cultural phenomenon	Flattens and fetishizes difference, obscures stratification

causes rather than effects of allegedly racial distinctions. They effectively reinterpreted race as a social product, politicizing difference instead of naturalizing or rationalizing it; and they promulgated this new perspective through sustained argument and through educational materials like textbooks. Very soon, the average white person's common understanding of race would bear little resemblance to its analogue in 1923.

The decline of classical racialism was even more evident in the structure of social life. Western nations gave up their colonies, mostly. Racialized schemes of labor exploitation, like sharecropping and contract labor, diminished in significance. Apartheid-style systems fell out of favor (except in the place that gave us the word, which chose just this moment to up the ante on white supremacy), as states eliminated *de jure* racial restrictions on immigration, naturalization, suffrage, mobility, property rights, employment, intimate affairs (like marriage), and more. And Western civil society uniformly began to frown upon private acts of racism.

In addition to these developments, global civil and political society began to celebrate the differences that white supremacy once demonized. A trickle of non-white people had almost always been able to win the admiration of the Europe-dominated world. Some did so for reasons we can now celebrate, like the great abolitionist Frederick Douglass. Others did so for reasons we should now lament, like Sara Baartman, better known as the "Hottentot Venus." But the late-modern period turned this trickle into a stream, if not quite into the flood we see now. From Louis Armstrong and Josephine Baker to James Baldwin and James Brown, black individuals and practices became more widely accepted and admired. Like these cultural icons, non-white political activists gained greater world recognition, from Gandhi and Nehru to W. E. B. Du Bois and Mary McLeod Bethune. At the same time, non-white identities became widespread instruments for political and cultural mobilization,as we can see from the emergence of race-based, pan-ethnic organizations like the Black Panthers, Yellow Seeds, and Brown Berets in the USA.

We could symbolize these developments with any number of watershed moments between the 1920s and 1980: India's independence from Great Britain in 1947; Australia's repeal of its Aboriginal "Protection" Acts by 1977; even the increasing visibility of South Africa's liberation movements after the Soweto uprising in 1976. But let's settle on the 1960s, during which most of Africa won its independence from Europe's former colonial powers. Let's focus further on the USA, where the Civil Rights Act of 1964, the Voting Rights Act of 1965, the immigration reforms of 1965, and the Indian Civil Rights Act of 1968 collectively disassembled US mechanisms of state-sponsored discrimination. These events not only symbolize the emancipations of late-modern racialism, they also register the work of one of recent history's most important and influential liberation programs, the US Civil Rights Movement.

The fight for civil rights is important here for three reasons. First, it reminds us of the bottom-up nature of emancipatory social change. The USA changed because some of its citizens forced it to. They did this not by taking up arms, though the thought that some might turn to violence gave the demands of the non-violent some added weight. Instead they marched and boycotted and conducted sit-ins – "occupied", we now say – and more, and were able to do all of these things because they cultivated and exercised the capacity for democratic mobilization.

The second reason to focus on the civil rights struggle has to do with the uneven legacy of that struggle. It did help bring about real change. But it also seems to have left untouched many of the conditions that many people in the struggle thought they were working to change. I'll offer more detail on this point in the next section. For now, suffice it to say that in a variety of ways, across a variety of measures of socioeconomic status, black and brown people still fare much less well overall than similarly situated whites. And they are still subject to certain indignities and harms – like being arrested or surveilled on the suspicion of being an illegal immigrant or a drug dealer – at much higher rates than their white peers. Or: the number of black elected officials in the USA grew from just over 100 in 1964 to just under 10,000 in 2006. But those 10,000 represent less than two percent of all elected officials – blacks make up around thirteen percent of the population – and, according to the source for this information, are concentrated in "the middle and bottom rungs of . . . government."[2]

The final reason to focus on the civil rights era has to do with some of the reasons for its spotty success. I mentioned above that the movement's democratic revolution created change from the bottom up. But there was also a top-down and less heartwarming aspect to this process. The USA *agreed* to change, and thereby insulated itself from additional, more revolutionary pressures. As Howard Winant puts it, the racial order shifted from domination to hegemony. White supremacy was politically dominant when it subordinated non-whites principally through sheer force. But after the late-modern period, direct coercion declined in importance relative to other mechanisms for maintaining racial hierarchies.

However, in invoking Winant's formulation I've gotten a bit ahead of myself. For people interested in what we can loosely call "racial justice," the middle 1960s were heady times. Political authorities had removed the most obvious formal obstacles to racial justice, and (some) epistemic and moral authorities had repudiated the most damaging metaphysical and moral commitments. Nevertheless, the impact of race-based expropriation and exploitation had distorted social opportunity structures in ways that would take years of concerted effort to correct – assuming there was sufficient political will to make and sustain the effort. In all these ways, racial justice was a live possibility for the first time in 500 years, but it remained precarious and unconsolidated.

The forces rather hesitantly set in motion during the late-modern period turn to egalitarianism developed into a more definite form by the 1980s. But one of the clearest keys to this shift in the USA, and the last watershed moment I'll invoke for the late-modern era, appeared much earlier, during the headiest moment of the egalitarian turn.

In 1965, a minor official in the US federal government named Daniel Moynihan wrote a report that quickly came to bear his name, but was eventually published as *The Negro Family: The Case for National Action*. The Moynihan Report traced persistent racial inequality to a "tangle" of black cultural "pathologies" – female-headed households, criminality, and dependency – rooted in the slavery experience. The report did discuss other factors, including the effect of high unemployment on the marriage prospects of black men. But Moynihan's willingness to explain racial stratification by appeal to culture got the most attention. Critics pounced on it for suggesting, as contemporary political scientist Adolph Reed puts it, "that persisting racial inequality in income, employment, occupation, and education was most crucially attributable to aspects of black culture . . . that under-cut development of the values and dispositions required for success."[3] Meanwhile, more sympathetic readers embraced the report, and enshrined it in the conventional wisdom of the policy elites that were its main audience, because of this same suggestion.

The Moynihan Report serves as a useful marker of the moment not because the denigration of non-white cultures was new – it wasn't – and not because its author, who would go on to become a respected US senator, was a racist – he probably wasn't, in any interesting sense. But the Moynihan Report marked the renewal of this mode of racist denigration for an era that had formally repudiated racism and racial explanations. In previous eras one could confidently claim that *these people are naturally inferior, and the proof lies both in their cultural backwardness and in their social, economic, and political weakness*. After the Moynihan Report – or, better, after the idea that the report is taken to stand for, which may or may not be what the report is – the claim could be more concise, though only a little less indifferent to the complex reality of the situation: *these people are weak (or poor, or unhealthy, or, or) because of their culture*. It was a short step from here to the thought that British analysts began calling "the new racism" during the era dominated by Prime Minister Margaret Thatcher: *if we shun them, or exclude them, or whatever, it's not because of their race: it's because of their culture.*

3.3 And after that: post-modern racialism

The thought that racial stratification has more to do with culture rather than with history or with still-distorted distributive mechanisms points us to the semantic and structural content for the period of post-modern racialism. During this period, we read race not as a social artifact but as a cultural phenomenon. We are in fact encouraged to dissolve it into discussions of culture, in ways I'll come back to. At the same time, we continue to distribute social goods along racial lines but with much less reliance on direct domination, and while denying that this is what is happening. In light of this, we can say that the distinctive ideological work of this moment veers even farther away from the determination to naturalize or rationalize difference that we saw in the early and high modern periods. Post-modern racialism even refuses to politicize race in the late-modern way, whether by expressly challenging the links between racial difference and social stratification or by mobilizing around race to mount such a challenge. Post-modernism here involves *flattening* difference, insisting on the unity of the human family and the declining significance of race, in ways that *obscure* the way various stratifying mechanisms continue to do their work.

Winant's idea of the shift from domination to hegemony will help flesh out this non-racial – post-racial, some would now say – racialism. As we noted above, the gains of the late-modern period were real and important. And to say, as I did above, that racial orders during this period – colonial empires, apartheid states – agreed to change is not to deny that some of the change from "above" proceeded in many ways from genuine moral convictions. There was a long history of white unease with white supremacy, and there were firmly established multi-racial traditions of resistance and anti-racist advocacy. Emancipation happened in part because these traditions and sentiments began to win out. But there was something else at work, too. Political communities established on white supremacist grounds sought to minimize the costs of maintaining themselves, by accommodating and co-opting resistance before it became too troublesome. This accommodation and co-optation signified the shift from domination, or rule by force, to hegemony, or, crudely, rule by consent.

If this sounds overly conspiratorial, rest assured that I don't need to posit "the Man" and his cronies in a smoky room making all this happen. I'm not thinking here of the self-conscious and unified mode of acquiring and wielding influence deployed by kings and queens. The point is just that where modern racial domination privileged whites through coercion, forcibly extracting labor, land, sexual access, and more from non-whites, modern racial hegemony privileges whites in other ways, using social reform to accommodate pressures that would otherwise disrupt the arrangements that ensure existing privileges.

If it *still* sounds conspiratorial, remember that social formations are like systems in stable equilibrium: their large-scale properties tend not to change over time, which is to say that if you subject them to pressure, they will right themselves in ways that maintain a steady state of the overall structure. (Think of a pendulum: you push it, and it eventually ends up back where it started. Now think of politics, where established, advantaged interests can insist on policies that work to their advantage.) The social systems we're considering were subject to many pressures. Some were psychological, involving the cognitive and moral dissonance of, for example, lionizing Martin Luther King, Jr while supporting apartheid South Africa. Some were material, involving the expense of, say, maintaining a colonial occupation force. Eventually these pressures combined with genuine moral convictions to motivate policies of accommodation, at which point the disequilibrating forces – moral criticism, military expenditures, and so on – diminished, allowing the existing patterns of privilege to remain more or less in place.

You might be wondering: What does it mean to say that rule by *consent* enabled all this to happen? And having detailed the emancipatory shifts of this era, how can I say that patterns of privilege remained even more or less in place?

The shift from force to consent means that what might have been or become dissent gets incorporated into the status quo, like this: Civil rights workers become legislators, eager to improve the lot of their disadvantaged cohort; but where they once planned to alter the relevant institutions, perhaps by abolishing them, they instead plan to manipulate the institutions, which is to say, to leave them intact. They come to identify the interests of their constituents, and their own interests as politicians, with the interests of the social order they once sought to change. Similarly, these legislators' constituents come to think of *their* interests in terms provided by the status quo. That is: the demand for racial justice can shrink to the desire for individual fulfillment, because racial justice is, at bottom (we are invited to think), about creating the conditions for every individual to be fulfilled.

This is how hegemony works. A hegemonic formation – the alliance between ruler and ruled that makes control without forcible coercion possible – encourages the disadvantaged to see themselves as stakeholders in the system that generates their disadvantage. It does this

in part by granting concessions to them, thereby winning their consent
to the system's continuation, and in part by getting them to accept a
description of the system that justifies or obscures their disadvantage.
Anti-colonial theorists like Amilcar Cabral and Frantz Fanon refer in
this spirit to comprador elites, by which they mean, to put it crudely,
post-colonial leaders who care less about the liberated ex-colonists
than about serving as local or "native" intermediaries on behalf of a
political system still shaped by and orbiting around the old colonial
metropole. And liberation theorists like Steve Biko explore in this
spirit the "colonized mind" – the capture of the oppressed person's
very consciousness by the forces that oppress him or her.

Of course, rule by consent is not in itself a bad thing. We might use
those words in a passable definition of democracy. The problem with
racial hegemony is that rule by consent *replaces* a system of domination, and enables that system to maintain many of its distinctive features. And this is why I can recognize the post-war trend toward racial
emancipation while also saying that patterns of privilege remain in
place.

Remember, one of the signs of white supremacy's decline was the
end of colonialism. But many places, like Puerto Rico, remain colonies
in fact if not in name, locked in quasi-colonial relations with their
former rulers. Places like the USA constitute the core of the global
system of political economy, while places like, say, Jamaica, constitute
a dependent periphery. (This core-periphery language is somewhat
misleading, as the "peripheral" nations are and have been essential to
the modern global economy, and as this periphery includes "white"
countries, for example in Eastern Europe. Clarifying the language in
this way makes it less likely to mislead, though, so I'll stick with it,
with the reminder that non-white countries disproportionately constitute the periphery.) At the periphery, livelihoods depend on goods,
tourists, and relocated low-wage jobs from the core, or on migrating
to the core to make money, often to send back home. This sort of
migration escalated during the post-war era, for reasons and with
consequences that put this and the other signs of decline in a different
light.

The movement of laborers from periphery to core, like the movement of factories in the other direction, signifies that people of color
are still over-represented in the West's global pool of cheap, mobile
labor. Illegal "guest worker" arrangements – officially proscribed but
unofficially given wide latitude – continue to pull workers into the
core, plugging them into undesirable jobs at undesirable wages while
denying them decent working conditions and political representation.
Of course, many workers come legally, many get good jobs, and many
become citizens. Many, in fact, start out as citizens, as subjects of the
ex-empire. But many of these continue to suffer demonization as

unalterably foreign, as we'll soon consider. At the same time, peripheral governments in the grip of neo-liberal economic plans tout their
non-existent labor protections and minimal environmental regula-
tions in the effort to attract low-wage, low-skilled, often dangerous
jobs. These jobs may be better than no jobs at all, though it isn't
obvious that sweatshops and unemployment are really the only
options. But I'll take no position on that. The point here is just that the
interdependence of the global economy makes different countries differently dependent. Some prosper, by marking up low-cost manufac-
tured goods and getting a tidy profit, while others just struggle along,
if that. This asymmetry effectively tracks the old asymmetries of the
colonial era.

The decline of colonialism seems even more overrated when we
move from economic to political causes of migration. Think of
Guatemala, and of the CIA-sponsored coup in 1954 that removed a
democratically elected leader, installed a military dictator, and
spawned a rebel movement. This led in turn to a brutal counter-
insurgency campaign, which led in turn to a wave of refugees making
their way to the USA. This pattern iterated elsewhere in Central
America, as well as in Southeast Asia and the Caribbean. No wonder
then that the US foreign-born population increased one hundred and
sixty-eight percent between 1970 and 1997, with about three-fourths
of the new residents coming from Latin America and Asia, and that
by 2010 over half of the foreign-born US population was from Latin
America and the Caribbean, while another 28 percent came from
Asia.[4] The core countries can make and enforce political decisions
about the black, brown, and yellow periphery, effectively annulling
democratic procedures, limiting prospects for self-determination, and
making life unbearable. That sounds a great deal like colonialism –
though to be precise, we might call it imperialism.

Jamaican poet Louise Bennett refers to the migrations we're considering as colonization in reverse, a phrase that brilliantly captures
certain post-colonial anxieties at the core.[5] These anxieties – about lost
jobs, and stretched-thin public resources, and being culturally overrun
– have helped revive racism as a political and cultural force. And this
revival, like the persistence of neo-colonial relations among states,
complicates the idea of late-modern racialism as a period of seamless
progress toward racial justice.

For example, many new immigrants arrived in Western Europe
after World War II, often, like Jamaicans in the UK or Algerians in
France, claiming their rights as citizens. In response, far-right extrem-
ism emerged from its post-war hibernation, supplementing its traditional anti-Semitism (in some ways rendered moot by the terrible
efficiency of the Holocaust and by the Israeli Law of Return) with anti-
African, anti-Arab, and general anti-immigrant prejudices. Mainstream

politicians have lurched rightward to keep up with this development, and now liberals and conservatives alike recycle familiar accounts of racial perils – disease, disorder, dependency, crime, cultural dissolution, and so on – in public policy arguments.

This *nativist* approach to difference – objecting to an internal population on account of its foreign racial connections[6] – is not the nineteenth century's classical racism. Instead of arguing that the unwanted races are inferior, it insists just that the alien peoples are different, perhaps irremediably so, and that a community has the right to exclude those who don't fit into its form of life. This is still a kind of racism, though, principally because it assumes that we can know who will and won't fit in, and, by extension, whom to include fully in the life of society and whom to disregard, just by looking. But it is, as some people call it, a new racism, a "post-racist" racism that denies itself recourse to claims about racial biology and hierarchies, and that often cloaks itself in neutral or even anti-racist language.

The phenomenon of coded or neutral appeals to racist sentiments brings us, finally, to the moment that I take as the opening signpost for post-modern racialism. In 1980, Ronald Reagan gave a campaign speech in Philadelphia, Mississippi, a town made famous by the abduction and murder of three civil rights workers only sixteen years earlier. At their trial, the murderers invoked a familiar justification for the peculiar institutions of southern white supremacy: they declared their support for states' rights. During his speech, Ronald Reagan also announced his support for states' rights, in what was widely perceived as a roundabout endorsement of the "peculiar institutions," or of the attitudes behind them. When Reagan's opponent, Jimmy Carter, gave voice to this widely held perception, Reagan accused *him* of race-baiting.[7]

Reagan's coded appeal effectively encapsulates the ideological key to postmodern racialism: establishing colorblindness as a political norm. This has two important consequences. First, superficial neutrality becomes an art form. Since overt racism is off-limits, coded appeals become quite useful, as does the pursuit of neutral goals with racially asymmetric policies (like shrinking government by cutting the budget for anti-discrimination enforcement). Second, the legacy of emancipatory struggle gets turned into a standing rebuke to any kind of race-consciousness – where "race-consciousness" is expanded to include ostensibly ameliorative policies, like affirmative action, as well as attempts, like Carter's, to criticize racism.

There's much more to say about colorblindness, and we'll get to some of it in later chapters. In advance of that, one parting thought is worth mentioning now. To speak of colorblindness is a trifle misleading, though it does track common usage. Post-modern racialism doesn't so much ask us to ignore race completely as to ignore what actually makes race matter. What we usually call "race" tracks a variety of patterns of advantage and disadvantage, but we're supposed to ignore these connections and think of race only as an aesthetic and cultural phenomenon. So we become multiculturalists, eager to celebrate different foods and holidays and dances, while we also become, in effect, anti-anti-racists, for whom the mere mention of race in ethics and politics is anathema.

There's also more to say about post-modern racialism, beginning with why I've given it that name. It will be easier to say most of what needs saying once we finish taking account of the racial order that modernity has left us – which is to say, after the next couple of chapters. I can say now, though, that the need to defer this discussion is itself a reason to invoke the idea of post-modernity in this context. Part of what it is to be post-modern, or, for that matter, to be post-anything, if the "post-" is used in a philosophical sense, is to stand in an ambivalent relationship to the past that shaped you and to the future that opens uncertainly onto the horizon. Crudely: we say we're post-something when we know where we've come from and we don't much like it, but we aren't quite sure yet where we're headed, or whether there's any "there" to head toward. Post-modern racialism involves, among other things, rejecting racialism while still being shaped by it, and embracing to some degree a world in which racial meanings are at best unstable. Once we're through the next two chapters, which should help clarify what this shaping amounts to and just what stable meanings we can expect it to yield, we can discuss what might be the clearest markers of the post-modern moment: the politics of immigration and the election of Barack Obama.

3.4 The US racial terrain today

One moral of the foregoing is that modern racialism has changed considerably but not fundamentally. Of course there have been real changes. It is not insignificant that the head of the UN at the dawn of the twenty-first century was a black African, or that the President of the United States at the close of that century's first decade is the son of a black African, or that this president has appointed the first Latina to sit on his nation's highest court. These changes notwithstanding, there are plenty of ways in which race still tracks advantage and disadvantage, and does so in the West in fairly familiar ways. (The story would be even more sobering if there were more space to explore racial projects that don't obviously track the old classical dynamics. I'm thinking of the racialization of Palestinians by Israelis, of Kurds by Turks, of Romani by Czechs and the French, of Hutus by Tutsis, and of the Ainu by the Japanese.)

In advance of the metaphysical arguments to come in this chapter, it will be useful to consider more carefully the correlations between race and social location. The different metaphysical pictures we'll soon consider are essentially philosophical snapshots of our current conditions. And since philosophic snapshots are less transparently about their subjects than photographic snapshots are, it will help to say in advance what these pictures are pictures of. Or: the populations that we think of as races tend to have very different life chances, and this may have some bearing on the metaphysical conclusions we draw. To ask about current racial conditions is to ask quite broad questions, which means that we should impose limits where we can. So I'll focus on a single specific and exemplary sociohistorical context – the contemporary United States.

Questions about racial conditions can be answered from many different perspectives, and by appeal to many different measures. But from most perspectives, US society still has at least the look of a place shaped by white supremacy. We still routinely think in terms of the four or five color-coded modern Races – brown, black, red, white, and yellow – and our statistics for income, wealth, poverty, and more depict a society in which these "colored" groups occupy quite different socioeconomic locations. Whites remain at the top, blacks, Hispanics, and Native Americans remain at or near the bottom, and Asians fall somewhere in between. (But do Hispanics, or Latinos and Latinas, count as a race? We'll come back to this in chapter 4.)

Consider that for the year 2006, 8 percent of whites fell below the poverty line, compared to 10 percent of Asians and over 20 percent of Latinos, African Americans, and Native Americans. Or that the three-year average rate of people without health insurance (measured over a three-year period for statistical reasons related to the small sample size of the populations) between 2004 and 2006 was 11 percent for non-Hispanic whites, 16 percent for Asians, 19 percent for blacks, 31 percent for American Indians and Alaska Natives (AIANs), and 32 percent for people of Hispanic origin. Or that in 2010, the median income for white households was over $55,000, while the figure was higher for Asian households (around $66,500) and much lower for Latinos (nearly $39,000), blacks ($33,000), and Native Americans ($35,000). (The numbers for the AIAN group are misleadingly rosy, in part because of changes in the way the Census Bureau gathered and presented the data between the 2000 and 2010 surveys. One thing to keep in mind: historical trends suggest that indigenous North Americans living outside of reservations probably have nearly *twice* as much income as those living on reservations. In 1990 the "off-reservation premium" was the difference between $18,400 in income and $30,500.)[8]

Consider further that non-whites are much more likely to be unemployed, to commit and to become victims of violent crime, to receive substandard medical care, or to live in inadequate housing.[9] We could go on, considering mortgage costs and likelihood of diversion into sub-prime loans (and, not coincidentally, of foreclosure), the so-called "achievement gap" in education (and the "discipline gap" that seems to track it), rates of incarceration and infant mortality, proximity of domicile to hazardous waste sites, and even the negotiated purchase prices of identical cars.[10] But you see the point: by any number of social measures, the populations that we think of as races remain differently positioned in society, with differential stores of and access to all sorts of social goods.

If this were a different sort of discussion, say, a sociological one, I'd take up in some detail the obvious question of how to explain this persistent racial stratification. Do the less advantaged groups suffer from intentional discrimination? Do they simply fail to cultivate the human capital – the habits, skills, talents, and knowledge – that it takes to prosper? Or are they the victims of social institutions and processes that work asymmetrically to the detriment of some races while involving little or no conscious discrimination at present? For good or ill, though, I'm – we're – doing philosophy, and we can only gesture at some answers. We can say in broad outline that persistent discrimination, wasted human capital, and institutional inertia all play their parts, though in proportions that we tend to misrepresent. Our mainstream political discourse tends to focus on discrimination and squandered potential, underemphasizing the first, overemphasizing the second; and it leaves little room for structural analyses of how impersonal social processes systematically but indirectly disadvantage certain people. In light of these patterns of emphasis, I'll speak only to the third factor, the cumulative and indirect production of systemic racial asymmetries.

Many of the aforementioned indicators of racial stratification are class-related, and hence only indirectly, or mediately, race-related. Being poor, or poorly educated, or unemployed correlates all too well with incarceration, lack of insurance, and much more besides; and being non-white correlates pretty well with being poor, poorly educated, or unemployed. And even where racial disparities appear at every class level, as with mortgage rates, stores of wealth, and certain health conditions, we can still appeal to indirect processes, this time the indirect results of historically racist conditions. Historically, blacks and Asians, for example, were prevented from owning businesses, or owning land; they were steered away from desirable neighborhoods, or forcibly expelled, or denied entry by redlining, restrictive covenants, or alien land laws. They were not extended the favorable mortgage terms that whites got from the Federal Housing Authority starting in the 1930s, nor were they (usually) granted the land that was allotted to Western settlers in the nineteenth century (land, to put it too swiftly, that was typically sold out from under the Native Americans to whom it had been granted, or who had been forced onto it). All of this, and more, created the conditions under which even a perfectly equitable present system for distributing wealth would continue to ramify the historical inequalities that would provide its starting point. Or, more simply: equality of opportunity is one thing, and a century of home equity is another.

Here's another respect in which the racial order has not changed all that much: intra-racial marriage, or racial endogamy, still occurs much more frequently than inter-racial marriage, or racial exogamy. And when interracial marriages do occur, they occur in distinctively patterned ways. As sociologists Zhenchao Qian and Daniel Lichter put it, "Historically, rates of intermarriage with Whites have been much higher among American Indians, Asians, and Hispanics than among Blacks."[11] As of the 1990 Census, the patterns looked like this: whites married whites 97 percent of the time, blacks married blacks 93 percent of the time, and Asians married Asians 70 percent of the time. Interestingly, where exogamy occurs, whites are, apparently, the more highly prized partners. In 1990, blacks married whites almost four times more often than they married any other out-group, and Asians married whites almost thirty times more often. Even more interestingly, Native Americans married whites more often than they married members of *any* other group, *including Native Americans*. This is in part a story about the history of "Indian policy," with its periodic reliance on forced assimilation.

More interesting yet: when we consider the difference that gender makes, we find, among other things, that black men marry white women much more often than black women marry white men. This is in part a story about the double bind of race and gender, and about the social capital and psychic income that a masculinist culture might confer on black men who could "marry up." These numbers had moved by 2008, but not much, and in equivocal ways. For example, black female-white male marriages increased from 1.3 percent in 1980 to 6.5 percent, and the percentage of black men marrying white women went from 4.7 to 14.4. But whites still married whites around 92 percent of the time, and Asians and Hispanics were actually significantly *less* likely to marry whites in 2008 than in 1980 (though they were marginally more likely to marry blacks).[12]

I've gone into all of this detail in order to lay the groundwork for this claim: a close look at our best quantifiable proxy for socially acceptable mating practices suggests that the USA still seems committed to producing and reproducing racially homogeneous populations. As with all of the other issues I've taken up, there is a great deal more to say about the causes, meaning, and propriety of this phenomenon. Also as before, this isn't the place to say it. We'll return to the issue of racial endogamy in chapter 5, but for now I'm interested in two points.

The first point has to do with the way I've come to these conclusions. I've focused here on "traditional" marriage between what we might call "traditional racial subjects" – men and women who identify themselves as members of only one race – and will do so again later because doing so seems the most likely way to get in the neighborhood of easily digestible information. There are interesting stories to tell about the racial dynamics of heterosexual domestic partner cohabitation, of same-sex relationships, and of committed relationships involving people who identify as bi-racial and multi-racial. But the practices of studying these dynamics is in its infancy, a fact which should not be surprising in light of the dismay with which each of these arrangements has, at one point or another, been regarded. As much as I lament the fact that marriage as an institution has been yoked to heterosexuality, and that we happily give public sanction and support to some identities and sexual relationships and not others, my feeble grasp of sociological methods – and the meager amount of space available to me to employ those methods – forces me to focus on the clearest, easiest, and best-studied cases.

The second point has to do with what this picture of a racially endogamous society tells us. The mechanisms that result in racial endogamy are complex, involving opportunity and other external constraints as well as preference and other internal conditions. But to the extent that preference and conscious choice are involved in selecting marriage partners and mates, our apparent horror of interracial relationships points toward deeply ingrained, subtly established, and thoroughly racialized convictions about the aesthetic and the erotic, the beautiful and the desirable, and the relationship between these and the social bases of self-esteem. Sociologists talk about all this in terms of racialized relationship capital, by which they mean that belonging to one race or another makes one more or less desirable, in general, as a potential partner or mate.[13] And relationship capital is racialized in part because we live in a world that has been defined by a pervasive system of racialized symbolic value.

We have for a long time valued different races differently, and we have expressed and refined this valuation in a social mythology of stereotypes and stock images. You know the system of ideas that I'm thinking of: Whites, at the top, are civilized but soulless, with rational men and beautiful women; blacks, at the bottom, are physically gifted but oversexed brutes; Indians, sort of in the middle but really off the scale, somewhere to the side, are noble savages, virtuously free of civilized impulses but childishly incontinent; and Asians, squarely in the middle, are a model but irreducibly alien and perhaps devious minority, composed of asexual men and submissive women. More broadly: whites embody Reason and Beauty, blacks represent The Body and Ugliness, Indians are Primitive Nature, and Asians are The Inscrutable Other. And the racially mixed Hispanic population slides between all of these positions, in ways we'll discuss further in the next chapter.

This is a complicated and ever-changing mythology, one that is always under challenge from the people it depicts, always mediated by intersecting ideologies like class and gender, and always on its way to becoming something else, especially in the late-modern era. But it used to be a mainstay, an axiom, of US literate culture; you could hardly read a newspaper or a novel until the 1960s without tripping over it. And it continues to shape our ideas about human worth, and not just in the spheres of bodily beauty and romantic compatibility.

3.5 Varieties of racialism: four accounts and ten questions

The preceding discussion shows that we still allocate (or countenance the allocation of) social goods along racial lines. More than that, it shows that our racial boundaries track the asymmetrical distribution of these goods. Relationship capital, wealth, income, symbolic value, and much more are all differentially distributed across our different race groups.

Once we would have concluded from these asymmetries that they result from something about the races, some talents or incapacities that are intrinsic to each group. But we saw in chapter 2 that this way of thinking is hopelessly problematic. And we've seen over the last two chapters that there are plenty of ways to explain these differences by appeal to external factors, like the exclusions and depredations of white supremacy.

So our racial boundaries don't enclose anything, and to distribute goods along racial lines is to respect social distinctions that don't mark or distinguish anything. In chapter 2 I argued that we should continue to explore racial discourse, the decline of classical racialism notwithstanding, in part because the discourse is still operative. People still use the language of race, and they thereby impose on us the burden of understanding how they use it and what they use it to do. But even if that's right, it doesn't tell us anything about the ontological commitments that come with this language. That is, it doesn't yet answer these questions: What does Western race-talk point to, what realities does it denote, if not the impossible populations of classical racialism?

There are two basic ontological options for critical – that is, post-classical – race theorists: either you think races exist, that race-talk refers to something real, or you don't. For want of a better vocabulary I'll refer to the first view as "realism" and to the second as "skepticism." (I'd like to use another pair of words here, something unburdened by associations that seem to pull in the direction of irrelevant considerations or other categories of discourse. Unfortunately, several centuries of debate about what's real and what isn't have left any language we might use with worrisome baggage. So between this language, warts and all, or some other language, with different warts, I choose this.) Racial skeptics conclude that, ontologically speaking, race-thinking is hopeless, period. Racial realists, by contrast, say that we just have to think more carefully about what "race" means if we want to find its referent in the world. Each of these views comes in different varieties, as we'll see below. I'll distinguish these varieties in part by appeal to what their adherents think the correct ontology requires of us. It will turn out, then, that I'm interested not just in ontology – in the right account of what there is – but also in the social diagnoses and recommendations for action that follow from finding the right ontology. The positions that I'll distinguish below result from putting ontology, diagnosis, and recommendation into different combinations. Joining Heidegger and others in a long-ish tradition of taking the word "metaphysics" to mean something more than "an account of what there is," I'll refer to each of these positions as a racial metaphysic. Each is distinguished by its answers to three questions, with the content of the second question determined by the answer to the first. (1) Do races exist? (2a) If they don't, what are we doing when we use race-talk? (2b) If they do, what are they? And (3) whether they do or not, what do we do – what should we do – now?

A final word before we get down to business: every time I start a discussion like this, I worry for a moment that it's passé. Philosophical race theorists seem to have established a kind of consensus racial metaphysic, though they differ over its precise content and limits.[14] My sense is that the heart of this consensus is what I call the CAMPS approach, which has five basic features.

1 It treats race *critically*, which is to say that it refuses the seductions of classical racialism.
2 It treats races as *artifacts*, which is to say that they are the results of the meaning-laden exercise of human agency, even if they still turn out, somehow, to be part of a responsible account of human biology. (More on this below.)
3 It treats race as a *modern* invention, which is to say at the very least that the most influential forms of race-thinking emerge during the modern period, and perhaps that the very idea of race is a modern innovation.
4 It treats race as a *political* phenomenon, which is compatible with a number of stronger or weaker claims about the connection between racial formation and political life.

5 It accepts the *social* dimension of race, which is to say that whatever
   else it is, race is *not* simply a matter of individual whim, choice, or
   preference. Individuals can make choices that affect their racialization. But these choices are conditioned by, and represent moves in
   a game that is defined by, social practices of racial identification
   and stratification.

There is room for much disagreement around the edges of the CAMPS
picture, but here we often agree to disagree. And if philosophers can
agree on this much (I find myself thinking), then surely people outside
philosophy, who have normal (rather than herculean) amounts of
tolerance and energy for hair-splitting and logic-chopping, can also
find some common ground. But just when I start to convince myself
of this, I run across someone who interrupts a conversation about
racial politics to exclaim, confidently and publicly, that "race is a lie."
So with all due respect to the consensus view, however we cash it out,
I'll press ahead with my attempt to map the conceptual terrain in
racial metaphysics.

3.5.1 What races are: a radical constructionist's story

You'll probably have already guessed where I stand on the question
of racial metaphysics. On my view, racial discourse not only has a
referent, it has a perfectly familiar one. Contrary to the view that
common-sense discourse about race is deeply confused or misguided
thanks to dupery or dimwittedness, I think that race-talk really is
about the populations and phenomena that it seems to be about, and
that most of us think it's about. We sometimes get the content of the
discourse wrong, or play fast and loose with the features that make
races races. But they really are what we think they are, and really do
include the people, more or less, that we think they do (though not
for the reasons some of us think). (For followers of professional football in the American style, call this the Dennis Green approach to race
theory: they are what we thought they were.) Statistical correlations
like the ones we discussed earlier pick out populations that overlap
considerably with the things we call races. This enables us to say that
a person we'd call black (to pick an example that I'll stick with) is
more likely to live in substandard or overcrowded housing, or lack
health insurance, or be unemployed, than someone we'd call white.
We've already noted that it also enables us to say that this same person
is more likely to be or to have been in the criminal system, or to
perform less well in school. And this makes some people worry, since
it seems to invite us to draw conclusions about black inferiority. But
the falsity of classical racialism prevents us from taking these correlations as evidence of some congenital incapacities or tendencies, and

requires that we look instead for social explanations – explanations that may avail themselves of facts about bias in law enforcement, and about the compound consequences of race, poverty, de facto residential segregation, and the problems of funding public schools with local property taxes. That is: the failure of classical racialism means that *"because they're black"* is no longer an explanation for anything. It becomes, instead, a gesture at a request for an explanation, or for an answer to a question like this: what is that links black people to these social conditions?

If the prerequisites for a racial identity, the body and bloodline that earn you a specific racial identity, correlate with certain probabilities of living well under, or in the wake of, white supremacy, then we can say that these statistical correlations make human bodies and bloodlines generically meaningful. More precisely: the correlations exist because political, economic, and cultural forces connect appearance and ancestry to social location, and the language that people like me use to point out these correlations is a device for expressing the meaning of a racial identity. The correlations certainly aren't foolproof: it obviously isn't the case that every member of a race has had the same experiences. This is true in part because race doesn't do its work alone. The interpenetration of social categories – we called this "the merger thesis" earlier – means that the experience of a racial identity will be defined by the experience of a certain class background, and in the context of a certain gender identity, and so on. But within each of these intersecting contexts we can specify the difference that being black is likely to make. Black women are more likely to bear low-birth-weight babies, at every income level. Black workers, of either gender, are more likely to be unemployed. And so on.

If social conditions assign probabilistic meaning to appearance and ancestry, then this is already a mode of racialization, as I've defined it. But this particular mode directly tracks the mode that we've developed over the last few centuries. So not only do social conditions create races, they give new content to the things that we were already thinking of as capital-R-Races. White supremacist societies created the Races they thought they were discovering, and the ongoing political developments in these societies continued to re-create them. Anti-racist activists turned them into political interest groups, cultural nationalists treated them as incubators for ethnic groups, shifts in immigration patterns problematized and expanded their boundaries, and economic changes redefined their relations to the productive forces of society.

All of this is to say: our Western races are social constructs. They are things that we humans create in the transactions that define social life. Specifically, they are the probabilistically defined populations that result from the white supremacist determination to link appearance and ancestry to social location and life chances. We no longer actively and intentionally maintain this linkage in the way we used to, but the effects of earlier efforts continue to shape our life chances in ways that disproportionately disadvantage specific populations.

To talk thematically about race, then – as in "race is an interesting philosophical subject" – is to talk about the field of forces and dynamics that produce and follow from the linkage between body and social location. To speak categorically, or taxonomically, of races – as in "what race does she belong to?" – is to speak of the specific populations that racial dynamics, or racial formation processes, create. And to speak of a racial identity is to speak of an individual's perspective and location on the field of racializing social forces.

There's much more to say about this approach to the metaphysics of race, and the easiest way to say it is to let the details develop under the pressure of criticism from other perspectives. So I'll consider some questions that adherents to alternative views might ask, both to clarify my approach and to introduce these alternatives. By the end you should see why I'll refer to my view as *radical constructionism*.

3.5.2 Ten questions

Question 1: How can you call these races? You said yourself that the idea was invented in the modern West, and it was used to mean something that can't exist. How can you just redefine it now?

The short answer to this question is that appropriation and redefinition are central parts of language use. They keep languages growing and vital, and enable us to create slang and dialects and jargon. We've taken all sorts of words – like "atom" and "snapshot" – and used them to mean things they didn't originally mean. My point about race is not that I should be allowed to redefine the term, but that we've already done it, and that our theories should reflect our usage.

Now for a longer answer: If you're inclined to ask this question, you're probably some variety of eliminativist. An eliminativist is a racial skeptic for whom race-talk is at best an egregious error, and at worst a pernicious lie. Not surprisingly, adherents to this perspective usually insist that we strike – that is, eliminate – race from our ontological vocabularies. There are many arguments for this view, and the best ones, as we'll see, are ethical. But there are two basic, sometimes related, non-ethical arguments, one building on the idea of objectivity, the other building on the meaning of "race." The second, semantic argument lies behind this question.

The semantic argument begins by adding two convictions to the challenge of human variation. The first conviction is that "race" just means what people in the modern West said it means; the second is that the dominant Western use of this idea has explicitly declined to treat race as a social construct. On this view, "race" just means something ontologically objective; it refers to the groups that people like Samuel George Morton and Thomas Jefferson had in mind. And this, of course, means that there are no races, since human biology doesn't determine culture, behaviour, capacity, or worth, and since the races aren't even biologically or physiologically distinct in the ways that nineteenth century or high modern race-thinking required.

But who says Samuel Morton has to have the last word on what "race" means? For that matter, who gave him the last word on the modern concept of (capital-R-) Race? Following the principle that I've dubbed Austin's Law – linguistic distinctions won't mark nothing – and adding to it my own principle of charity – if a linguistic distinction marks its domain murkily or unclearly, refine it to make it do better – I've defined race-thinking as a way of assigning meaning to human bodies and bloodlines. The modern West inaugurated the most far-reaching, ambitious, and thoroughgoing program of race-thinking in human history, but other peoples in other times assigned meaning in the ways I've described, which is to say that they engaged in racialization. I don't know of a better word than "race" to indicate this fact, which it can't do if we reserve it for the race-thinking of the moderns.

But even if we stick with the moderns, we've seen that different approaches to Race held sway at different times. In *Color Conscious*, the philosopher K. Anthony Appiah suggests that we settle questions about what Race means by focusing on the ideas of intellectual elites. These are the people who play the role of society's semantic experts: they are the ones we go to, either in person or by exploring the knowledge they've stored in books, lectures, and such, when we want to know what, say, "proton" means, and when the impressionistic ideas we've retained from high school science classes just won't do. Just as there are proton experts – and, to stick with our earlier example, money experts, who tell us when paper counts as legal tender – there are, or were, Race experts, and Appiah says these experts were people like Jefferson and Morton. (Matthew Arnold is his preferred example, but Morton, whom we have discussed, stands in well enough.) So Morton tells us what "Race" means, and, as we've seen, the things he was talking about don't exist.

But why pick these experts? There were other people with other ideas – Samuel Stanhope Smith, for example, or, later, W. E. B. Du Bois. Perhaps the answer is that Jefferson, being Jefferson, had more influence than others, or that people like Morton expressed and refined the conventional wisdom while Smith and others were lonely voices in the distance. But why doesn't that just mean that more people were wrong than right? It's been known to happen – in the history of every science, for example.

Maybe Jefferson, or Morton, or any expert on classical racialism, is to race-thinking what Galen is to biology, or what Wilhelm Wundt is to psychology: an important founding figure whose work and ideas we've completely left behind. Maybe we had to have the social sciences or, more broadly, social theory before we could understand the role of race in human life. If social theory has just started to show us how to use our ideas about race productively, then races don't have to be what Jefferson and Morton said they were. Maybe they are social facts, in the sense of the expression invented by pioneering sociologist Emile Durkheim, and maybe they require analysis by social theorists. And if that's right, then the collapse of classical racialism doesn't entail the non-existence of races.

The philosopher Naomi Zack streamlines the semantic argument in a way that to some extent avoids my appeal to the possible evolution of race-talk. Taking a cue from the same ordinary-language approach that I've repeatedly embraced, she says simply that we should take "race" to mean what most people mean by it, and most people mean, more or less, what Samuel George Morton meant. Zack is of course not the only one to hold this view: several empirical studies even seem to confirm the point. But there are competing studies, and the overall picture, as one sociologist puts it, "suggests that enough variation in racial conceptualization currently exists that talk of a consensus view on race in the American public is inaccurate...."[15] (This is distinct from the consensus among philosophers that I mentioned some while ago.) So while Zack and I share the intuition that our language practices, and other practices, indicate some commitment to race-thinking, I'm not confident that we have a settled view about the metaphysical foundation for these practices. So I'll continue to tease out some options, undeterred by the eliminativist attempt to equate racialism with its classical variant.

Question 2: Even if you want to use the race concept in this way, how can you say that it refers to something real? Real things, things that exist, have to be objective, the same for everyone, everywhere. Races manifestly and famously fail to satisfy this requirement, and so fail to achieve the status of real things.

This question points to the second eliminativist argument, the appeal to objectivity. We should say something about what "objectivity" means before we go any farther. "Objective" is an example of what the philosopher Ian Hacking refers to as elevator words. These are words, like "reality" and "truth" and "knowledge," that raise the conceptual altitude and the stakes of any discussion into which they find their way, seeming to indicate depth and profundity while mostly just causing us to spin our intellectual wheels.[16] Until philosophers get ahold of them, though, these words tend to have more or less straightforward and familiar meanings. Most simply, something is objective when it is valid, whatever validity comes to, from any perspective; otherwise it is subjective, or dependent on an individual's perspective. Journalists aspire to objectivity, which means that they set aside their private agendas and biases and simply report the news; similarly, philosophers have often aspired to objectivity, which means that they've argued for notions of truth, beauty, goodness, and so on that do not depend on the contingencies of cultural location or on personal inclination.

The eliminativist argument from objectivity begins by noting an important fact. Race clearly fails to be objective in at least this way: people who belong to one race in one place and time may belong to another race in another place and time. The meanings of terms like "black" and "white," when applied to humans, seem to shift with locale and culture. By contrast, paradigm cases of real things – rocks, trees, the sun, wombats – are what they are, wherever they are, whatever we say about them. We might tell idiosyncratic stories about them in different places and times: we might think of the sun as a god here but as a ball of gas there. But the basic underlying reality is whatever it is, and we're just right or wrong about it. With race, there doesn't seem to be an underlying reality. Whatever the people around you say you are, is, pretty much, what you are, since it's hard to see how they'd be wrong without some biological story. And since classical racialism collapsed, we know that no biological story is in the offing.

So far, so good: there are no races because the things we call races aren't objective, and hence aren't really, well, things. But do things have to be objective to be real? And objective in what sense? The green pieces of paper in my wallet are instances of legal tender. Each one really is worth a dollar. But is that an objective fact about these pieces of paper? If I visited a Stone Age people, or a camp of radical Luddites, would my little papers mean anything to anyone? If all human societies everywhere collapsed, a rock would still be a rock. But what happens to my dollar? (The "paperless" dollars in my bank account, such as they are, would vanish, but that's another problem, as is the fact that I hardly have enough of them to make this example work.)

We can use the example of money to refine our talk about objectivity. Some things are ontologically subjective but epistemically objective. Money, for example, unlike wombats, depends for its existence on human agreements, which is to say, on human mental states, like belief. It is ontologically subjective. But once we've established the networks of convention that bring money into being, then there are facts about money that are entirely independent of my individual beliefs. That is, money is epistemically objective. I can't just decide, unilaterally, that my green pieces of paper will be worth a thousand dollars each. Or I can decide this, but if I tell anyone, they'll rightly reply that I'm wrong; and if I try to act on this decision, I won't get along too well in the world.

Race is in these respects like money. Race-thinking varies from society to society, which shows that it depends on local human conventions for its existence. But once the conventions are established, once we've put in place and routinized the practices that tell us who counts as what, then there are facts that exist independently of any individual's particular judgments and beliefs. I can't just decide, unilaterally, that my dark skin and curly hair mark me as white, or as having no race. Or I can decide this, but if I tell anyone in the United States, they'll likely think I'm wrong, and perhaps a bit confused. They may not tell me that I'm wrong, either because we now, as a matter of state policy, give people wider latitude for self-declaring their racial status, or because of politeness, or because of sympathy with my apparent political or ethical motives. But it will be clear that I'm swimming upstream of something like the facts, even if they are facts-for-us-here, like facts about money.

So there are things, like money, that seem real without being ontologically objective. And it seems that much of what we say about money we can also say about race. Just as money-thinking, or dollar-thinking, takes pieces of paper and assigns them value as legal tender (or just as we, in the grip of dollar-thinking, create pieces of paper that we will assign value as legal tender), so race-thinking takes human bodies and assigns them racial identities. We may use our dollars while thinking erroneously that they are backed by piles of gold somewhere, or without thinking much about what makes them worth what they're worth; similarly, we may interact with members of races while erroneously thinking that racial identities turn on biological facts, or without thinking much at all about what racial identities mean.

The objectivist may want to insist at this point that no social construct, money included, is real. If so, I'd be inclined to say that she's changed the subject, or that, as Charles Peirce might say, she's simply pretending to engage in serious talk. And then I'd invite her to write me a big check for all of those illusions in her bank account. Ever-persistent, she may insist that I'm the one who's changed the subject, that "race" in fact means an ontologically objective phenomenon, and has meant this since maybe the seventeenth century. Unfortunately, this is just a restatement of the semantic argument that we just disposed of.

Question 3: But isn't race-thinking ethically dangerous? How can you insist that we hold on to it?

Without question, race-thinking is dangerous. Of course, so are hammers and knives. A little later I'll argue that the practice of race-thinking, like hammers and knives, is in some ways useful enough to keep around, provided that we attend to its risks. But right now we're engaged in a metaphysical inquiry. Ethical questions are important, but they have little bearing on the argument in question here. Notice the logical structure of the discussion. The eliminativist argues that races do not exist, either because they fail to be objective or because they've been falsely posited by hopeless theories of human difference. These are ontological arguments. By contrast, the ethical arguments we're being invited to consider tell us why race-thinking complicates the pursuit of important goals, but not why it fails to accord with the facts. And this sort of argument can figure into an ontological claim about facts only if the facts are ones we bring into being. If I ask you whether widgets exist, there's no reason for you to tell me how bad widgets are unless I have some say in their prospects for existence. That is, if they are artifacts, things I or we can create, like money, then your admonition may encourage me to rethink my, or our, creative project. So with these arguments eliminativism either concedes the ontological dispute by lapsing into a kind of social constructionism, or avoids the metaphysical question altogether.

Question 4: What do you need metaphysics for? There's no conflict involved in using race-talk and denying that races are real. You just have to under-stand how the language works.

If you ask this question you might be what I'll call a quasi-racialist, or a racial skeptic who doesn't accept eliminativism. Instead of saying that racial discourse is false in the same pernicious way in which lies are false, which is to say that, like lying, it ought to be eliminated wherever possible, the quasi-racialist says that it's false the way myths are false. Myths are false narratives that help constitute and explain distinctive cultural forms and modes of social arrangement. They offer explanatory accounts of the sort that get displaced by science, but in the process they help unify social groups by dramatizing ethical pre-cepts and inviting attachment to customary practices. If we want to understand a form of social arrangement, then, we should probably take seriously the myths it uses to justify and explain itself.

On this view, the literal falsity of myths isn't their most important feature. There are many progressive Christians who aren't terribly interested in the question of whether a man named Jesus really lived and did the things we think he did, and who refuse to take literally the story about God creating the world in six days. But these same people continue to take comfort in the Gospels and Genesis, taking the stories as occasions for convening and celebrating their communities – at holidays, say, or at church functions – and using them to illustrate and insist upon the importance of virtues like mercy, forgiveness, love, and obedience. Many more people take the Bible as the literal truth, and use it, or try to use it, to govern their lives: the story of Sodom and Gomorrah means that "unnatural" sexual practices are wrong, and the fact that Adam came first, and that God made the world, including Eve, for Adam's benefit, has implications for everything from environmentalism to gender relations. But even if we disagree with these people about the truth of their cosmology, we can see the connection between their beliefs and their practices. (Myths needn't, of course, be religious, or wholly false; every country surrounds its origins with explanatory stories that motivate customary practices and dramatize basic norms. Here in the USA we have Founding Fathers who were real, but who've come to be larger than life. Religious myths just provide the clearest cases.)

The quasi-racialist argues that race-thinking works like a myth, and that we should work through the details of the myth and the culture that it supports before we demand a moratorium on the myth's falsehoods. On this view, classical racialism was a false account of human variation and differentiation that nevertheless served as the cornerstone upon which much of US culture, society, and political economy have been built. If we want to understand the USA, and if we want to participate in some of the practices maintained by its residents, we should probably take its generative myths seriously. This means that we might need to act as if there are races. We might continue to engage in race-talk the way the progressive Christian accepts Bible-talk, as a condition of entry into certain communities. This is one way to think of the NAACP's refusal to trouble itself with the question of whether colored people really exist. Similarly, we might continue to engage in race-talk the way a cultural anthropologist accepts talk of deities she doesn't believe in: as a way of putting oneself in position to understand ongoing practices and social arrangements.

Having recognized the social power of race-thinking, quasi-racialists are not so eager to eliminate the practice. As I've noted, some might have an open-ended commitment to using it in its mythic capacity, as a device for doing political or cultural work. Some quasi-racialists do join the eliminativists in wanting to get rid of, or as they often say, abolish, race-thinking. But these abolitionists eschew imperatives to eliminate racial discourse immediately, typically because they believe that getting rid of race-thinking and its effects will require a long struggle, and because they believe that the early stages of this struggle should use the resources of race-thinking to highlight the still powerful legacy of white supremacy. This leads the abolitionists to endorse both parts of a seemingly paradoxical position, one that we can illustrate with quotes from historian David Roediger.

First the abolitionists say things like this: "race is . . . [an] 'ontologi-cally empty' and 'metaphysical' category." Then they say things like this: "[anti-racists] must pursue a political strategy 'caught up in the very metaphysical categories it hopes finally to abolish.'"[17] Here are the two claims together, this time from philosopher David Theo Goldberg: "Races have no ontological status. In the case of race . . . there is literally no object referred to." Nevertheless, he says, "the issue is not the fact but the terms of asserted reference."[18] The issue is not the fact, any more than the essence of Christianity for progressive Protestant theologians lies in the historical facts of the life of a man named Jesus (which wouldn't have been his name, anyway). The issue is what people meant, and mean, and do, in asserting their "facts." So races aren't real on this view: they have "no ontological status" and the race concept is "ontologically empty." But we have to act, at least for now, as if – *quam si* – races do exist, and as if "race" does refer to something.

Quasi-racialism is a fancy name for a familiar and plausible view. Anyone who has said that ideas about race still shape social life, that this is true and important whether races exist or not, and that this is reason enough to keep talking about race, is a quasi-racialist. Anyone who says all this is, moreover, surely right. Similarly, anyone who has spoken without hesitation of their race, fully mindful of the fact that they don't mean what someone in the nineteenth century would have, is probably a quasi-racialist. And they are, in addition, not obviously irrational or cognitively impaired for behaving this way.

But once we've conceded all that we have to concede to make quasi-racialism work, it appears that we're entitled to something stronger than just quasi-racialism. Once we say that race-thinking shapes social life, we can say that it is constructive – not in the sense of being positive or useful, but in the sense that it creates new condi-tions and states of affairs. Among the new states of affairs that race-thinking creates are the groups into which it sorts the human population. And since, in our discussion of eliminativism, we've detached the race concept from its nineteenth-century incarnations, since we've hitched it to its subsequent development in social theory, why not simply say that these groups are races?

Question 5: Aren't you afraid of that treating race metaphysically will encourage us to forget its processual, political, and social nature?

This question also comes from the quasi-racialist perspective, and points to a quite reasonable reluctance to embrace any kind of racial realism. The reluctance comes first of all from the fact that quasi-racialists tend also to be racialization theorists, or people who focus on the processes by which states of affairs become racialized. Perhaps the best known racialization theorists in the USA, Michael Omi and Howard Winant, put it in a way we've already encountered: "race is a concept which signifies and symbolizes social conflicts and interests by referring to different types of human bodies."[19] Omi and Winant are most interested in the processes that result in groups getting identified as races; they study the social dynamics that link situations (or events, or behaviours, or whatever) to one race or another, and the political mechanisms that connect race to the distribution of social goods. This focus on process and on dynamic events pulls against an emphasis on products and on durable entities.

The focus on dynamic process leads to the second reason for quasi-realists to reject full-fledged realism. If beliefs and ideas, for example, about race, can shape the social world, then we have to pay attention to the consequences of certain ways of thinking. The race concept has usually been used to naturalize social hierarchies, or to make it appear that existing social arrangements are in some sense inevitable or necessary, as if encoded in the nature of things. Quasi-racialists are eager to debunk this idea, to highlight and shield against its dangers. As a consequence, they often adopt the strategy that we find explained in the beginning of historian Matthew Jacobson's book, *Whiteness of a Different Color*: "It has become customary," he says, "to set words like 'race,' 'races,' 'Anglo-Saxons,' or 'whiteness' in undermining quotation marks. The practice certainly suits the spirit of this book, whose central theme is the social fabrication of 'race' and 'races.'"[20] If, like Jacobson, you're interested in how race gets fabricated, and you're troubled by a history in which realism about race usually came with the conviction that races and racial hierarchies were natural, then you'd also be less than enthusiastic about describing races, or "races," as real.

This worry about nature leads to a third reason for the reluctance to embrace realism. Quasi-racialists tend to be social scientists of one sort or another, which is to say, they're not philosophers. As such, they lack, to their credit, the philosopher's often-perverse determination to turn every question into a deep question about the nature of something. For them, "nature" is one of the elevator words I mentioned earlier, and unlike many philosophers, social theorists are often quite sympathetic to intellectual traditions that call elevator words into question. Often drawing on the work of figures like Michel Foucault and Jacques Derrida, these theorists are highly suspicious of notions like "true" and "real." "Metaphysical" is one of the original elevator words, coming down to us from Aristotle (for whom it wasn't elevated at all, but that's another story). And we can see Roediger tarring it with the same skeptical brush in his complaint about race being a metaphysical – a "metaphysical" – category.

This suspicion of "the Real," as many now put it, actually aligns the theorists I have in mind with an older philosophical tradition. Philosophers of various stripes have railed against metaphysics for centuries, depicting it as the province of unfettered and unproductive speculation, or of incoherent aspirations to profundity. (Both targets of this critique survive in the "metaphysics" sections of many bookstores; that too is another story.) But while many philosophers, like me, have rediscovered a willingness to talk at least sometimes about the nature of reality, people in other fields have, for various reasons, inclined in the direction of a kind of agnosticism-cum-skepticism: they just don't care to talk much about the nature of things, and, in fact, they're pretty suspicious, for good reason, of any attempt to do so. This isn't surprising, since the whole point of being a social theorist is to study the artifacts – that is, the non-natural, human-made things – that constitute our societies, practices, and cultures, and since we have so often pretended that these artifacts – hierarchies of governance, gender roles, and so on – were handed down to us from on high.

Having said all that, why should quasi-racialists give up their hard-won middle ground between realism and eliminativism? Moreover, I've said that quasi-racialists are entitled to stronger conclusions than the ones quasi-racialism endorses. I haven't yet said why they should act on this entitlement. After all, I'm entitled to go sing karaoke at the neighborhood pub, but I have several quite good reasons not to exercise this right.

One reason to push quasi-racialism into some kind of racial realism is that elevator words don't have to be as problematic as they've been made out to be. The worry is that we'll see or hear "true" or "real" and think that whatever we're talking about was woven into the tapestry of the universe, as if by some divine power. But five hundred years after the scientific revolution began, and several decades into the televisual and infotainment revolution, we're surely more savvy than this. We know that there are provisional and circumspect ways of using elevator words. I'm rather inclined to worry, with feminist theorist Susan Bordo, about the opposite problem. People have become so jaded by competing truth-claims, claims tendered, for example, by news outlets, advertisers, and political campaigns, or, more prosaically, by hair weaves, techniques for editing digital imagery, and aesthetic surgeries, that the more pressing problem involves getting people to abandon their reflexive skepticism and believe anything.

Another reason to drop the "quasi" from quasi-racialism is that the political and explanatory work of the view might be done more effectively by fully developing its underlying conceptual resources. I'm thinking here of their willingness to talk about the fabrication of race, and the construction of social realities, and the artifactual nature of political and cultural arrangements. I'm thinking in particular about how these ways of speaking converge with my earlier argument against eliminativism, the argument that races, like money, result from social practices and conventions. Quasi-racialists say with Roediger that they have to "confront" race to abolish it because they want to highlight the role race has played in shaping arrangements that many of us take for granted. How better to do this than to talk explicitly, straightforwardly, about what human agency has made? Why stop with talking about what it has "made"?

We might take a more concrete approach to this last argument for turning quasi-racialism into racialism tout court. The abolitionists I've been talking about – like some eliminativists – tend to be in favor of tracking racial statistics, for example on police activity – traffic stops, arrests, and so on – and on general demographic questions – to see who lives and works where, and under what conditions. They tend to be provoked to this view by advocates for colorblindness, an aggressive version of eliminativism that calls for the immediate renunciation of all racial identifications, especially by the state. If pressed on the point, and pressed long enough, advocates for colorblindness will eventually say that there aren't any races anyway; so what kind of sense does it make to track them? Quasi-racialists insist that there are many good reasons to record racial statistics – which isn't to say that it's always a good idea, or that we always interpret the data properly. They could more easily keep this debate about racial statistics focused on the real question, the question of whether the statistics do important and permissible work at an acceptable cost, if they disposed of the red herring presented by the colorblind advocate's ontological argument.

Question 6: If you're going to say that races are real, why do you limit yourself to talking about the "probabilistically defined populations" that white supremacy created? Aren't races really cultural groups?

If you're moved by this question, you may be the kind of racial realist that I'll call a racial communitarian. This is someone who thinks that we construct races by creating cultural groups. There are stronger and weaker ways to make this point. The strong version tends toward ethnic or cultural nationalism, while the weaker version tends toward what we might paradoxically refer to as social-naturalism.

The strong communitarian might say that races are like ethnic groups, composed of people who share or have some claim on a common culture. We could make the view even stronger by saying that these ethnic groups deserve a certain kind of reverence or commitment from their constituent members, such that the people who don't participate in the culture ought to do so, on pain of punishment, criticism, or psycho-emotional derangement. This is the sort of view we find in the Afrocentrism of Molefi Asante.[21]

There are several insights connected with this ethnic or cultural-nationalist account of race, but there are some problems as well. The first problem is that it's usually stated in ways that militate against even discussing it here. Remember, we're talking now about the metaphysical options for critical race theory, a field that emerges after the decline of classical racialism. Often enough, the cultural nationalist derives his ethical and political imperatives, his ought-statements, directly from the presumption that people who look a certain way or who have a certain ancestry just naturally belong to certain groups. This is a classical racialist assumption, and one that our friends in anthropology (both physical and cultural) strenuously urge us to set aside.

Fortunately for the cultural nationalist, it's easy enough to detach the insights behind this view from the classical racialist baggage. The nationalist rightly recognizes that people are often treated badly because of the generic meanings that get assigned to their appearance and ancestry, and that this mistreatment has spawned long-standing traditions and institutions that have profoundly shaped the world. He recognizes that people who are treated in similar ways might do well to join forces to resist their common oppression. And he recognizes that individuals tend to need things to identify with, causes and collectives larger than themselves, communities to belong to, systems of meaning by reference to which they can orient and esteem themselves. These recognitions seem to point in the direction of organizing into race groups, both for mutual defense, as some nineteenth-century black liberationists put it, and for the existential sustenance of mutual affirmation in a hostile society and world. As I say, this is not the usual mode of argument here; think of this as a kind of practical cultural nationalism.

We could make the practical nationalist argument from any number of perspectives, from "Asia-centrism" to Zionism. But these would surely be arguments about how we ought to construct races: they would be what Omi and Winant have taught us to call racial projects, attempts to reinterpret the discourse of race in order to shift the distribution of social goods. Our aim here, you'll recall, is to evaluate accounts of the groups that engage in and result from racial projects, descriptive accounts; it is not, or not yet, to consider prescriptive recommendations about how to reshape those groups. And to the extent that the nationalist argument is a descriptive one, it collapses into nationalism or ethnicity and so runs afoul of the conceptual considerations we raised in the previous chapter. Amadou Diallo and Vincent Chin died because of how they looked, not because of the cultures they participated in; and the racist realtor who helps distribute housing opportunities along racial lines can do so, and thereby enact a racial project, without participating in any nationalist project.

So if the core principle for a racial communitarian is that we construct races by creating cultural groups, the strong reading of this claim fails. It is simply incorrect to describe the groups we call races in terms of ethnic groups or national units. As we saw in the previous chapter, ethnic groups can become racialized, and race groups can become ethnicized. But the notions are distinguishable, and there are racial phenomena, like the killing of Vincent Chin, that seem to have little to do with cultural questions. Chin was killed because his assailants identified him with what was widely perceived as a Japanese hijacking of the US economy, which is of course a cultural matter. But he was singled out not because of his clothes or his religion or any other cultural attribute, but because he looked Asian. His assailants read his body as a sign of national origin, which is a mode of race-thinking.

Question 7: Okay, so race isn't cultural the way ethnicity is cultural. But there is still a culturally richer story to tell than we get from your talk of "probabilistic" populations. What about the way culture mediates the production and reproduction of these populations? To put it crudely: what about things like beauty and the erotic?

This question points us to another way to be a racial communitarian, a way that begins with the realization that races are culturally mediated breeding populations. On this view, in the words of philosopher Philip Kitcher, races are human collectives in which "patterns of acculturation maintain the genetic distinctiveness between groups."[22] To claim from this perspective that we create races by creating cultural groups is to claim that our social practices lead us to act in ways that create and maintain reproductively isolated populations. For this reason, we might join philosopher Lucius Outlaw in referring to this view as a kind of social-naturalism.

We can see the motivation for the social-naturalist claim about reproductive isolation by reminding ourselves of the earlier discussion of racialized relationship capital. As we've seen, radically divergent rates of interracial and intra-racial mating are characteristic of US society. This means that our races have in effect become breeding populations, which in turn means that there is some warrant for thinking of races as genetically distinct, since they do not exchange genes at substantial rates. This is not a claim about overall genetic variation, which is much greater within races than between them, as eliminativists and physical anthropologists are rightly eager to point out. Rather, it is a claim about the reproductive isolation of human groups, and it builds on two facts: that the groups we now think of as races were geographically isolated for quite a long time, and that after this isolation ended they remained, to a large degree, culturally isolated, even when in close physical proximity to each other. There were of course exceptions, including the odious and systematic practice of European slave masters forcing themselves on enslaved African women. And while we might point to this long-lived practice to undermine the claim that the members of a race resemble each other more closely than they do the members of another race, that's not the claim at issue here. The point here is just that these groups have usually been and are now relatively isolated breeding populations.

So far this appeal to socially mediated reproductive isolation should seem uncontroversial. The most influential forms of racial ideology, after all, have been famously concerned – one might say obsessed – with preventing interracial sexual activity. But there are different ways to develop this point, and some are more responsible than others.

The less responsible forms flowered near the end of the twentieth century, when a series of conceptual and methodological advances in the 1960s and 1970s gave new confidence to researchers who sought to explain social phenomena in biological terms. Popular texts like Edmund O. Wilson's *Sociobiology: The New Synthesis* (1975) expressed this confidence publicly, and created room in public discourse for speculation on the biological roots of human social life. Wilson and other scientists sometimes made what one commentators describes as "rash generalizations about human nature," despite being concerned most often in their scholarship with lower animals like bees and ants.[23] Also, as sociobiology's many contemporaneous critics vigorously argued, these generalizations too swiftly reduced complex social phenomena to single-factor biological accounts, and were easy to coopt into public arguments for racist and sexist political agendas. What's more, the zealous pursuit of evolutionary explanations left the sociobiological program open to the same worries that can arise for any evolutionary argument – worries about the speculative invention of "just-so" stories, the failure to define the unit of selection with sufficient precision, and so on. But the real problem with the sociobiological synthesis was the space it opened in public discourse for the renewal of racist myths, just when the formal transition to late-modern egalitarianism was creating a market for new ways of justifying racial inequality.

Among the texts rushing in to fill this space were popular books like *The Bell Curve* and *Taboo: Why Blacks Dominate Sports and Why We're Afraid to Talk About It*. The first book was concerned with the racial gap in performances on intelligence tests, while the second was concerned, as its title makes clear, with the preeminence of black athletes in US major sports. But both adopted the same strategy. Focus intently on capacities that seem to distinguish our contemporary race groups from each other – performance in athletics, on standardized tests, and so on. Innocently suggest that differential achievement in the areas marked out by these capacities could be the result of selection pressures operating in recent human history on human populations that really are physiologically distinct. Then equably point out that having once been selected for, these traits would have been passed down from earlier to later generations. And there you have it: an all-purpose explanation for everything from the achievement gap in education (enslaved Africans would, after all, have been chosen for their strength, not for their critical reasoning abilities) to the alleged dominance of the black athlete (consider the conditions of chattel slavery, again, and the fact that the bodies of East Africans seem to be built for winning marathons).

Serious inquiry undertaken in the sociobiological spirit (which most often now appears under other names, like "evolutionary psychology") must walk a fine line. It must try to trace complex social behaviors to evolutionary imperatives without forgetting the dangers noted above or the role of the environment – which, for humans at least, includes the social environment – in shaping the expression of genetic traits. And researchers in this area have come a long way in these areas since the early days of working in the shadow of eugenics. Pop sociobiology, by contrast, stomps over this line in seven league boots. How much less could one do to avoid a unit of selection problem than to put umbrella terms like "intelligence" or "athletic excellence" at the heart of an inquiry? And what bearing does the lung capacity of the average Kenyan marathoner have on the freakish gifts of LeBron James? Especially if the marathoner does not inherit this capacity but develops it by training at high altitudes, and if Mr James developed his gifts under the tutelage of a highly organized system for finding and cultivating basketball skills, a system that for straightforward sociopolitical reasons does most of its work in African-American communities?

Fortunately for science, popular science, and society in general, the interest in applying pop sociobiology to racial phenomena eventually waned. Less fortunately, the deep roots of racist discourse in Western societies leave us in perennial danger of relapses. Consider, for example, Mr Kanazawa's aforementioned speculations about the objective ugliness of black women (chapter 2), which in some ways echoed, while lagging far behind, a small surge of interest in the evolutionary psychology of human bodily beauty.[24] I've devoted the last few paragraphs to the irresponsible modes of social naturalism more to promote awareness of this danger than to represent this mode's current influence in the field. Much more relevant to the field, and quite distinct from these less responsible forms of social-naturalism, are the philosophical efforts of people like Kitcher and Outlaw. Where some sociobiologists would have explained the formation of race groups by appeal to an evolutionarily advantageous predisposition to fear or evade unfamiliar others – Wilson's "xenophobia" – Kitcher says that "[t]he sources of the low rate of black–white intermarriage lie ultimately . . . in the history of slavery and colonialism, and, more proximally, in socioeconomic inequities."[25] And he develops this thought in ways that have inspired a number of philosophers of science and biology to take seriously the thought that some concept of race may yet play a useful role in biological science.

Outlaw reaches similar conclusions, but from the direction of critical theory rather than the philosophy of science. He agrees that the basic causes for the reproductive isolation of our modern Races have to do with sociopolitical and cultural factors. But he also argues that this kind of sociocultural differentiation is native to the human condition, and generates racial differences even apart from modern conditions. Humans are social animals, Outlaw reminds us, joining others in society to find and create meaning and order. Part of this process involves giving ourselves templates for assigning meaning to the human body. We learn to use body-types to distinguish between in-group members and out-group members, between Them and Us: They (Hutus, Turks) look like that, while We (Tutsis, Greeks) look like this. But we also learn to see which kind of body earns someone consideration as a potential mate (consideration by whoever does the choosing). Different cultures always have, and have always had, different ideas of human beauty and attractiveness. These ideas influence who mates with whom, which in turn shapes the genetic profile of subsequent generations. For Outlaw, the career of Western race-thinking is just an instance of this broader phenomenon. "Raciation," as he calls it, or the process of dividing ourselves into groups and racializing the dividing lines, is, on his view, a natural accompaniment to, or instrument of, human social life.[26]

So the question remains: why do I talk about probabilistic populations instead of social-natural kinds? First I have to point out that I did have in mind something like what Outlaw and Kitcher discuss, not least because I've learned to think about these things in part from reading their work. You may recall that I insisted on the importance of a conceptually autonomous racial discourse in part because it helped highlight the connection between human bodies and the distribution of social goods. The social-naturalists develop this picture in rich and incisive ways. They stress the ways we connect bodies and bloodlines to the condition of belonging to a state or society, and they highlight the interpenetration of race-thinking with questions of beauty, desirability, sex, and reproduction. These instances of conceptual and affective connection are unavoidable features of any adequate account of race in the West, as well as of US history and society.

My only worry about the social-naturalist account, and my main motivation for adopting a different account, is that it fails to distinguish between groups and populations, and treats races mostly as groups. I talk about populations because groups and populations are different, and the difference matters. I've been happy to leave the distinction murky to this point, but now it has to do some work.

A group, strictly speaking, is a collective in which the members are aware of whatever binds them together. When we take a walk together, we are a group, because we've oriented ourselves toward a joint project that we share. By contrast, when I look out my window and point out all the strangers who happen to be walking down my street at the same time, I've picked out a population. To take examples of less transient social collectives: all of the red-haired people in Yankee Stadium during a baseball game constitute a population – the population of red-haired people, who happen to share a phenotypic trait that I've taken as the basis for lumping them together. By contrast, the Bronx Redhead Coalition, if there were such a thing, would be a group, because its members have come together out of a common interest in the condition or experience of being a red-haired person. (This is not a point about how we in fact use the words "group" and "population." I'm appropriating the words to mark a distinction that some words ought to mark, and that social-naturalism declines to find words for.)

Populations result from sorting processes that can work without the knowledge of the people who get sorted, processes that appeal to traits that the people in the populations may not even know they have – think, for example, of the population of people with the gene for Tay-Sachs disease. Groups, by contrast, are the object and result of what philosophers call we-intentions (there are different accounts of what groups are, but this will do for my purposes). When I'm in a group, or when I act in my capacity as a member of a group, I act with other people on intentions that we share, intentions that have our collective as their object. When we go to dinner as a group, we intend not just to eat but also to share an experience. This means that our actions are coordinated in a way that they would not otherwise be, and that the motives behind those actions are not my motives but ours. I can unknowingly act in ways that mirror those of a group, as when my afternoon walk down Fifth Avenue finds me in the middle of a group of people who are strangers to me but who know each other and continue their conversation around me. And I can unwittingly act in ways that further the project of some group, as when my innocent request for directions keeps a police officer from noticing the thieves robbing that sidewalk vendor. But I can't be in a group and not know it.

I said not long ago that our common linguistic habits tell against the attempt to collapse race into ethnicity: Diallo and Chin, we're inclined to say, were victims of racism, not of ethnocentrism. Something similar happens if we try to treat races entirely as groups or communities. On some occasions we treat races as populations, or we use racial language to pick out populations. At these times, race-talk points us to individuals who don't see themselves as bound together, or who are bound together in ways they don't entirely appreciate. And it isn't clear how social-naturalism will tell an adequate story about these cases.

Question 7a: What the heck are you talking about?

Maybe some examples will help.
Example 1: John is the fourth generation son of Irish immigrants to the USA, and he's decided that he's not white. To counter his seamless Irish heritage, his pale complexion, and his straight, sandy hair, he cites the difficulty that his ancestors had in achieving the status of whiteness, and he insists on the uselessness of biological racialism. To press the point further he argues that the surest way to defeat racism is to abolish the idea of race, and, in particular, to abolish the idea of whiteness, which has caused so much trouble over the years. So, he says, he's not white. He cultivates a multi-racial circle of friends, all of whom agree with his reasoning and admire his ethical convictions. Nevertheless, they send him to the street to hail the taxis that would pass some of them by, they make sure they stand close to him in department stores, so they'll get waited on more quickly, and when they rent a house together, they send him to fill out the application and pick up the keys.

Example 2: Regina is a dark-skinned woman of African descent, born into a family that has lived in Tennessee since her newly manumitted great-great-grandfather moved there from Alabama just after the Civil War. Like John, Regina is a committed eliminativist; what's more, she treats her identity as a matter of personal style. She denies any deep attachment to African-American culture, which she says has been eclipsed by her fondness for Thai cooking, Indian saris, white men, and French furniture. And she feels no sympathy with the causes that galvanize black nationalists. Injustice comes in many different forms, she says, and there are lots of ways to fight it, if one is so inclined. Still, when she goes clubbing with her white and Asian female friends, she finds that they have much better luck with the white men than she does, though she does well enough; and when she finds her ideal (white) man – John – and marries him, she finds that his parents are able to contribute a bit more toward their first house than her parents, despite having precisely the same class background (both fathers worked in factories, both mothers were teachers). When she confronts her parents to demand an explanation, they point out that John's grandparents were able to get a federally secured mortgage in the 1940s, while her grandparents were excluded on racial grounds. John's family grew the equity from that first house and passed it across the generations, while her family built wealth much more slowly, starting with a higher-rate mortgage in a less-desirable neighborhood.

In both these cases, there is a sense in which we could say with considerable plausibility that Regina and John really are what they claim not to be. John's whiteness is what his friends count on when they make him their advance guard in social transactions. Talking about his whiteness, more precisely, is a way of describing what is surely a fact about him: his ability to enjoy the privileges of white supremacy, even when he specifically disclaims any racial identity. Similarly, Regina is black in the sense that her life chances are negatively impacted by anti-black race-thinking, both directly, in the clubs, and indirectly, in the wake of generations of pro-white racial preferences. And talking about her blackness is a way of indicating the socioeconomic location that a history of racial practices leaves her in.

Of course, there is also a sense in which it seems quite strange, perhaps even oppressive, to insist that these people are what they say they aren't. The sense of strangeness intensifies if we take seriously the idea developed above, that race, whatever it is, depends on a network of conventions and tacit agreements for its existence. If there are races only by agreement, or, better, convention, then how can we shoehorn people into groups whose existence they specifically deny or ignore?

This is a question about the gap between identification, or how I see myself, and ascription, or how society places me. And it'll be easier to answer this question once we've developed the conceptual resources that constitute the last metaphysical approach to critical race theory. For now, the point is just this: if we treat races just as groups, or communities, even in the manner of the social naturalist, then it's hard to see what to say about John and Regina, both of whom explicitly try to opt out of "their" racial groups. More precisely, it's hard to see what to say about what we say about John and Regina, both of whom we could describe racially without doing violence to the way we use the language.

In fairness to the social-naturalist approach, we should note the sense in which Regina's difficulty on the club scene actually attests to the utility of thinking about races as breeding units. After all, her experience reveals the prevalence of the sorting mechanisms that the approach requires, and even if she exempts herself from these mechanisms, their predominance, their operation by and large, should be enough to make the point. Still, though, these breeding units result from the operation of forces that also shape Regina's life and experiences. There is a sense in which these social forces mark her as a black person, personally and directly, instead of simply creating a breeding group that she then belongs to, no matter what she does individually. If that's right, then race membership can't entirely be a matter of membership in the breeding group. It must have something to do with being positioned by the forces that produce these groups. To say that is to say that the forces in question, the forces of what we've seen people refer to as racial formation and racial fabrication, produce states of affairs apart from these groups: they do things to us, individually, as well. The metaphysics of critical race theory should account for this fact.

So here's the punch line: The communitarian believes that we create races by creating cultural groups. The social naturalist in particular believes that these groups are breeding communities, whose members by and large see each other as appropriate candidates for mating. On this account people like Regina and John belong to their races only derivatively: their membership is parasitic upon the fact that other members of the group comport themselves in certain ways. But we tend to act toward and speak about Regina and John in ways that call for a non-derivative story about their racial identities.

Question 8: Granted, racism sorted us into populations –

Loosely.
     – "Loosely"?
Loosely. In the sense that the correlations that define them are statistical instead of deterministic: they don't hold always and everywhere for everyone in the alleged race.

– Okay. And, sure, you can call these populations "races" if you want, using your little definition. But what's at stake? Why not define race-thinking in terms of classical racialism, and let them both expire together? To return to the question you postponed before: why would you bother holding onto race? Why insist that races are real?

We've already considered a couple of answers to these questions. First, as the quasi-racialists say, there is some value in inhabiting racial discourse at least for a time, because it still drives so much of what happens in the world. And second, as the social-naturalists remind us, the idea of race has an intimate connection to, well, the intimate affairs of human social life. Using the race-concept is a simple way to evoke certain of the embodied and erotic aspects of social organization.

Question 8a: So you want to say races are real because it's useful to say so. Well, it's useful for me to say I'm the most successful person in the world:

makes me feel good, you know. But that doesn't make it true. (Though of course it is.)

Just so. And if I were urging you to *pretend* that races are real for the sake of some further end, the point would be germane. But that's not what I'm urging. The suggestion is not that if having certain objects around would be useful, then we can act as if the objects exist. It's that we take usefulness as a motivation for choosing between competing world-descriptions, not as a motivation for inventing one. I'll have to take a bit of a detour to explain this.

Remember how we talked about money depending on human agreements for its existence? It turns out that there are lots of things like this. Let's call them institutional facts, and let's make a short list of some examples: money we've talked about; but consider marriages, touchdowns, and torts.

The force of calling these things institutional facts is to indicate their reliance on a network of conventions, agreements, institutions, and practices. A tort is a nonconsensual harm that is actionable under civil law. (This is different from a torte, unless the torte is very bad, or grossly misused.) If I hit you in the head with a frying pan, I've committed a tort: you could sue me for battery, or something. I should say, my hitting you is a tort provided that the right network of practices is in place – provided there is such a thing as the civil law.

A touchdown is what someone playing American football gets when they enter a part of the field called an end zone while carrying the football. Scoring a touchdown gives the ball-carrier's team six points. But going to the right place on the field counts as a touchdown only if there is a football game in progress – and if there is such a thing as football, with its constitutive conventions and rules. Otherwise I've just taken a stroll, or a jog.

Finally, if you say "I do" at the right point in the right kind of ceremony, you become someone's bride, or groom, or newly minted spouse. If you say it at the wrong time, or in the wrong institutional context – you should see a pattern developing here – then you've just said a couple of words, and you're still the same old you. But in the right context you become a Newlywed, with all that that entails.

Notice what happens in all of these cases. Thanks to the ontologically transformative power of social conventions, some entity or event for which we have a perfectly straightforward common-sense description undergoes transfiguration (in something like the sense of this term that philosopher Arthur Danto uses to talk about art). Human agreements, usually tacit or implicit ones, establish contexts within which things enter into new relationships, take on new properties, and participate in new schemes of interaction. When this happens, things of one sort undergo transfiguration and become things of another sort. The existence of civil law means that in the aftermath of my wild swing of the frying pan, I become liable, or duty-bound to compensate you. You can truthfully say of me, when you awaken, that I have the property of being liable, where otherwise I would simply be remorseful, or satisfied, or purged of bloodlust. The existence of civil law also means that my "I do" can be a causal force: after I say it, in the right context, with the right authorizations, and so on, I have duties that I didn't have before; and I've entered into relationships that I was not previously a party to, not just with my spouse, but with her family as well.

All of this relates to race in the way we started toward in the critique of eliminativism. Just as institutional context turns a properly produced piece of paper – a paper with the right causal history and physical features – into legal tender, institutional context turns a person with the right ancestry and appearance – the right causal history and physical features – into a member of, say, the Asian race. So the proposal is not that we simply slap racial labels on things to accomplish some putatively laudable goal. The claim is that race-talk is well-suited to the task of noting the ways in which people are already, and really, implicated in schemes of social interaction. These schemes of interaction have real consequences for their lives, as we've seen; and if we are willing to say of a piece of paper that is properly implicated in certain social relations that it really is worth a dollar, then we should be willing to say that a person who is properly implicated in certain social relations really is, say, a white person.

Question 9: You want to use utility to choose between competing descriptions of the world? Fine. Now you've got your competing descriptions. On the one hand, JJ's friend Lisa is a woman who looks the way she looks, descended from people from Japan. On the other hand, she's a member of the Asian race. But where is the alleged utility in choosing the second description? Why not just say that she's an individual, sometimes affected by the false beliefs of other individuals?

Of course, she is an individual, just like a dollar bill is a piece of paper. But for the purposes of tracking the paper in its career at the institutional level, we're better off focusing on it as a dollar. Similarly, if we want to track individuals in certain institutional contexts, we're better off seeing them as members of races. Think of the paper in the book you're holding –

– Is this another detour?

Yes, another detour. Think of the paper in the book you're holding (I'll assume you're not reading an e-book or some such). I could say that you're not really interacting with paper, but with a distinctive aggregate of protons, neutrons, and electrons. There isn't really any such thing as paper, I might continue, nor are there really any trees for paper to come from. Subatomic particles are the Alpha and Omega of existence, I thunder, oblivious to your increasingly puzzled stare. This is when you say something about having to catch a bus, any bus, and walk away.

We don't insist that physical objects are complex arrangements of smaller constituent elements, even though they are, because we usually set our metaphysical sights at a higher level of analysis. If we focused only on protons and the like, we'd have a pretty hard time talking about different kinds of paper, to say nothing of the stuff that's printed on the paper. We'd all be chemists, drawing little diagrams to represent the molecular structure of everything we want to talk about. And we'd all be exhausted after trying to link our diagrams to higher-level entities, like fonts, dependent clauses, or card stocks.

Sometimes it's important to stay at a higher level of analysis, even where reductions are available. If you don't like the paper-proton example, we could conjure up many more. A photographer will usually decline to point out that her print of Mount Vesuvius is really an arrangement of silver compounds in a gelatinous emulsion. (The photographer I'm imagining is the last living holdout in the transition from film to digital.) Musicians tend to think of themselves as interacting with themes, chords, harmonies, or scales, rather than with systems of overlapping vibrations in a fluid medium (the air). And a therapist, of a certain sort, anyway, will set aside the fact that the patient's behaviour proceeds from the operations of an electro-chemical processing system, and focus instead on what the patient believes, thinks, desires, and remembers.

All of these cases have the same moral, and the same explanation. We are ontological pluralists in the general course of events, because it is often important to us to focus on what happens at a specific level of reality, even if we can resolve that level into something more basic. This pluralism is important because different levels of reality highlight different kinds of forces and interactions.

Just as there are contexts in which it makes sense to treat aggregates of subatomic particles as instances of paper, there are contexts in which it makes sense to treat aggregates of individuals as races. When particles (or clumps) relate to each other in the right ways, they create higher-level entities that interact or behave in ways that we can more easily describe and analyze at the higher level. Similarly, when individual people relate to each other in certain ways, they create higher-level entities – races – that interact and behave in ways that we can describe only with difficulty at the lower level.

I want to say that racial populations are real things built from individual agents and behaviours, in something like the way that pieces of paper are real things built from protons and their ilk. Both resist reduction or resolution into their constituent elements, because staying at the aggregate level reveals patterns and phenomena that we might otherwise miss. If I focus just on atoms I'll look right past, or beneath, or through, the paper. Similarly, if I focus just on individuals I might not notice patterns of residential segregation, or of occupational concentration, or of governmental inattention or over-attention. If I focus just on individuals, I might be strongly inclined to say that black unemployment is entirely a problem of motivation and initiative, that *those people* just don't have the pluck to succeed. There might be something in this sort of explanation for some individuals: there are good apples and bad apples in every bunch, after all. But it is surely too quick simply to decide, *a priori*, that no more systemic explanation is available. If I start more generally, locating individual experiences in relation to systemically operative social forces, then I might find that certain social arrangements routinely generate situations in which jobs and people are not likely to find each other. I might even find a more systemic explanation for the cases of squandered human capital – an explanation appealing, as it might be, to the enervating experiences of despair, hopelessness, and alienation.

So race-thinking is useful first of all in the way that motivates one typical argument against doing away with racial classifications. If you stop letting yourself notice, statistically, who's Asian or black or whatever, then you'll have a hard time noticing patterns that may point you to systemic problems, like the economic fallout from years of alien land laws, or the public health fallout from the discriminatory delivery of medical services. These will not be the only interesting patterns, surely, but they are still worth knowing about.

Question 10: Now tell me why I, as an individual, should accept the racial description of myself. You've convinced me that I can use race-talk in connection with populations. If I were an epidemiologist, I might want to look at racial statistics, to keep track of how the mechanisms of racial stratification affect public health (although this is not as straightforward as it sounds). So you've motivated an external description of racial individuals. But why should I apply that description to myself, as it were, internally?

Good question. (It sounds like you've been talking to philosopher Robert Gooding-Williams. He distinguishes between being black and being a black *person*, where the latter corresponds to your internal description or self-conscious embrace of a racial identity.)[27] So far we've talked about racial formation on a macro-level, in terms of how it affects and creates populations. But there's a great deal to say about how it impacts individuals. Racial formation creates identities along with populations. There are existential aspects to this process that

we'll explore in the next chapter. Here we can focus on the metaphysical aspects.

The basic point is that a racial description of a person effectively
locates that person in a racialized scheme of social interaction. It indicates, provisionally and defeasibly and in connection with all sorts of
other social categories, the sorts of things that are more or less likely
to happen to her or be true of her. If she could easily extricate herself
from the network of practices and relations that defines the contemporary racial situation, then there wouldn't be much point in insisting
on the racial description. But some practices are so ingrained in the
general workings of a society that one can't opt out of the practice
without opting out of the society. I might unilaterally decide that I
want to stop using money (*it's just paper*, I say, or *bits of information on
a server somewhere*, or *notations in an accounting ledger; it isn't REALLY
worth anything*). But I'll have a difficult time acting on that decision
while also remaining connected to my current social context. Or,
better: even though I very much want to stop being a debtor, I can't
just unilaterally opt out of my relationships with my creditors. That
would ruin my credit rating – another of these almost compulsory
institutional facts. Race after white supremacy, like money under capitalism, seems to define a pervasive institutional context, one that we
can opt out of only with great difficulty.

(Of course, this raises once more the ethical questions I've been
putting off. Just as the right sort of socialist might say that the dollar
system is morally illegitimate and therefore ought to be abolished, the
right sort of eliminativist might say that the system of racial construction is illegitimate, and should be abolished. Let's call this the position
of an ethical eliminativist, as opposed to the metaphysical variety we
encountered before. We'll examine this position in the next chapter,
after we finish with the metaphysics.)

Now we can restate the question: what good does it do an individual, any individual, to locate herself on the racialized social landscape? First of all, there might be cultural considerations. As the
quasi-racialist suggests, race-thinking defines certain forms of life in
the West. As an African-American person of a certain age, background,
and temperament, it is an important part of who I am that I am black.
Not just that I am African American, which is an ethnic identification,
but that I am a member of the black race, in my sense. To say this is
to say that certain connections exist or can be made between my ethnic
and cultural background and the background of a black person from
Kenya, Ghana, or Haiti. This isn't to say that black folk everywhere
share a common culture; it is to say that various African-derived cultures may be similarly oriented toward the idea of a black race, or
toward the idea of being similarly situated vis-à-vis the history and
practice of white supremacy. Yes, the connections that result from this

will in a sense be artificial, and chosen; they may be the result of our common immersion in pan-African ideas. But they are connections, nonetheless. And yes, I can make other connections too, for example to my fellow *estadounidenses*, or my fellow southerners. People can identify with all sorts of things; and the way I've been encouraged to inhabit African-American – and American – culture encourages me to make blackness one of the things with which I identify.

Of course, not everyone has these cultural motivations. So as a second approximation, consider that a racial identity can also be a bundle of predictions regarding one's path through a racialized social terrain: it can be a theory about one's social positioning. Call this the bundle theory, or the theory theory, of racial identity. The West African immigrants we encountered in the discussion of Amadou Diallo said they were learning what it meant to be black in the United States. This means at least in part that they have recognized that certain kinds of things are more likely happen to them just on account of how they look, and they're using the racial label as shorthand for – as a bundle of predictions or a theory about – that fact. In a similar spirit, W. E. B. Du Bois said in 1940 that to be a black person was to be someone who had to ride in the segregated Jim Crow car in Georgia. This was not the whole story for him, as he went on to offer a political and cultural theory of pan-African identification. But parallel social locations were a key element for him in constructing that identity as specifically racial.

Literary theorist Paula Moya helps us locate this "theory theory" in a discussion of what she joins others in calling, a bit clumsily, the post-positivist realist theory of identity.[28] She argues that identities are ways of approaching the world. They are theories, she says, that help us make sense of what happens to us, and that help us prepare for what's likely to happen to us. For this reason, some identities – some ways of describing ourselves – can be better than others. An identity, a description, that points you to the dynamics and forces that are most likely to shape your experiences, is a useful instrument. It helps you navigate the world, not just by making it easier for you to describe yourself, but by making it less likely that you'll overlook aspects of your environing conditions that are relevant to your prospects. Moya reports that she once thought of herself as Spanish, and so was unprepared for the anti-Mexican prejudice she faced when she got to college. If she had thought of herself as Mexican, or, better, as Chicana, she probably wouldn't have been as surprised or perplexed by the behaviour of her fellow students.

Moya's embrace of a Chicana identity points to a third respect in which a racial identity may be valuable at the micro-level. In addition to marking my place in a cultural form of life and providing me with a bundle of predictions about the experiences I'm likely to have, claiming a racial identity may be the first step on a political journey: it may be the beginning or the product of a consciousness-raising experience. For Moya and many others, Chicana is to Mexican–American as (again, for many people) African American is to Colored: using the first term in each pair signifies one's social identity *and* one's acceptance of something like the theory theory. On this approach, Colored folks and Mexican–Americans simply occupy the place that white supremacy assigns them in society, perhaps without thinking much about how they got there. But Chicanas, Chicanos, and African Americans insist on the political, historical, and social processes that have created their social locations. To identify as a Chicana is to recognize that every component of the term "Mexican–American" is problematic, not least because the hyphen embodies tensions that the hyphen in, for example, "Italian-American" no longer does (and some say it never did). And to identify as an African American is to insist, perhaps, on the African ancestry and cultural background that drops out of "Colored," and that refutes the charges of cultural vacuity that have dogged darker peoples since the onset of modernity. Similar arguments also show up in the critical whiteness literature. White people can claim whiteness, people like Noel Ignatiev say, as a way of recognizing the racial privileges that they still enjoy, and as a first step toward disclaiming those privileges, all in the spirit of justice that animated radical abolitionists like John Brown.[29] So accepting a transfigured description of myself may be a way of announcing the truth of the theory theory, of steeling myself to face the challenges that critical race-thinking predicts for my future, and of preparing myself for the political work of responding to those challenges.

3.6 Conclusion

As metaphysicians of race theory, we could respond to the fall of classical racialism in different ways. We could ignore it, perhaps by decrying all the arguments from the physical anthropologists and the multiculturalists either as propaganda put forth by timid or corrupt epistemic and political authorities, or as irrelevant to the distribution of power and resources that we wish to maintain or create. This would align us with white supremacists and certain black nationalists, as well as with advocates for the new racism of the late-modern era. On the other hand, we could try to shore up or replace the nineteenth century's grounds for believing in deep, essential differences between our Races. This would make us, well, classical racialists, neo-classicists if you want a new name, and it would align us with the authors of *The Bell Curve*, and many others.

The burden of this chapter has not been to explore and summarize the views of these old and new classical racialists. Our subject here has been the metaphysics of critical race theory: we've tried to see what follows for racial ontology and for our racial practices once we accept the arguments against classical racialism. And we've seen that one might try to explain and respond to the ontological commitments of critical racialism in a handful of ways.

The skeptic says that classical racialism takes race with it when it falls, so that there are no races. This leaves race-talk devoid of its referents, and leaves the skeptic the burden of telling us what the persistence of racial discourse means. One kind of skeptic – the eliminativist – says that we're misguided or malevolent, lying either to ourselves or to each other; while another kind – the quasi-racialist – says that we're either participating in or provisionally accepting the consequences of a kind of myth-making, where literal falsehoods serve social functions that we want to promote or understand.

The realist, by contrast, says that race-talk is a lie only on an unduly narrow conception of what "race" means, and that myth-making is a way of bringing social realities into being. The communitarian realist says in effect that racial myths – the nineteenth-century falsehoods, and the forms of organization that remain in their wake – did what all effective myths do: they created communities, cultural groups whose members think of themselves as having embarked on a joint project of some sort. The nationalist defines the joint project politically and prospectively, using the myths to build a community with aspirations to some level of self-determination, and with internal ethical relations. The social-naturalist locates the joint project at the intersection of culture and biology, by showing how we've used cultural norms – concerning beauty, and who counts as an appropriate mate – to constrain our processes of biological reproduction.

My view, which I promised to call radical constructionism, extends the insights of social naturalism by emphasizing the array of conditions that connect the morphological prerequisites for racial identity to social goods like erotic and romantic interest. For the radical constructionist, our social practices create populations as well as breeding groups, by connecting certain bodies and bloodlines to certain social locations and modes of treatment. On this view, races are probabilistically defined populations. If we pick out subsets of the US population by focusing on bodies and bloodlines in the way that race-thinking suggests, we'll find that the members of these subsets tend to be – *tend to be* – similarly situated with regard to certain social conditions, including the mechanisms and measures of social stratification. Since these mechanisms assign meaning – a statistical relation to certain measures of social stratification, for example – to bodies and bloodlines, we can speak of them as racializing, and of the populations they create as races.

Radical constructionism also introduces the idea of transfiguration, as a way of calling attention to the way racializing practices create distinct contexts of interaction, defined by distinctive relations and dynamics. Race-talk is a way of capturing or describing people and populations from the standpoint of these contexts. And the utility of this mode of description and of the stance that generates it, when and where they are useful, recommends them over other stances and descriptions. This is an aspect of radical constructionism that we might think of as instrumentalist.

When one emphasizes the reality of race, even, or perhaps especially, in the constructionist manner I've endorsed, it is important to be clear about what one isn't saying. I don't mean to suggest on behalf of radical constructionism that individuals are only or most saliently members of races. One might adduce considerations like the ones raised here for identifying oneself by reference to other principles of social differentiation, like gender or class. The point has just been that the metaphysics of race is a contextual affair, that race-talk highlights the relations, forces, and dynamics that characterize and distinguish certain important contexts, and that individuals who find themselves embedded in and affected by the relevant contexts have reason to attend to the truths, the propositions about existing relations and dynamics, that race-talk points to. That certainly doesn't mean that they can't attend to the ways in which they are implicated in and by other contexts, and by the ways in which their environing contexts interact and shape each other.

Also, I'm not rejecting the idea that races ought to be abolished, or race-talk ultimately eliminated. Radical constructionism explores the processes that eventuate in the social construction of race; but something once constructed can certainly be troublesome and worth demolishing. Just as we can say of an already completed building that it is an eyesore, or an environmental hazard, or an urban planning nightmare, and should therefore be torn down, a radical constructionist can say with the eliminativist that our races are ethical hazards, more dangerous than useful. The important thing, though, is to be clear that the eliminativist can't get this conclusion strictly on metaphysical grounds. (*Tear that construct down*, the eliminativist says. Why? *Because it doesn't exist. . . .*)

Finally, I'm not saying that racism is the only thing that creates races. I am claiming that white supremacy created the conditions under which the modern Races came into being. But once those conditions were in place, the process of racial formation began, with its continual contestation over the meaning and import of racial discourse. The people in the disfavored groups were not passive objects of racist manipulation; they did what people always do, everywhere: they made lives for themselves using the cultural resources they had at hand. Races, as I've defined them, are not cultural groups, strictly speaking. But they are features of the social landscape around which social groups can form.

All of this leads us back to the ethical question, or questions, that I've been setting aside until we had the language to deal with them. Should we abolish races? Even if races are social constructs in the sense elaborated above, might they not be problematic constructs, like the flawed building? And if they are, shouldn't we strive for the eliminativist's ultimate aim, if perhaps at the quasi-racialist's deliberate pace: a ban on the practices of racial identification? I'll take these questions up, finally, in the next chapter.

Part II
Practice

4

Existence, Experience, Elisions

Prologue

"Hey, Boyd. When you get rich and famous, don't forget your nose."

"I think you mean, 'don't forget your friends.' Or 'don't forget where you came from.'"

"No, I mean don't forget your nose. I'm tired of black folk striking it rich and then hiring plastic surgeons to make them look white. Just think of how poor Michael Jackson used to look, God rest his soul. Him and his whole family, just about. Ain't a one of them still got the full Africoid nose that God gave them. Hell, Michael hardly had any nose left at all by the end."

"Africoid?"

"Yes, Africoid. As in from Africa. As in –"

"I know what it means. It's just a little weird. Anyway, aren't you being a bit judgmental? Lots of people in entertainment get plastic surgery, not just black people. Maybe it's not even about race."

"Mm-hm. Did you ever see Michael Jackson?"

"Okay, so he was a special case, with the hair and the skin and everything. But –"

But nothing. Black folk have always had the nose thing. When my baby niece LaMarque was born, my grandma was always pinching the poor girl's little nostrils together. Like millions of black grandmas did to millions of black babies before. Like that was going to keep her from developing the wide, glorious Semple nose. Michael just inherited this old nose complex and replaced his grandma with a bunch of doctors.

"I'm talking about self-hatred, brother Boyd. About people changing themselves to look different. To look like a different kind of person. I'm talking about people looking in the mirror, thinking 'If only I weren't like this.' What kind of mess is that? Back in the day, maybe, when if you looked white enough you could *pass* as white and get better jobs and whatnot. But now?"

"I still think it's not just black people. Asian people get eyelid surgery, and the plastic surgery business got started on Jewish noses and Irish ears."

"It's not just black people, but it's still about race. Maybe people aren't thinking, 'I wanna look like a white person.' But their ideas about how they should look have been shaped by a world where white is beautiful and everything else is ugly."

"It's self-hatred, I'm telling you. And it was written all over Michael Jackson's face. I hate to speak ill of the dead –"

"But you will anyway," I said.

"But he had the nerve to sing about how he didn't want to be black or white, or any color. He sure looked like he was aiming to be white. If he didn't wanna be any color, he'd a had to turn transparent. Otherwise, he shoulda told his doctor to make him look like a brother from the Dominican Republic, or from Hawai'i. Or somewhere else where everyone is all mixed."

"We're all 'all mixed.' "

"Don't start that. You know what I mean. I mean mixed like, black parent, white parent. Mixed."

"If Michael had thought to go for that look, he might have remembered that being mixed in the USA means being invisible."

"Invisible? Tiger Woods is invisible? Mariah Carey? All them light brown fashion models? They got the bronzed, exotic looking ones, the freckled, wild-haired ones, the –"

"But what about the people who aren't stars or models? What about the school kids who feel like they have to choose between the black side of the cafeteria and the white side? Or between Mom and Dad?"

"Aw, this is the best time ever to be mixed. They got the census people to change the categories for them back in, what was it, '97? They got organizations and magazines, they got Halle Berry and the Rock and Vin Diesel. They even got President Obama, for goodness' sake. And what do you care, anyway? You're not mixed, you're just light-skinned, right? Right, Boyd?"

4.1 Introduction

So far this book has been an extended exercise in what philosophers call conceptual analysis. I've tried to take the presuppositions behind certain widespread practices of racial identification and distill them into a coherent philosophical account. This process of distillation is not a matter of reading people's minds and explaining what they are in fact thinking, for at least a couple of reasons. First of all, people are in general pretty unclear about the principles that govern their behaviour and their conceptual discriminations. This is not a swipe at the rational faculties of the average person, but a generalization about how we think and act. We have habits, after all, that practically think for us much of the time; this is (in part) why it's so hard to explain how to do things that we can do with ease, and why people give such bad driving directions. (It is also why we have therapists, and cultural critics.) So even if there were perfectly consistent principles behind our adventures in race-thinking, it would take some effort to locate them.

As it happens, though, and this is the second reason why the analysis of race is not a report of explicitly held beliefs, we haven't allowed ourselves the conceptual resources to explain our racial practices. Our practices of racial identification have developed in ways that race-talk drawn from the nineteenth century can't countenance, even when that vocabulary is put in the service of critical race theory. But the idea of race still captures some aspects of the contemporary social landscape better than any other way of thinking. This simultaneous obsolescence and relevance produces a peculiar but familiar ambivalence; this is what moves Appiah to say that races do not exist but racial identities do, and what encourages Roediger to say that anti-racist work must remain "caught up in" the same racial categories it aims to abolish. I've tried to bring race-talk up to date, to reconcile the theory with our practices, to take race seriously in words, and, eventually, in the ontological world-pictures that the words represent, the way we take it seriously in society and politics.

So in chapter 1 I interpreted our practices, including our linguistic practices, in a way that refined the often-inchoate distinctions that mark "race" off from other ideas. Chapter 2 explored the ethical, conceptual, and sociohistorical settings for racial discourse, gradually zeroing in on the cultural context that is my here and now – the early twenty-first-century United States – and the distinctive version of modern racialism that comes with it. And chapter 3 began with more history, before examining the metaphysical and epistemic implications of taking race-talk seriously. These implications led me to three suggestions: that races are institutional facts, involving statistically defined relations between bodies, bloodlines, and mechanisms of social stratification; that they have as good a claim to the status of reality as dollar bills, tortfeasors, and players in football games; and that we have ample epistemic warrant for accepting them into our social ontologies, and for accepting the descriptions of ourselves that a racial level of social analysis makes available to us.

If this radical constructionist approach is right, then races are aspects of real systems of social interactions and forces – systems that I'll denote with the single word, "race" – just as physical objects are aspects of real systems of physical interactions and forces. This may just mean that metaphysics is cheap, that all sorts of things can count as real if we're willing or determined to interact with them in certain ways. In either case, whether radical constructionism is interestingly true or whether it follows trivially from deflating the pretensions of metaphysics, we've cleared the way to address some questions that I've repeatedly put off, and to shift from analysis to other modes of thought.

Most of the postponed questions were ethical in nature, and related to the suspicion that race is a problematic social construct, one that we should stop building and using. Now that chapter 3 has removed the metaphysical window-dressing for this idea, we can address this ethical eliminativism on its own terms. I'll do that in section 4.2.

Some of the postponed questions were more existential and phenomenological in nature. I mean by this that they touched on two interlocked aspects of the human condition: that we aspire to find and give meaning during our time in the world, and that we spend our time in the world immersed in the medium of experience. Race inflects these basic realities in distinctive ways, ways that we almost took up in earlier discussions of passing, of the gap between ascription and identification, and of the racial and cultural hybridity of the Latino and Latina population. Those discussions sped past such deeper issues as double-consciousness, mixed-race identity, and invisibility. The remainder of the chapter will take up these issues in earnest, pausing along the way to consider the gaps and elisions in the model of US racialism that I've been working with.

4.2 Ethical eliminativism, for and against; or, the anti-racist challenge, take 2

We've already noted three arguments for ethical eliminativism, in the discussions of racism and eliminativism. The first argument is that race-thinking leads to racism (along with, we may now be inclined to say, races), and even if it doesn't always have this result, the risk is too great to take. Call this the slippery slope argument. The second argument is that race needlessly complicates struggles for justice, either by dividing what might be effective political coalitions, say, against poverty, along racial lines, or by encouraging activists to ignore the complexity of the issues that their constituents face. Call this the argument from political realism. And the third argument complains that race-thinking constrains us in our individual pursuits by imposing racial scripts that limit our horizons. Call this the argument from self-realization. I've been saying all along that we wouldn't be able to evaluate these arguments until we'd worked out more precisely just what race-thinking involves. Having done that, now we can see if we should continue to accept the way of thinking I've been describing.

4.2.1 *The slippery slope and the argument from political realism*

The history of race-thinking does provide ample motivation for the slippery slope worry. The modern world has been irrevocably and tragically shaped by race-related oppression, exclusion, exploitation, and genocide. And even if we could somehow guarantee that there would be no more large-scale, world-historical tragedies like the Holocaust and the displacement of the indigenous Americans, the notion of race would still make possible all the small-scale exclusions and slights that can poison the atmosphere of daily life.

History also provides plenty of motivation for both forms of the argument from political realism. In terms of race working to obscure intra-racial complexity, advocates for civil rights in the mid-twentieth century often ignored the gender and class conditions in light of which racial oppression worked differently for different people (remember from earlier? All the blacks are men . . .). And in terms of working as a wedge, race has often contributed to political divisions, in ways that we can appreciate from many different perspectives. A Marxist might note the way race-thinking has frequently blocked, or been invoked to prevent, the development of class solidarity, as when white labor unions excluded non-white workers. A feminist might say that only misguided racial nationalism could have prevented so many black women from seeing O. J. Simpson and Mike Tyson as agents of a system that systematically uses violence to keep women in their place. A liberal might worry that race-based affirmative action programs reveal a willingness to throw over our commitment to truly human values and rights in favor of campaigns for group rights. And a conservative might worry that such programs require meddling with time-tested cultural devices for protecting individual freedom, for encouraging initiative, and for rewarding merit.

Looking back at the history of race-thinking does reveal these and other ethical problems. But if we look forward to the continuing need to traverse the social terrain that's been shaped by racially motivated wrongs and tragedies, we may find it more useful to hold onto race than to abolish it. This is not an a priori conclusion, meant to catch the ethical critic in some fallacy; it is a hypothesis, meant to offer countervailing recommendations for practice. Social policies, campaigns, and movements are always elaborate experiments, based on projecting into the future our best estimates of existing conditions and of the prospects for intervention. My sense is that we're better able to right the wrongs of classical racialism if we hold onto race-thinking.

I believe this in part for the reasons I gave in discussing the quasi-racialist and the radical constructionist metaphysical perspectives: because we need the concept of race to help us note and track the consequences of racism. Past instances of racism still shape current social conditions, not least by setting in motion mechanisms of routine economic stratification; and current instances of racism can be mediated by such deep-seated psychological attitudes and well-established institutional arrangements that they can easily avoid casual detection. In both cases, it would be useful to adopt a racial stance, in light of which bodies and bloodlines give us defeasible insight into the social location of an individual or population.

But my conviction here, to be honest, also has something to do with the pessimism that I share with the people from whom I've borrowed the name, "critical race theory." Legal scholars like the late Derrick Bell insist that racism is an integral part of US social and political life, and that even well intentioned efforts to address this fact face overwhelming obstacles. In light of our inability to maintain a robust public sphere against the depredations of waning civic participation and debased political discourse, I'm inclined to think that there's considerable value in leaving ourselves recourse to Edmund Burke's "little platoons," the smaller associations that make up civil society and shelter us against the failures and incapacities of the state. And as things now stand, these "platoons" are often race-based interest groups and the ethnic communities that often find shelter inside them.

After that flirtation with pessimism, here's a more utopian consideration against the slippery slope argument and the argument from political realism. Race is a social construct, which means that we've taught ourselves how to make races. We may not have invented the practice from nothing; there does seem to be a basic, though certainly defeasible, impulse to racialize human difference (though just how basic it is remains an open question). But we have invented the specific ways of acting on this impulse, which means that we could unlearn our distinctions between the colored races, if we could summon the political will. The crossover successes, if they are that, of popular culture icons and trends, and the growth of the mixed-race identity movement, with its multi-racial individuals, trans-racial families by adoption, interracial couples, and hard-won concessions by the census bureau both attest to the instability of our current color-coding. But the lingering inequalities and exclusions of US society and culture attest to the staying power of our particular conceptions of Race. Unlearning our version of Race-thinking would require a massive effort at public education, and anything related to public education won't go anywhere unless it works through a variety of racial neuroses and through an assortment of issues in ethnic politics that we misleadingly think of as racial. So at the very least, the quasi-racialist program for abolition is right. We'll have to go through race to get rid of it. (Sorry, that wasn't so utopian after all.)

4.2.2 *The argument from self-realization*

The third ethical complaint against race-thinking is that it encourages individuals to imagine their life-plans in overly narrow ways. It encourages them to think of themselves, their prospects, their personal styles, and their relationships in accordance with oppressive racial scripts. We eventually developed this worry by introducing the gap between ascription and identification, between what I think of me and what society encourages people to think of me. From that perspective, and returning to our earlier examples (from section 3.4), the problem looks essentially like this: John and Regina deny that they are what we say they are. She says she's not black, he says he's not white. In addition to the motivations we gave them above, they both might say that these racial labels are too constraining, and don't adequately represent the way they think of themselves. We've seen that whiteness involves an assortment of unsavory things that John wishes to distance himself from, and that blackness doesn't capture Regina's diverse cultural sensibility. How do we resolve this tension without oppressing these individuals and without doing violence to the intuitions we explored above, intuitions that invite us to say that these people really are what we say they are?

One perhaps facile response is to say that the John-Regina problem is just a special case of a much broader difficulty. It is always a struggle to get people to see you the way you want to be seen. That's why we have the capacity to feel slighted and to worry for our reputations and to suffer embarrassment, and why politicians and celebrities have public relations campaigns. It's not obvious to me that critical race theory has to produce a solution to this quite general existential worry, which, if people like Hegel, Sartre, Freud, and, in a different way, Hobbes are right, may just be a condition of living in human society.

A second, more substantive response to the race-theoretic version of the problem of reconciling our public and private selves begins by distinguishing two senses of identity.[1] Individual identity corresponds to or reflects the way I see myself, while social identity appeals to some principle of social differentiation to reflect, as we said above, the way social forces position me. Social identities are, as we also said above, ontologically subjective but epistemically objective. They depend on human beliefs for their existence, but this dependence is conventional and systemic, and operates on such a large scale that individuals can opt out of the relevant system only with great difficulty. Just as I can't unilaterally decide to print my own money, I can't unilaterally decide to be a white person. I can make a decision that I articulate with the words, "I am white," but whiteness is a position on a social landscape, it is a global property that I possess, or not, in virtue of my role in a system of relations and forces. And I can't just unilaterally decide how I stand with respect to all that.

The two senses of identity are dialectically related in much the way ideals and realities are related. I have ideals concerning what I would like to be and what ought to be possible for me, and I would like to have those ideals respected by society. I also have ideas about what the world really is like, and how I have to comport myself in order to achieve my goals safely and effectively. My sense of reality tempers my sense of the ideal, but my ideals also motivate and shape my encounters with reality, and my attempts to reshape it.

Radical constructionism, especially in its instrumentalist aspect, calls for reasonable balance in this dialectical process. It heartily endorses the view that individuals are free to shape their own life-plans and senses of themselves, and that we should not ostracize and assault individuals who violate our expectations about such things as race and gender. But it also insists that we can effectively work on shaping our lives and our selves only if we accurately gauge the conditions under which we do this work. Race-thinking is a way of pointing to these conditions. It is easy to turn our rightful dismay over some of these conditions into an aversion to race; but it may be more productive to use race to identify and alter the conditions.

All of that to say: the ethical demand for self-realization is important, but it doesn't obviously trump the practical, political demand for a realistic sense of the context in which the self takes shape. One still has to determine just where to draw the line between real and ideal, and where and how to press reality in the direction of the ideal, and when to use already-existing avenues to pursue and shape one's conception of the ideal. But once again, that's an occasion for ethical experimentation: there is no a priori solution or key.

4.3 Existence, identity, and despair

My quarrel with the argument from self-realization touches on one of the oldest sources of philosophical and human perplexity: the problem of human existence. You know the problem I mean, and the questions it entails. Who am I, really? What should I do, or aspire to? And What's the point, anyway? Or, why bother asking these questions, or aspiring to do or be anything? Let's call these the questions of identity, agency, and meaning, and let's follow Lewis Gordon in saying that they define an area of inquiry called the philosophy of existence, or existential philosophy.[2] The philosophical movement known as existentialism has pursued these questions to surprising depths, providing us with important conceptual tools along the way. But many people have addressed these questions and engaged in existential reflections from other perspectives, as we can see from a cursory examination of any religion, or from a slightly less cursory examination of human cultural life.

The institutions and ideologies of modern racialism, like the elements of any broad cultural formation, purported to solve the problems of existence. But they did so in ways that often raised the basic questions anew. We've already caught glimpses of the questions of identity and agency while considering the tension between individual identity and the racial scripts of social identity. In this section we'll consider further the specifically existential import of this tension, and we'll consider how the question of meaning arises when societies force compliance with racial scripts and demand submission to racial hierarchies. Along the way, I'll help myself to some of the tools provided by the existentialists, but only in order to sketch a quite general picture of the existential implications of race. (I herewith absolve myself of the obligation to be faithful to some particular approach to existentialist terminology or procedure. There are many, and that's not what this book is about.)

4.3.1 The basics

Let's say that humans exist in an existential condition with four basic aspects: thrownness, absurdity, freedom, and responsibility. At birth we are thrown, as it were, without explanation into a world not of our making, including a social world of practices and institutions that were likely in full flower before we arrived, and that will likely continue without us. Our presence here is absurd or groundless because the universe offers us no rationally verifiable guidance or guarantees for living our lives, and because what guidance we do receive, from the social world, with its religions and cultures and ethical systems, is ultimately groundless also. So we are responsible for ourselves, forced to be free in a sense even deeper than Rousseau's: we have to choose who and what to make of ourselves, whether and how to accept or revise the paths that have been laid down for us by others. Our freedom consists largely of this capacity to excavate and come to some accommodation with societal influences, so that we chart our life paths not blindly but truly knowing what we are about, even if we finally decide to follow a well-worn path.

The realization that freedom and existence are groundless can be dizzying, like looking down from a great height (hence the force of "groundlessness" as a metaphor). The existentialists took this existential dizziness seriously, and analyzed it in terms of such notions as dread, anguish, and nausea. Even worse, the awesome responsibility of creating the meaning of one's own existence can be overwhelming, and the absence of guidance and certainty can be disheartening and

disorienting. This is how dizziness turns into nihilism, or the despair-
ing belief that life is pointless. It is also why existentialists are often
caricatured as depressive types.

Human cultures and institutions try to insulate us from this dizziness, but often at the cost of allowing us to evade responsibility for
ourselves. Institutionalized religions, for example, provide conceptions of the good life, of who we are and what we should do; they
mitigate the shock of thrown-ness by explaining our place in the universe; they buttress our experiments – our attempts to act and create
in the absence of guarantees – with faith; and they make freedom
significant by stressing the risk of momentous error, or sin. But, like
other human institutions, they often do all this by seducing us into
thinking that our paths in life are already charted, that our preferences
and ambitions, our values and desires, are determined or ultimately
ratified, somehow, by something not of our choosing.

We might raise two kinds of worries about this evasion. We might
cite the danger of living an undifferentiated or inauthentic life, in
which we fail to wrest control of our lives from the hands of society.
Or we might cite the danger of acting in bad faith, which is to say, of
lying to oneself about one's existential condition, in this case by trying
to shirk the responsibility for self-creation.

The philosophy of existence concerns itself with identity, agency,
and meaning in the face of absurdity, and with the dangers of nihilism,
inauthenticity, and bad faith. There are two obvious ways to connect
a view like this to the conditions of modern racialism. First, we can
locate the challenge of nihilism in the experience of white supremacist
terror and domination. And second, we can continue to explore the
questions of identity and agency as they arise in the tension between
individual and social identity.

4.3.2 Despair and terror

As we've frequently noted, for much of its history the USA formally,
explicitly, and severely limited the aspirations of its non-white peoples.
In so doing, it also prevented them from accomplishing the basic task
of existence. How can I create meaning for myself if white mobs can
destroy my home and business (or neighborhood, as in Tulsa, or town,
as in Rosewood) and lynch me with impunity; if an overseer can kill
me, rape me, or sell my children on a whim; or if empty treaties fail
to regulate the state's appetite for the land I think of not necessarily
as property but as home? Under these conditions, in the face of
powerlessness and organized terror, why should I bother? Why not
despair? Or, to put the point in a way that speaks more directly to
current conditions (though not in a way, at this point, that argues for
this description of the conditions): How can I create if my efforts are

blocked by generations of accumulated disadvantage; by pervasive, public, and official doubts about my ability to learn, to follow the law, or to speak English clearly; by disproportionate criminal sentencing and public school funding; or by the asymmetric and effectively unregulated exercise of police power? Why not despair?

This despair born of impotence has analogues for whites as well. Think, for example, of the feeling behind what's usually parodied as liberal guilt: the sense that one's white skin suggests to others that one is somehow ethically or politically compromised. This sense can lead to the impulse to assert one's anti-racist, or at least non-racist, bona fides, sometimes in a defensive and preemptive tone. But it can also lead to a sense of hopelessness, and to the unwillingness to participate in anti-racist organizing.

Liberal guilt is a contemporary phenomenon, available to us only after emancipatory racialism incorporated non-white perspectives into mainstream US racial projects. But the official and routine violence of classical racialism also caused white people to experience race-related feelings of meaninglessness and despair. Historians tells us that white southerners before the end of slavery lived in almost irrational fear of slave revolts, and that this fear fueled brutal assertions of dominance and power. We might speculate that this fear was an expression of a deep-seated guilt or ethical uncertainty, a stress-laden reaction to the dimly perceived truth – perceived more vividly by some than others – that some reprisal or radical moral shift was warranted. And we might speculate further, moving from the psychological realm to the philosophical, that this uncertainty shaded into the existential problems of groundlessness and anxiety, as the ethical foundations of a comprehensive form of life became unsteady. But this sort of speculation is done more convincingly in the manner of historians, in close proximity to the sources, the journal entries and letters and newspaper editorials, that show the texture of everyday experience and provide the data for the argument. So I'll content myself here with noting two things that we've unfortunately come to understand more clearly of late. First: a long-standing, low-level fear for one's life can sap the will to go on. And second, while a vivid, heightened fear for one's prospects can be similarly enervating, it can also lead to violence, to a general indifference to human life and suffering, and to authoritarian political mobilizations.

The experience of non-Anglo Europeans in America presents us with a second example of white anxiety under the terror of white supremacy. The non-Anglos were, in effect, and as we've discussed, just barely white when they started to come to the states in large numbers. Consequently, many of them suffered much the same treatment – in particular, lynching and forcible exclusion and expropriation – as the non-whites with whom they sometimes allied themselves (early on). Still, they did have the advantage of being officially white, however tenuous their claim to the title; and this meant that they were never slaves (after the mid 1600s), that they could own property, and that they were ultimately able to chart paths to upward racial mobility that were closed to non-whites. Just by changing their names (from Mihaly or Mikhail, say, to Michael, from Cohen to Cone, from Tejada to, of all things, Welch, as in Raquel), smoothing out their accents, helping to clear Indians from the path of westward expansion, and refusing to work with "Negroes" and "Chinamen," they could buttress their claim to whiteness.

But in adopting these techniques for minimizing their exposure to racist terror, the probationary whites created additional existential trials. Think of the familiar themes of the Euro-American immigrant experience. Think of how people forgot languages, refusing to speak them or pass them to younger generations; think of how they ignored traditions, expurgated family names, shifted world-views; think of how individuals and families floated in the cultural and experiential limbo between being "American" and being whatever they were before. All of this is a recipe for what I referred to above as existential dizziness, as the European "ethnics" stepped away from the cultural foundations that supported them and ventured onto the new and untried ground of American whiteness.

4.3.3 Double consciousness

I'm gesturing at the conditions that we associate with being, or becoming, what we call a hyphenated American, and this leads me directly to the second respect in which race implicates the philosophy of existence, and back to Du Bois's idea of double consciousness. Double consciousness is an old notion in philosophical psychology, available in Emerson and Goethe and elsewhere, connoting a kind of double personality or internal duality. At the beginning of the twentieth century, Du Bois applied this notion to the condition of African Americans. Perhaps the best-known example appears in this passage from his 1903 classic, *The Souls of Black Folk*:

> [T]he Negro is a sort of seventh son, born with a veil, and gifted with second-sight in this American world – a world which yields him no true self-consciousness, but only lets him see himself through the revelation of the other world. It is a peculiar sensation, this double-consciousness, this sense of always looking at one's self through the eyes of others, of measuring one's soul by the tape of a world that looks on in amused contempt and pity. One ever feels his two-ness, – an American, a Negro; two souls, two thoughts, two unreconciled strivings; two warring ideals

in one dark body. . . . The history of the American Negro is the history of this strife, – this longing . . . to merge his double self into a better and truer self.[3]

This reflection on the experience of mediated self-perception is complicated, relying on a number of assumptions and making a number of overlapping claims. Some of these are questionable, and have little to do with what I'm after here. There's the idea that being a Negro carries with it distinctive thoughts, strivings, and ideals (philosopher Paulin Hountondji calls this "unanimism"); there's the identification of blackness and manhood; there's a hint of the elitist identification of American Negroes with *the* Negro that Du Bois makes explicit elsewhere. But other assumptions and claims bring us closer to some important points in this introduction to the existential philosophy of race.

First, there's the potentially paralyzing nature of this inner turmoil and dissension, as the agent vacillates not just between, as we sometimes say, serving two masters, but also between two visions or conceptions of who he or she is. We can generate a version of this problem by returning briefly to the ethical eliminativist's argument from self-realization. The worry there was that racialism enlists us in the cause of stunting our own spiritual and psychological growth; that it provides us with scripts that tell us how we should act and where our affections and loyalties should lie, without regard for our individual preferences in these matters. To make matters worse, these scripts often come with tacit or explicit evaluations – the "amused contempt" of Du Bois's passage. I might chafe under the constraints of my script, if I feel a countervailing obligation to myself, or, for that matter, to some other script, like the one provided by my nationality or my class. And I might feel the conflict between a negative valuation of my racial identity and my own positive valuation of myself. All of this would inevitably take an existential toll on me, perhaps making me diffident and insecure in my journey toward self-creation, certainly sapping energy that I could use to fight other battles and solve other problems, maybe even weakening my resolve to keep answering that most basic question, why bother?

A second important point from Du Bois's discussion concerns the source of the internal duality. It is in part cultural for him, as Negroes are torn between their American aspirations and the cultural aspirations that the early Du Bois equated with racial identity. But a more interesting aspect remains even after we strip away this cultural nationalism. I'm thinking of his comment about "always looking at one's self through the eyes of others." I said earlier that the existential condition involves coming to some accommodation with societal

influence. This is what's at stake in Du Bois's discussion. Many subsequent writers have unpacked the idea using resources from philosophers like Hegel, Sartre, and de Beauvoir, but the basic point is
straightforward enough. Identity is always a relational affair: my
sense of myself is something that I come to while interacting with
other people. I try to see myself the way they will see me – that's why
we have mirrors in public bathrooms – and I try to constrain and
guide their perceptions of me – that's why we think so hard about
what to wear on that first date, and why we don't bring batting
helmets to business meetings. There is always some give-and-take
over our identities, especially where people we care about or who
have influence over us are concerned; and this give-and-take shapes
who we are. Identity is, in this sense, dialectical.

The dialectical nature of identity is especially evident where race
is concerned, and even more so when a negative conception of one's
racial group is widely held. Negative conceptions, of course, abound
in the modern West. Ideologies of non-white inferiority were key elements in the attempt to justify white supremacist institutions; and
ideologies of white moral depravity have been key elements in certain
modes of anti-racist resistance. So over the last few centuries, Western
cultures have produced racialized mythologies of symbolic value, like
the dominant Western model we saw in chapter 3. On this worldview
whiteness is rational, intelligent, brave, industrious, beautiful, civilized, and temperate; blackness is whimsical, stupid, timid, lazy, ugly,
savage, and licentious; and everyone else falls somewhere in between.
Native Americans were seen as savages, but as noble savages, and
sometimes beautiful. Asians were seen as timid, or lacking individual
initiative, but also as industrious and, in some inscrutable way that
put one more in mind of bees or ants than people, civilized.

If I know that I'm seen as a member of a population that is thought
to embody negative traits, then a handful of existential problems
follow. I may subordinate my journey toward self-creation and
meaning-making to the externally given mission of proving that the
stereotypes don't apply to me. Worse, I may struggle internally with
the thought that maybe they really do apply to me. Even worse, I may
find myself hesitating over concrete choices, paralyzed by the question of whether I'm acting for my own purposes or just trying to
change someone's opinion of me. And perhaps worst of all, I may
simply find myself pushed toward despair and nihilism by the persistent awareness of being undervalued and unappreciated. This dia-
lectic is the subtext of the stigma argument against affirmative action,
to which we'll return. The non-white person who benefits from some
race-based affirmative action program is, on this view, supposed to be
psychologically disabled by the knowledge that others feel affirmed
in their prejudices against her. If she weren't inferior, she feels them

thinking, why would she need this help? And this, the argument continues, makes her hesitant, and resentful, and distracted. So, the argument concludes, there are two reasons to eliminate affirmative action: we don't want to encourage people to think less of others than they should, and, more to the point just now, we don't want to subject people to situations in which they have to fight through the distracting knowledge that others look down on them. (As I say, we'll return to this argument. But I can't let it pass without insisting that we note its reliance on facts of empirical psychology: it is an empirical question whether people respond in these ways.)

4.3.4 Micro-diversity, part 1

A third point to glean from Du Bois's discussion of double-consciousness derives from his juxtaposition of double-consciousness and 'second-sight,' or clairvoyance. As before, there's a great deal to say about this idea that I won't cover here. For example, we could consider the "seventh son" language, with which Du Bois metaphorically invokes New World African traditions of conjure or vodou, the syncretic family of religions and mystical practices that helped enslaved Africans and their descendants forge common ties and carry forward West African traditions. Or we could explore the idea, systematically highlighted these days by people like bell hooks and David Roediger, that white supremacy turned non-whites into covert anthropologists, studying the ways of white people in order to help secure their own survival.[4] For now, though, I'll take this idea of second-sight just to indicate that the condition of double-consciousness, of self-perception complicated by racialization, needn't be debilitating. It can be productive. (Hence also Du Bois's "solution" to the problem of double-consciousness, as he says just after the passage I've reproduced: "In this merging he [the American Negro] wishes neither of the older selves to be lost.")[5]

We can see the potential productivity of double-consciousness by turning again to the condition of whiteness. Philosopher Linda Alcoff suggests that "white identity needs to develop its own version of 'double consciousness.'"[6] She argues that white identity might be productively suspended between, on the one hand, an awareness of the history of privilege and exploitation that has so shaped contemporary conditions, and, on the other, an awareness that many white people struggled against the grain of this history. Each side of this double sensibility is necessary. Without the awareness of privilege white identity becomes ahistorical, and the status quo, with whites on top, appears to be a natural occurrence rather than the outcome of centuries of social engineering. This encourages whites to see privilege as an entitlement, and to block campaigns for racial justice. On the other side, without an awareness of the white "race traitors" who fought against white supremacy, white identity may start to seem wholly negative, and that implicates once more the problems of guilt, despair, and nihilism.

We might broaden Alcoff's idea beyond the confines of white identity – and trace it to one of its sources – and say that her mode of double-consciousness encourages us to think from the underside of modernity. I've borrowed this phrase from the Latin American philosopher Enrique Dussell, who uses it to talk about the condition of non-whites under the quintessentially modern project of white supremacy. This condition provides a distinctive perspective on modernity, a perspective that calls into question the omissions and interpretations of the victors' stories. This is important for at least a couple of reasons. First, let's say that we're serious about instantiating the values that the victors in this case (and others) espoused, such as equality and universal rights and the continual development of human capacities into an open-ended future. More adequate, comprehensive stories, ones that supplement the victor's partial perspective with those of the vanquished, can tell us more accurately how things got to be the way they are, which can help us bring about change. Second, modernity, with all of its many and quite real benefits, came into existence at the cost of immense human suffering. This suffering constitutes the basic condition of modernity's underside, a condition toward which basic humaneness demands some sensitivity.

Moving back from white double-consciousness to the more general phenomenon, we might also note that in highlighting this inner duplicity we remind ourselves of the unavoidably messy process of fashioning identities and cultures. We – that is, we moderns – used to think of the self as a coherent entity, the stable core and source of our lives and activities. Then Freud, Marx, and others came along and dashed those hopes, suggesting that we end up the people we are, doing what we do, thanks to all sorts of forces that usually escape our notice. The self, it turns out, is a fractured and inconstant mess, and one of the burdens of life is to pull it together long enough, often enough, to accomplish anything (and to decide what accomplishment means). Similarly, we used to think of cultures as coherent and pure, self-contained and self-guided, often enough coterminous with racial groups. But there are no pure cultures, and there are no pure races: we're all mixed up. (Here I can't help but think of Elvis bringing what we call black music, but what was always a hybrid blend of Scotch, Irish, West African, and other musical influences, to a de-ethnicized white audience; or of a dreadlocked Don Byron playing klezmer-jazz; or of the Lebanese-descended, Colombian-raised, Caribbean-identified, US immigrant named Shakira Isabel Mebarak Ripoll – known to the many fans of her music simply as "Shakira.")[7] And since we're all mixed-up, only temporarily fixed in place – fixed in different places in different contexts – by our various identities, it may be useful to commemorate that fact by cultivating a sense of our inner heterogeneity. Naomi Zack has given the elegant name "micro-diversity" to an idea like this (soon we'll come to exactly what she means), and that seems exactly the right name for an emphasis on our inability to keep the seams in our identities from showing.

4.3.5 Micro-diversity, part 2

Zack uses the idea of micro-diversity to discuss another kind of inner heterogeneity, which expresses the racialized tension between self and society in a slightly different way. She has in mind the self's inner mirroring of the racial complexity of our diverse societies. Zack's target is the idea of racial purity, especially as it came to be understood in the USA after the 1890s. On that approach, capsulized in the rule of hypodescent, a single drop of non-white blood makes one non-white, as if by contamination, so that the people we now think of as white are supposed to have nothing but white ancestry. (This rule does not apply to everyone; it does not, in particular, apply to Native Americans, about whom more in a moment.)

As a sorting device for social purposes, the hypodescent rule works tolerably well, provided that the people in power commit themselves to it, as they did. But as a description of the US population, and as a way of tracking the sexual history of the population, the idea is a miserable failure. Attraction, desire, and procreation have always crossed racial lines, which means that the families and individuals that resulted from these transgressions also crossed the lines. Hypo-descent meant pushing these transgressors back to one side or another – and if white "blood" was involved, it (usually) meant staying on the non-white side. This wasn't always the case in the USA, which had a "mulatto" category on the census as late as 1890. But soon the rule took root, and after mixed-race African-American activists embraced it and strategically aligned themselves with clearly (!) black people, the "pure" groups absorbed the mixed-race population.

In recent decades a vocal and vibrant movement has emerged to try to reclaim some space for the micro-diverse, with considerable success. As we saw, the census now allows individuals to identify with more than one race, in part thanks to strenuous urging by the members of this movement. Also, social networks for the mixed-race commu-nity have proliferated in recent years, complete with magazines, con-ventions, and terms of art, like "Hapa" (a Hawaiian word for mixed-race people, specifically those with partial Asian heritage).

Mixed-race activists often employ a frankly existential line of argu-ment. It sometimes goes something like this: It is inappropriate to force someone of, say, white and Asian ancestry to choose between the two sides of their heritage. This is like, or more than like, asking them to choose one parent over the other. It is a demand that they suppress some part of who they are to fit society's arbitrary boxes. They shouldn't have to choose, and they shouldn't be faced with pressure, from society or the government, to declare one way or the other. And the only way to remove this pressure is to grant official status to mixed-race identities, perhaps by establishing mixed-race boxes on official forms, perhaps by giving people the option of checking more than one of the traditional boxes (the census solution, more or less), perhaps by abolishing box-checking altogether.

This sort of argument for mixed-race identity causes some people to worry, especially when the argument moves so quickly from considerations of identity, meaning, and bad faith to questions of policy. Some worry, for example, that granting official recognition to mixed-race people will create a new mixed-race community, and that this will diminish the ranks and political power of the mono-racial groups that would have counted the micro-diverse among their constituents. This is a concern about racial politics, about how best to respond to the various forms of exclusion that modern racism has brought into being. And it seems to me to be a real worry only on an unduly narrow conception of racial justice work. If you need racial solidarity as a necessary precondition for organizing people against injustice, then yes, micro-diversity may be a challenge. But if you think of racial solidarity as a starting point, as a useful but quite limited tool, then you'll need to build coalitions across racial boundaries in any case.

Other worries relate specifically to the move from mixed-race politics to eliminativism, especially in the practical form that wants to free us all from the burden of publicly declaring any racial identity. Some racial justice activists see this as just another rearguard action against racial classifications, an action that may raise both familiar and distinctive worries. A familiar concern about this practical eliminativism is that it may deprive us of the tools we need to notice and respond to continued racial discrimination.

Another less familiar concern, one with a special, more distinctive resonance in the context of a proposal based on micro-diversity, has to do with reinforcing or giving freer rein to colorism. This is a name for the view that lighter is better, a view that tracks and reinforces the hierarchy of racialized symbolic value that we've talked about, with black people at the bottom and whites at the top. In addition to separating racially defined populations, colorism also works within the communities that have grown up within white supremacy and internalized some of its principles. African-American communities, for example, once had brown bag and blue vein tests, on which complexions lighter than paper bags or light enough for veins to show through were made conditions of entry to social institutions. These tests have mostly disappeared, but lighter skin still carries with it significant relationship capital, and confers an advantage in many social and, apparently, professional settings. A critic of mixed-race eliminativism might worry that abolishing racial categories will not abolish colorism, which means that people who look less like white people will still be vilified, while people – mixed-race people – who come closer to being white will be more easily assimilated to the privileged racial position. To put the worry cynically: the mixed-race argument for eliminativism may simply be a way of claiming whiteness for the micro-diverse.

I don't propose to explore the merits of all the approaches that take micro-diversity as an argument for eliminativism. My sense is that whatever its source, eliminativism has certain limitations that I've already discussed. The interesting thing about those approaches just now is that they don't reveal any special link between micro-diversity and, say, the racial privacy initiatives from chapter 2. An interest in micro-diversity may be one way to motivate such an initiative, but declaring that interest in terms of something you're willing to call mixed-race identity actually presupposes a commitment to race-talk. Zack, for example, correctly argues that we're all racially mixed, and uses this fact in her argument against race-thinking. But then she concedes that some sort of race-thinking may be a practical necessity, especially for micro-diverse individuals who want to gain some measure of peace in a race-obsessed world.

So the existential concerns of the micro-diversity movement don't translate directly into eliminativist policy. They may not even translate directly into any policy regarding racial classifications, since we don't have to take bureaucratic categories as expressions of our cultural or individual identity. I can check "Asian" or "black" for political purposes, while fully embracing and celebrating my multi-faceted heritage in the aspects of my life that fall outside the purview of state bureaucracies. Still, there are many other reasons to want official state recognition, some related to the pervasive influence that the contemporary, bureaucratized nation-state has over civil society. To put it much too crudely: the state shapes public discourse in quite profound ways, and finding oneself written out of the official narratives of national life that this discourse disseminates may seem less like an opportunity to celebrate oneself and one's community in private than like an erasure.

This discussion of micro-diversity points us to some of the many gaps in the dominant model of US race-thinking. Conceptually, this model presupposes notions of racial purity and of tainted, and tainting, "blood." And socially, it shores up the illusion of purity by excluding the possibility of mixed-race people. In effect this leaves mixed-race people betwixt and between, stuck in a kind of social and existential limbo. US racial discourse, with its obsessive focus on black and white, also leaves certain other groups in between, in various ways. In the next, suitably intermediate section, flanked by discussions of the existential and phenomenological aspects of race, I'll explore this peculiar condition of interstitiality.

4.4 In between: illusions of purity and interstitial peoples

The earlier chapters of this book were meant to clarify the US version of Western-style race-thinking, and to shore it up, or to shore up something like it, for certain limited purposes. On my view, races are not cultural groups, though they can serve as incubators for them; and they are not self-conscious political entities, though they can produce conscious interest groups in the same way that any population can (think cancer survivors, Gulf War veterans, and so on, all with lobbyists and political action committees). On my view, the modern Races are probabilistically defined populations of people whose lives are affected by the operations of white supremacist institutions.

Since that's my definition of Race, you should not be surprised to find that I have no illusions about the existential limitations of race-thinking. It certainly does not point us to every interesting aspect of a person; it does its work only in combination with all of the other social forces that position us and shape us; and it is only sometimes useful or even relevant to our lives. In many contexts we are much more saliently other things before we are bearers of racial identities. That said, I of course still say that race-thinking has its uses, that holding onto the idea of race can help us identify, understand, and cope with the schemes of social interaction and stratification that exist in the wake of classical racialism and its nostalgic postmodern evocations. But I also say that we can reap these benefits only if we highlight the elisions and blind spots in our racial discourse.

The elisions I'll focus on here derive mostly from the US practice of identifying race relations with black and white. This practice has equated The Race Problem with The Negro Problem, and it has obscured the role that other races have played in the drama of the US racial order. There are at least a couple of quite straightforward reasons for this short-sighted binarism. First: thanks to the genocide and forced assimilation of indigenous peoples, the exclusion of Asian immigrants, the assumption that problematic Europeans were still white, and the steady importation and "breeding" of enslaved Africans, blacks and whites for the longest time constituted the largest racial populations. It was natural, then, that the problem of black folks under white supremacy should be more prominent. And second, blacks in the USA occupied a strangely paradoxical position, as social and political outcasts who were integral, in large numbers, to the economic and, in the South at least, to the private life of the nation. Simultaneously despised and essential, alien and intimate, African Americans were made a part of the country in ways that Indian wars and Asian exclusion acts made impossible for those populations.

There are, then, reasons behind the black–white binarism, but they are not reasons to perpetuate it. So I'll focus here on the populations that this binarism ignores or makes interstitial in one way or another. In the process, we should start to see more clearly that different groups get racialized differently. Blacks were racialized, usually, as subhuman brutes; whites, as the height of human achievement, as virtuous and beautiful angels. And the others fell in between.

Perhaps the most obvious elision in US race-thinking, apart from the question of micro-diversity with which it is closely allied, involves Latinos and Latinas. These populations are interstitial because they represent an alternative racialist model, the one that holds sway in the former Spanish and Portuguese colonies of the Americas. In these places racial hybridity is a widespread and openly accepted condition, as the European conquerors, the indigenous peoples, and the enslaved Africans mingled more or less freely (with some mingling more or less freely than others). There are many different explanations for the distance between the Iberians and the English on their openness to what we sometimes still call miscegenation. Some appeal to the different historical experiences of the two groups – one at the center, more or less, of a multicultural Roman empire, the other at the margins, seeking to maintain its political distinctness. Some appeal to the different techniques of settlement – one group sent settler families, the other sent military men without women or families. There are other views, and choosing between them is beyond the scope of this project. The point just now is that there is a sense in which Latin America is, as writer Richard Rodriguez so eloquently points out, brown, through and through. It consists in large part of racially mixed peoples, who have increasingly made their way to, or been engulfed by, a United States that doesn't quite know what to make of them.

In practice what this means is that Latino and Latina peoples in the USA are unevenly racialized. Sometimes we treat them like an ethnic group, though this course of action is commonly frustrated by the many, quite real, quite evident political and cultural differences between, say, Mexicans, Cubans, and Puerto Ricans. But at other times we treat them like a distinct race, a race of brown people who sometimes count as white, and who appear somewhat lower on the scale of racialized symbolic value that we've had a couple of occasions to mention. It is worth mentioning that this scale of value applies even on these more fluid models of race-thinking. Some have claimed that places like Brazil are more racially egalitarian, for example because, to put it crudely, the possibility that my family members might be of any race, or a mixture of all of them, makes me less likely to demonize the members of any one race. Unfortunately, a look at the rhetoric and reality of Brazil's racial terrain belies this claim. As is the case in every place that's been shaped by modern slavery, there is a pro-white colorist continuum: lighter is better. Wealth and prestige can "whiten" darker individuals, but for the most part the importance of color is literal, as when marrying someone lighter is treated as a blessing for you and your progeny. And, perhaps most tellingly, the Afro-Brazilian population – that is, those people who are unambiguously or predominantly black – are overrepresented among the poor and destitute, and underrepresented, as elsewhere in Latin America, in government and the media.

But to return to the USA: The dominant theme in current Latino and Latina racialization is a mode of what's called outsider racialization: this is what happens when a racial project constructs a group as alien or foreign. The contemporary moment presents all sorts of unprecedented possibilities: think of the postmodern mutability of (light-skinned) Jennifer Lopez, mentioned in chapter 3; or of the Texas ties of the Bush political dynasty, whose patriarch once crowed publicly about his "little brown" grandchildren. (It is difficult to imagine this crowing if the brown had come from mixing white and black!) But, as our quick visit with the census showed, the Latino and Latina people mostly suffer a kind of economic marginality that puts them quite close to blacks. It is morbidly fitting that they now dominate paid domestic work – cleaning, housekeeping, and so on – the way African Americans once did.

Asians also constitute an interstitial population, in ways that are in some respects similar to Latinos and Latinas. The fortunes of both groups are closely tied to the politics of outsider racialization, migration, refugees, and citizenship, especially in the context of formal and informal "guest worker" arrangements. These try to meet labor needs without upsetting the ethno-racial citizenship mix, either by formally proscribing the employment of undocumented workers while tacitly permitting it, or by turning desired workers into special classes of legal migrants. Asians in America, though, are also subject to model minority racialization, which is what happens when a minority group is racialized in a way that constructs it as exemplary, as a model for other groups in their quest to live up to mainstream or majority values.[8] Perhaps surprisingly, this mode of racialization does create problems. It glosses over the real cleavages in the Asian population, obscuring, for example, the differences between relatively affluent Japanese immigrants and relatively disadvantaged Vietnamese communities. And it overlooks the cultural and social differences that sometimes inflate the measures of Asian economic well-being – like the larger than average households, the greater percentage of residents in the workforce, and the higher proportion of foreign-born professionals, all of which inflate the household income statistics and conceal the sometimes difficult economic circumstances under which many Asian Americans live. I say that Asians – which, you'll recall, is my name for the people who occupy a certain position on the landscape of US racial politics – are an interstitial population because their model minority racialization places them squarely between blacks and whites. They are often held up as models of what blacks ought to do, and have failed to do. But they are also held apart from whites as irremediably foreign.

Native Americans are not so much interstitial as multiply anomalous, and hence in some ways outside the scale of US racial value. They are interstitial, though, in the sense that their specific mode of racialization involved the not entirely dehumanizing ideology of savagism. According to this idea, the Native, as a primitive version of modern humanity, is a harbinger of human possibilities as well as a reminder of what natural human goodness looked like before the corruptions of civilization. In the nineteenth century this meant extolling the virtues of the Indian, lamenting the impending extermination of the native ways of life, but actively seeking to bring extermination about. In the twentieth century and beyond this meant celebrating native bravery with ethnological sports mascots – the Washington Redskins football team, the Atlanta Braves and Cleveland Indians baseball teams, and so on – and extolling native nobility on film – *Dances With Wolves* – while continuing to treat Indian tribes as wards of the state.

The practice of using Native Americans as mascots points to just one of the respects in which this is an anomalous population, subject to a mode of racialization that the black–white model doesn't capture. Indian groups and individuals are divided on the question of these mascots; some find them dehumanizing, others don't care. But it is at least interesting that the only other ethnological mascots we still have – the Boston Celtics, the Syracuse Orangemen, and the Notre Dame Fighting Irish – celebrate, or "celebrate," the European people to whom the English first applied their ideas of innate savagery, the Irish. ("Celt" means more than this, denoting the language-culture group that inhabited lands in contemporary Wales, Ireland, Scotland, and elsewhere. But in the context of nineteenth-century US immigration politics, it came to denote a particular kind of non-Anglo immigrant, one that was easily racialized, and mostly equated with the "savage" Irish.) This use has become archaic, resonating now with the fully whitened Irish Catholic culture of places like Boston and Syracuse.

Bostonians identify with the Celtics, more or less. Do any Native American groups identify with the Cleveland Indians? As comedian Chris Rock once asked, can you imagine a team called, say, the New York Negroes? (Rock's language was somewhat more colorful.)

Native Americans experience a distinctive form of racialization also in that the USA treats the tribes, the recognized tribes, as subjugated sovereign nations, marginally self-governing but subject to the exigencies of US Indian policy. (They are not completely anomalous in this respect, since they share this at least quasi-colonial status with the peoples of the various US "possessions", like Puerto Rico and Guam.) And, finally, when the rest of the US racial order was moving to the one-drop rule of hypodescent, the US government declared that Indians had to be at least "half-bloods" – half-Indian – to count as Indian for official purposes. This is because the rule was linked to a policy of land allotment that distributed formerly tribal lands to Indian individuals. Since whatever land was left over could be sold, there were substantial economic interests to be served by finding as few Indians as possible. (Take this as another argument for chapter 2's merger thesis.)

We've been looking at interstitial populations, or populations whose members are racialized in ways that point to the gaps and rough edges in the dominant styles of US race-thinking. These examples also serve as a reminder that any general account of race-thinking will have to cover a number of different kinds of racial formation processes, often unfolding simultaneously and in a dialectical relationship. As a final example, we should consider a case that points both to the vexed history of race and to its developing future. We saw earlier that a conception of distinct and ranked white races was once popular, until shifts in immigration policy gave the probationary whites time and space to claim their status in full. I told that story mostly with European whites in mind, but the US government, which I take here as a codifier of common-sense attitudes (it is of course more than this), thinks more broadly about whiteness. According to the people behind the census, the "original peoples of the Middle East and North Africa" are also white. The morphology of many of these peoples has made it possible for them to submerge their cultural differences beneath their whiteness. But in the wake of the last World Trade Center attacks and the second *intifada*, we've become increasingly sensitive to the presence of people who "look Arab," especially men. This sensitivity is still most often mediated by cultural factors, like clothing and Arabic names. But in our determination to create a terrorist profile for use in restricting entry to sensitive locations, we've started to pay more attention to putatively Arab faces. And we've continued to refine a terrorist variation on the theme of outsider racialization, as we can see in any number of terrorist-attack films from the 1990s, including *The Siege*.

4.5 Experience, invisibility, and embodiment

So far we've approached race from the standpoint of a philosophy of existence. This has enabled us to uncover race-related problems of despair, and to find both positive and negative forms of double-consciousness. It has also enabled us to start registering the peculiar nature of the experiences of living under white supremacy: the experience of having one's self called into question, of wrestling with society over who and what one can be, and so on.

It seems, then, that there is also a phenomenological side to taking race seriously, in a sense that is articulated by but not limited to the philosophical movement known as phenomenology. We saw earlier that the philosophy of existence asks three questions: Who am I? What should I do? And why bother? As I'll use the idea here, a phenomenological standpoint adds a fourth question: what is it like to be that way (to be that person, doing those things)? Or: what is it like to be a being that can ask these questions, and to have the experiences this being has? As in the discussion of existential philosophy, I'd like to start toward a non-sectarian application of these ideas to the phenomenon of race; specifically, I'd like to introduce, in a non-sectarian manner, beholden to no Canonical Figure, the idea of a phenomenology of race. First we'll get the basics, then we'll see the application.

4.5.1 The basics

Asking the experience question points us in the direction of the three main elements in a philosophy of experience. First, there's a reorientation toward the immediate feeling of our experiences. These philosophies begin, as experience does, with the pre-theoretical perspective of practical agency, which finds the world populated not by the bare and abstract things that science describes, but by everyday things with meanings for us. Science turns our meaningful things, the things we love and value and fear (a photograph, a concerto), into meaningless things, made of particles and motions and chemical relations (an arrangement of silver compounds in a gelatinous emulsion, a complex of vibrations in a fluid medium). But we pursue the denuded objects of science and reflection using techniques shaped by our values, aims, and fears. And we often do this for the sake of forestalling our fears and ensuring our values.

For the philosopher of experience, the meaning and meaningfulness of our experiences is basic and only provisionally eliminable.

This approach provides an important check on the hubris of cognition – or, should I say, on the amnesia of cognition, which sometimes forgets that thinking is only one of many ways to interact with the world, and that the cognitive way often serves the other ways. Focusing on immediacy also helps us remember what's at stake, existentially, in the process of experience: the burden of assigning meaning to one's life.

The two remaining elements of a philosophy of experience, emphasizing environments and embodiment, follow pretty directly from the focus on immediacy. Experiences are highly circumstantial affairs, shaped by our moods, by the intellectual and expressive resources that we use to interpret and respond to what happens to us, by the societies that shape our intellectual and expressive repertoires, and so on. Or, to put it more in the spirit of the preceding point: experiences are themselves the contexts out of which our world takes shape. A philosophy of experience reminds us to take all of this into account, and, in this respect, has an environmental focus.

Experiences are also corporeal affairs, partly registered, for example, by sense organs, and reflected upon by minds that depend on (or are identical with, or whatever your favorite philosophy of mind tells you to say here) the condition of such bodily things as our brains. The body, then, seems to be an ineliminable condition on creatures like us even having experiences. This means that the body is not, as I said earlier in this book, just the thing our souls (or minds, or whatever) ride around in; it is the point of view from which the "soul" encounters the world, the physical precondition and realization of mind. My body is, in a rather fundamental way, my self, which is why, in the general course of affairs, I treat it as me rather than as something of mine. True enough, I can objectify it, and doing so isn't even that unusual: I've done it in the last two sentences; I do it when I lift weights or diet to change how I look; I do it when I complain about age and injury leaving me unable to do the things I'm used to doing. But even this familiar body-mind distance plays a much smaller role in our lives than the casual, instinctive ways in which we identify with our bodies. (*Get away from me*, we say, not *Get away from my body*. Unless we're dead, in which case we're typically in no position to make demands.) This is what I mean in speaking of embodiment, and this is the third focus of a philosophy of experience.

4.5.2 Invisibility and the other mind–body problem

By directing us toward immediacy, environments, and embodiment, the philosophy of experience is a useful perspective from which to examine the existentially loaded phenomenon of race. Race-thinking is a matter of assigning meaning to human bodies, and under classical racialism this meant explicitly and systematically connecting physical appearance to the distribution of important social goods. In such conditions, and under subsequent conditions, as the connections become more implicit and less systematic, the body becomes a crucial and conspicuous bearer of meaning, in at least two ways.

First, the body under classical racialism becomes a nexus for the basic existential conflict between self and world. If the bodily aspect of me is what excludes me from the jobs I want, what prevents me from living where I'd like; if what I see in the mirror when I look at myself is the mythic creature – the rapist, the illegal alien, the white supremacist – that keeps people from seeing me and treating me the way I'd like; if all of that is the case, then racist exclusions will translate quite directly into my lived experience, perhaps blossoming into what feels like a conflict between my self and my body. This conflict often expresses itself in our perennial pursuit of bodily beauty, which we'll take up in the next chapter. In this connection it motivates a tradition of intellectual work that I've elsewhere referred to as anti-racist aestheticism, which counts Toni Morrison's remarkable novel, *The Bluest Eye*, as one of its canonical works.[9]

The post-colonial theorist Frantz Fanon is perhaps the most famous analyst of this collision between body, self, race, and world. He describes it well in this 1951 meditation on having his race publicly noticed:

> "Dirty nigger!" or simply, "Look, a Negro!"
>   I came into the world . . . and I discovered myself an object among other objects. . . . Then we came to have to confront the white gaze. . . . I was all at once responsible for my body, responsible for my race, for my ancestors. I ran an objective gaze over myself, discovering my blackness, my ethnic characteristics, and then I was deafened by cannibalism, intellectual deficiency, fetishism, racial defects, slave ships.[10]

Fanon here reports the interpenetration of self and body, the easy slippage between self-conceptions and public mythologies, the way public responses to his body assail his sense of himself. In this and other places he deepens Du Bois's picture of the negative modes of double-consciousness by adding an explicit focus on the body. Like Du Bois, Fanon traces a kind of self-doubt, or self-consciousness, to the experience of seeing himself through the eyes of another. But he explicitly relates this to such dynamics as, in his words, the "epidermalization" of difference.[11]

Fanon's conflict – between self and racialized body, between embodied self and racialized world – leads to a second sense in which the body becomes a bearer of racialized meaning. In speaking above of how the swirl of racial meanings prevents people from seeing me, I focused on the internal struggle with my body that results. But the first step is important too: one of the recurring themes of anti-racist literature and art, or of the branch of critical race thinking that expresses itself creatively, is the idea of invisibility. When racial mythologies come between me and other people, or between me and my mirror image, I become invisible. The "I" that I wish to present to the world apparently becomes indiscernible, and the people around me seem to be interacting with some mythic avatar. Ralph Ellison's classic novel, *Invisible Man*, is of course about this condition, and begins with this description of it:

> I am an invisible man. No, I am not a spook like those who haunted Edgar Allen Poe; nor am I one of your Hollywood movie ecto-plasms. . . . I am invisible, you understand, simply because people refuse to see me. . . . It is sometimes advantageous to be unseen, although it is most often rather wearing on the nerves. . . . [Y]ou're constantly being bumped against by those of poor vision. Or again, you often doubt if you really exist. You wonder whether you aren't simply a phantom in other people's minds. Say, a figure in a nightmare which the sleeper tries with all his strength to destroy. It's when you feel like this that, out of resentment, you begin to bump people back.[12]

Speaking of invisibility may seem an unduly dramatic way of talking about being stereotyped, or of having other people pay insufficient attention either to my unique qualities or to the limits of excessive generalization. But the point of a philosophy of experience is to start with the meanings of experience as they present themselves, and to attend carefully to the way some bit of existence is immediately lived, to the way it feels. And after being followed in enough stores or being turned away, for no apparent reason, from enough jobs, one's experi-ence starts to develop a specific phenomenological texture that sterile talk of stereotypes and generalizations can't capture. One feels effaced, elided, *invisible* – and, eventually, willing to bump back. It is part of the function of works of art like Ellison's that they help us to imagine the lived experience of circumstances that we might otherwise simply describe or fail even to notice. Works of philosophy and theory, armed with the right metaphors, can do this too, as we can see from pieces like Michele Wallace's *Invisibility Blues*.

Another kind of invisibility returns us to the phenomenon of white racial experience. Many critical race theorists writing on whiteness highlight a kind of invisibility that comes with dominance – I'll call this camouflage, to distinguish it from Ellison's invisibility. The basic idea here is that whiteness under white supremacy, as a privileged position on the social landscape, has the privilege of centrality. It is the center around which everything else revolves, for the convenience and benefit of which the rest of the world is set up. This means that whiteness becomes normal, and things that are normal can often enough go unmarked and uncommented upon.

It's easy enough to illustrate the basic idea of this normative invisibility: just think about any domain in which you fit the average, think about how you can move around there without thinking, and then think about the extra lengths people who aren't average, or normal, have to go to. In a world sized for average adults, children stand on tiptoe to peer over counters that are just right for me, and their feet dangle from the chairs they've climbed into; if I were to visit a first grade classroom, though, the desks that seem just right to the students would seem startlingly tiny to me, especially if I tried to squeeze myself into one.

There are innumerable examples of the racial version of this normative camouflage in literature. Just think of all the occasions on which US writers have gone on describing events in their fictional worlds, recounting the passage of dozens of unmarked men and women, only to shift gears suddenly and announce the lone Negro or Oriental who makes his or her way into the scene. Here's an example from Walker Percy, for whom the racial meanings are not incidental. The speaker is Binx Bolling, the main character and narrator of Percy's novel *The Moviegoer*, set in Louisiana in the 1960s.

> The bus is crowded with shoppers, nearly all women. The windows are steamed. I sit on the lengthwise seat in front. Women sit beside me and stand above me. On the long back seat are five Negresses so black that the whole rear of the bus seems darkened. Directly next to me, on the first cross-seat, is a very fine-looking girl.[13]

Binx never racially identifies the women beside and above him. He goes on to give a lengthy description of the various virtues of the fine-looking girl, and never explicitly mentions her race. Of course, he doesn't need to tell us in either case. (Imagine: "Directly next to me is a very fine looking white girl." Easy enough to say, and natural enough now; but completely obvious to old Binx.) Women and girls are white, especially when they're on the front of a bus in the South before the Civil Rights Act of 1964. Non-white women are Negresses, or Orientals, or whatever they are. I point this out not to criticize Percy, or even to criticize Binx; nor do I mean to suggest that this camouflaging always happens. The point is just that it happens with some regularity, though with less than it used to, and that when it happens it indicates the way we register the centrality of whites under white supremacy by making their whiteness invisible. We'd be hard-pressed to find a contemporary writer of repute reproducing lines like this without something more in the way of irony. But there are all sorts of other examples. I'll limit myself to two. We can still describe minor characters in Hollywood movies like this: "There was the plumber . . . the banker . . . the girlfriend . . . and the black guy." And we can still find restaurant listings that identify purveyors of "ethnic foods," which is supposed to mean the foods that mainstream, which is to say white, *estadounidenses* find foreign or exotic or otherwise distinguished by some markers of identity. (What isn't an ethnic food? Hamburgers? Deli sandwiches? Apple pie and ice cream?)

A third form of invisibility comes into focus if we recall our discussion of the typical black–white binarism of US race-talk. It is still the case that when we hear or read about race, in the news, say, we're usually being told about some conflict between black people and white people. The overall effect of this is to remove Asian Americans, Native Americans, Latinos, and Latinas (about whom more, shortly) from the US racial mix, subjecting them to a kind of concealment. As we've seen, there are some reasons for the invisibility-cum-concealment of people who are neither black nor white; the best ones point to ways in which the black–white dynamic has been peculiarly central to the racial drama of US history. But that drama is certainly not as uniquely central as I was taught to think while growing up. Talking about race just in black and white encourages us to overlook the long histories of collaboration and cooperation between people of every race, histories that might be encouraging and inspiring in an increasingly cynical and mean-spirited age.

4.5.3 From the ontic to the ontological

The black–white dynamic may have the appearance of being unique due to its role as a widely applicable structuring dynamic. In speaking of a structuring dynamic I mean the sort of thing that a post-structuralist might call a binary opposition: a fundamental and asymmetrical dichotomy, with one side valued over the other, that shapes our thinking about some domain. You know: male–female, light–dark, nature–culture, religion–science, and so on.

A black–white opposition of this sort seems to frame the conceptual space of white supremacy, in ways that take us far outside the geographic and political boundaries I've repeatedly imposed on this book. The black–white divide is central in Australia, where the blacks are indigenous peoples, not of African descent (not any more than the rest of the human race, anyway). It is also central in the United Kingdom, where the Asian population tends to be from South Asia – Bangladesh, Pakistan, and India – and where these Asians are often considered, and called, black (or some, ah, colloquial equivalent). And it even goes beyond the boundaries of what I've been calling white supremacy, with its connection to the institutions and ideologies of the West. As we've noted, the caste system in India seems to some degree to be racialized, with darker skin often signifying lower caste background; and there seems to be a color bias, at least among the Hindu population, much like the one we found in Latin America, with lighter skin being valued in children and potential mates.

We see a pattern here, with the condition of blackness, in its various forms, firmly established at the bottom of several modes of social organization. This pattern encourages some analysts, like Lewis Gordon and Linda Alcoff, to explore ideas like blackness as basic ontological positions. To make sense of this we have to take the idea of ontology in a different sense than we have been. So far we've used the word in the fashion of analytic philosophers, to denote simply the set of entities that one is willing to count as real. In this new sense, derived from philosopher Martin Heidegger, ontology has to do with the modes of intelligibility that we adopt as self-interpreting beings: it is a basic interpretation of the human way of being. (And what we were doing before becomes an inquiry into the ontic, not into ontology; but this is immaterial since we won't need to take up either term for much longer.)

In this new sense of "ontology," we can say that our color-coded ideas about race express basic ontological positions. Blackness is a way of being, as is whiteness; and they are ways of being that frame the field of racial positions that defines not just Western social life but also, as we just saw, more besides. In this spirit, authors like Richard Rodriguez (*Brown*) and Richard Dyer (*White*) have written books detailing the mode of being that some racial position represents.[14]

The widespread development of anti-black sentiments – as opposed to anti-African sentiments, which are a proper subset of the first – suggests to some people that there are basic psychological mechanisms at work. We humans, the idea goes, are endowed with perceptual mechanisms that have evolved in ways that bias us against dark-skinned peoples. This is an empirical claim, and I'll let the scientists hash it out. My sense, though, is that if a sizable chunk of the human race is dark-skinned, as it is, then this mechanism will be have to be much more parochial, and much less deeply hard-wired, than an evolutionary or cognitivist explanation would like. And in any case, it would have to be an extremely plastic predisposition, like most human predispositions, which means that we may still be better off focusing our resources on the social causes of racism and exclusion.

4.6 Conclusion

The two parts of this book have quite different aims. Part I was an extended abstract reflection, an attempt to explain the philosophical content of a version of critical race theory, conducted mostly in the idioms of analytic philosophy. That's why it consisted of chapters on the meaning of race-thinking, on the ethical, conceptual, and sociohistorical contexts for racial discourse, and on the metaphysical and epistemic implications of taking race-talk seriously.

Now we're halfway through Part II, where something else is supposed to happen. This chapter remained quite abstract, but began a discussion of the issues that usually animate popular and artistic treatments of race: issues of double-consciousness and identity, of invisibility and embodiment, of experience and interstitiality, and, at the beginning, of ethics. The next chapter will continue this move, taking up some of the concrete issues that have arisen on the racialized US social landscape.

This chapter also adopted a less analytic idiom and reached out to other philosophic resources. If the analytic-continental-pragmatist philosophic schism means nothing to you, that's fine. The details of it aren't crucial here. Just know that there are shifts afoot. Part I tried to unpack common-sense intuitions, locutions, and practices, and tried to offer a revisionary metaphysic or precising definition of "race." This chapter introduced Part II by highlighting some of the experiential dynamics of a racialized mode of existence. The next chapter will shift once more, to highlight some of the political dynamics of a racialized mode of existence. And the preferred idiom there will be modeled on John Dewey's idea of philosophy as criticism.

5

The Color Question

Prologue

"Boyd, do you think I should be colorblind?"

"Do you have a choice? Either you can tell when the stop light changes or you can't."

"I don't mean colorblind like I can't tell my blue socks from my red ones. I mean colorblind like Dr King said: judge people by the content of their character, not by the color of their skin. I mean colorblind like, should I get serious with Inga."

"Inga?"

"You know, *Inga*. We've been hanging out, going to movies and whatnot, and I think I really like her, man. And I know she likes me, too."

"How could she not? So what's the problem?"

"The problem is, her name is *Inga*. She's Swedish, for goodness' sake. Can you imagine me taking a blue-eyed, Swedish blonde home to meet dear old Ma and Pa Semple? I might get run out of the house. I haven't even *thought* about *her* parents yet. And even if they're all okay with it, I'm not sure I am. I mean, Dr King's rule is important and all, but it has its limits. All these beautiful sisters out here, and I'm gonna be courting a white woman? I'd feel like I was letting them down somehow, like they've got me under some kind of duty. Besides that, Inga and I would never be able to go out. You know how sisters get when they see brothers out with white women. I'd be scared for my life."

"You're being overly dramatic, as usual. I don't think people care anymore about interracial relationships. And since when do you care what people think about you? Are you sure the problem isn't with you?"

"What do you mean?"

"I don't think you really believe that 'content of their character' stuff. I certainly haven't seen any evidence of it before now. Remember your little adventure on the bus last week?"

"You just have to bring that up, don't you?"

"Yes. Yes I do. Because you're the only person I know who gets off a city bus when a guy wearing a turban gets on. Because I don't know anyone else who would decide not only that such a man is not only an Arab, and not, say, a Sikh, but that he is an Arab *terrorist*, and that he is on that bus, of all places, to kill you, of all people, with a suicide bomb. And having made this decision, what did you do?"

"I did what any rational person would have done. I got off at the next stop."

"Mm-hm."

"Don't look at me like that. If you heard someone blew up a bus, you wouldn't picture an Arab?"

"Around here, I'd picture Timothy McVeigh. If I told you someone mugged me, would you picture a black man?"

"Hell yeah. I been in this neighborhood all my life, and I know how these Negroes act. Life is too precious for me to mess around trying to be politically correct."

"This is my point. You don't believe in colorblindness."

"Oh man, that's different. Before we were talking about love and whatnot. Now we're talking about life and death. And that's where Dr King's rule ceases to apply. Now we are in the province of the Semple Principle: survive first and ask questions later."

"And that justifies racial profiling?"

"Who was profiling? I didn't have a gun or a badge, I didn't shoot the brother or arrest him, and I didn't round up everyone in a turban and put them all in lockdown. I just got off a bus."

"Okay. What about affirmative action? It's not about life or death, it violates Dr King's rule, and you support it anyway."

"Who says it's not about life and death? Since when are jobs and schooling not about life or death? Affirmative action has to do with how you're gonna put food on the table and a roof over your head. And that, my friend, is life and death. So the Semple principle kicks in, and it's a-okay."

"Aren't there some questions about fairness here? I mean, is it fair to blame all South Asians and Arabs for what a few of them have done? Same thing with affirmative action: is it fair to make . . . Hey. JJ. Hey. What are you looking for?"

"Sorry, man. Inga's supposed to meet me here. I'm trying to keep an eye on the door. You know, I really like that girl."

The faraway look in JJ's eye made it very clear that our debate was over for the day. "So," I said. "What do you think you'll do about her?"

"Tell you what," he said. "If she doesn't hog the wifi, she's the woman for me."

5.1 Introduction

Is JJ right when he declares that affirmative action and racial profiling are both permissible policies? Is he right to place prudential limits, or limits of any sort, on the colorblind ideal? And does he really have some duty to date women of the same race?

Ethical questions like these have to be part of our philosophical introduction to race because questions like these make race a controversial subject, and one worth pushing in the direction of the clarity to which philosophy sometimes aspires. The process of racial formation generates or implicates a number of ethical controversies, from the appropriateness of placing limits on hate speech to the role of identity politics in new techniques of warfare and new patterns of global migration. Working through any one of these issues with the care it deserves would mean vastly exceeding the scope of this little book. So I'll use somewhat less care in simply introducing a couple of familiar and hopefully representative issues: conjugal choice and affirmative action. Together, these issues provide us with windows onto the ethics of US racialism in both the more or less private and the more or less public domains.

These representative controversies jointly define what we can call the color question. We can call it this not just because we have the habit of using "color" as a metonym for "Race," but also because the norm of colorblindness has come to occupy such a central place in our ethical deliberations. Most people agree that there are spheres within which race is not an important consideration, and that in these spheres we should act on the principle that Dr King and JJ recommend: focus on character, not color, on persons, not races. Unfortunately, there is considerably less agreement on just how expansive this Kingian sphere is, and on just how much ethical space is available to the countervailing norm of color-consciousness. In light of this disagreement, and in light of the fact that it was an ideal even for Dr King, rather than a rule for immediate and absolute application, we should add a *ceteris paribus* clause: *other things being equal*, we should focus on character rather than color. Now the burden is to interpret the duty of colorblindness so that we know how to say when other things are equal.

So to ask the color question is to entertain queries like these: Should we appeal to race in distributing social goods like wealth, job opportunities, and relationship capital? If we already distribute some good along racial lines, whether through conscious choices, institutional inertia, or unconscious prejudices, is this pattern permissible or is it ethically problematic? What role can race-thinking play in cementing our social bonds, in our attempts to fashion just communities and fulfilling relationships? And, above all: what does colorblindness mean? In what follows we'll explore two areas in which these questions have been particularly pressing. These particular areas are no longer at the center of the action in racial politics, in ways we'll discuss in the next chapter. But they have the virtue of familiarity and of raising the relevant issues quite clearly.

5.2 Color and "courting": the ethics of miscegenation

The statistics we saw in chapter 3 make it clear: when it comes to what JJ calls courting, or to marriage, anyway, we are determinedly color conscious. You remember the situation: The members of each race marry within their races much more often than they marry outside, which is to say that racial endogamy is the rule. And when non-whites marry outside their race, or exogamously, they marry whites much more often – up to thirty times more often, as of 1990 – than they marry members of some other non-white race. Which is to say: white identity seems to carry with it substantial relationship capital.

I want to use these marriage patterns as a window onto a rather larger domain that I'll refer to as the conjugal world. This world comprises the elements of human experience that sometimes lead to marriage, including eroticism, romance, sex, sexual attraction, bodily beauty, domesticity, and procreation. Marriage statistics are not a perfect barometer of our attitudes about these things, for several reasons. Not all committed couples get married, not least because not all of them can, legally. (I'm thinking here of the state's insistence on heterosexuality; I am not thinking of the many people who are under some other, more defensible legal impediment, like already having a spouse, or like being in love, or whatever, with a child.) Also, not all the people who get married stay that way. And people get married for many different reasons, only some of which have to do with love or sexual attraction. Still, patterns of endogamy and exogamy give us some idea of how race impacts our intimate lives. And the impact appears to be substantial. (It is declining, as we can see from the steady increase in interracial marriages since the state laws that prohibited such unions were ruled unconstitutional in 1967. But if the percentage of whites marrying whites is in the low nineties as late as 2010, then the endogamy rule has not lost that much of its hold on us.)

Of course, patterns of racial endogamy don't mean that every individual who declines to pursue an interracial relationship is directly motivated by color-consciousness. There are at least three factors other than consciously held individual preferences that might play a role. First, and of course, there is the way that race-thinking can shape our ideas, preferences, and choices at an unconscious level. A person who sincerely believes himself free of racial prejudice may find that he just doesn't find people of a different race attractive; *nothing wrong with them*, he says, *got nothing against, wish them the best*, and so on. But this aesthetic judgment may well be shaped by his experience of a community that cultivated his preferences in racialized environments, or, if he is white, by his experience in a society that is still trying on the idea that black, for example, can be beautiful (which is why 1960s activists had to assert the point so vociferously). We'll return to this.

A second factor is that in matters of conjugal relations, as in so many things, we can succumb to social pressures, from family, friends, or anyone whose opinion matters to us. If the people whose approval we crave are likely to frown on relationships of a certain sort, then we are that much less likely to undertake such relationships. And if those of us who were born before 1964 (or so) spent part of our lives in a world officially and pervasively defined by classical racialism, how many people in or approaching what we think of as a marriageable age have parents or grandparents who are at least uneasy about the idea of interracial relationships? (Here's some help answering that question: Alabama has just gotten around to removing its anti-miscegenation law from the books, in the year 2000. The vote to repeal the unenforceable law managed to win the approval of just 60 percent of the participating voters. On the cusp of the twenty-first century, forty percent, or *two-fifths*, of Alabama voters believed that interracial marriage should be against the law.)

Finally, there are also considerations of opportunity, as we see when sociologists who study these things speak of marriage markets, or the settings where people meet potential spouses. To the extent that US social life remains profoundly segregated, as members of different races work and play and live in different settings, marriage markets will be skewed toward endogamy. One can participate in these markets, and have one's conjugal choices shaped by them, without ever considering any racial prerequisites for beauty and romance. Dating within one's class or income group, or looking for someone with a similar background will often enough lead to racially endogamous choices. (I can't help thinking here of the well-received moving picture franchise, *Sex in the City*. The main characters, four white women, were involved with many, many men during the show's run on HBO, and then during its resurrection on the big screen. Vanishingly few of these men were anything other than white, or Anglo, or gentile; but the women were clearly not racists.)

But even if endogamy has these indirect causes, we still openly countenance the social conditions that turn races into breeding populations. We can see that racial endogamy is the rule, and we seem not to be troubled by this. No one, or almost no one, invokes Dr King's ideal when talking about courting. But why not?

It is tempting to contrast our overt color-consciousness here with our eagerness to insist in recent years on colorblindness in the political sphere. But the difference between political society and civil society, between the state and the individual (or the family, or the voluntary association) may be relevant here, as it is, in the USA, anyway, when we talk about endorsing a religion. We'll come to the question of when the state can be color-conscious soon enough; for now let's raise the color question as an ethical problem for individuals. How can we justify our overwhelming commitment in the conjugal sphere to the otherwise troubling norm of color-consciousness? What makes it permissible here?

I'll consider this ethical question without endorsing the standpoint of any particular ethical theory – Kantianism, say, or utilitarianism. Instead I will assume what I have assumed elsewhere in this book: that we share a broad sphere of discursive commonality, and that the philosopher's job is to assume that he or she is representative enough to call on that commonality without leaving the armchair. We tend to agree on quite a lot, ethically, in part because of the shared public and political cultures that unite people in the USA, and in the West, and in the Modern world. I'll rely in what follows on intuitions that I think I find in this area of agreement. Like I said in the first chapter: if you don't agree, take this as a provocation to tell a better story.[1]

5.2.1 Endogamy and the elements of ethics

Is JJ right about having some duty to date within the race? There are many different ways to argue for this point, and none of them seem to work. Still, working through them should shed a little light on the way race intersects with this most affecting domain of human experience, and with the project of ethical deliberation.

An advocate for scientific racialism might claim that races are originally and naturally distinct populations, that this makes race-mingling unnatural, and, therefore, that color-conscious endogamy is not only justified but obligatory. But every step of this argument fails. Races are products of human artifice, not of nature; they are, as Du Bois once wrote in a related context, exasperatingly intermingled, not pure; and it is not at all obvious that unnatural activities are necessarily bad – think of flying, or taking Viagra, or eating Twinkies.

Someone who thinks of races as cultural groups might choose to dispense with ideas about racial biology and develop a cultural pluralist argument. If cultures are in general worth preserving, then we ought to preserve the races that have nurtured their cultures into being. And this might mean blocking any sort of defection, conjugal or otherwise, from the racial community. But races aren't cultural groups; and even if they were, a concern just for the cultures they've produced ought to move us to recruit anyone we can get, of any color, to learn and participate in the practices that define this intrinsically valuable way of life.

Someone who thinks of races as political entities might make a similar argument, with similar results. It could go like this: To the extent that we want to end, say, black oppression, we must create the conditions under which black people will stand or fall together. And this means creating strong black families to serve as the bedrock of a strong black community; or, less ambitiously, it means encouraging conjugal ties that will help bind the community together. But this argument presupposes that black people have some privileged access and connection to the cause of black advancement. Without that assumption, one might conclude that the way to end black oppression is to create coalitions, and to get as much support for the cause, among all people, as possible. And if you think conjugal relations are the key to political solidarity, then you might argue that the real key to equality and ethical progress is as much exogamy – race-mixing, miscegenation – as possible. After all, advocates for this view have said, why would I discriminate against my own relatives? Or, since this consideration seems not to have registered with Southern slave-owners or their descendants: how can we discriminate by color if we're all the same shade of brown? (This is an argument from what some call "the browning of America." As philosopher Ron Sundstrom makes clear in his thoughtful treatment of this and related questions,[2] this phrase refers to the demographic shifts, due mainly to immigration and racial intermarriage, that will eventually make the USA a "majority–minority" country. The argument that these shifts will make us more egalitarian, which Sundstrom eloquently calls into question, resurfaces every now and again in racial discourse. The last one I noticed was in Warren Beatty's 1998 film, *Bulworth*, which means we're probably due for another dose.)

The arguments that we've considered so far fail to support any duty to remain endogamous, mainly because they presuppose problematic ideas about race. In light of this failing, they also fail to justify any other sort of ethical demand on us. I say this because duties are not the only components of the ethical sphere. We have rights to do things that we are under no duty to do. And we can earn ethical praise for doing something more than meeting our obligations. To exercise our rights is to act permissibly, and to earn praise for going above and beyond the call of duty is to engage in supererogation, or supererogatory acts. None of the arguments considered so far even generate a right to color-conscious endogamy, since we can't justify rights based on false assumptions. Just as the invitation of the goblin who lives under your porch gives me no right to enter your home, the natural solidarity of race groups gives me no right to deviate from our baseline assumption in the ethics of race, Dr King's principle of colorblindness. And they certainly give us no motivation for praising such deviations.

Another class of arguments dispenses with problematic ideas about race, and fares a bit better with respect to the ethical positions other than duty. Perhaps the most familiar of these arguments is an inferential one. Interracial relationships are often said to be ethically problematic because they simply reveal the self-hatred of the people involved. The Asian man who marries a white woman hasn't violated some duty of racial fealty; he has simply revealed, in his determination to move outside the marriage markets that make Asian women his most likely partners, his hatred or distaste for, or alienation from, Asian-ness. The charge of self-hatred works as an ethical complaint, as opposed to a psychological diagnosis, only if we insist on problematic views about racial loyalty. But apart from those views, we can say from this perspective that people who engage in interracial relationships have in effect revealed themselves as racists. There is no duty to be endogamous, but there is a duty not to be endogamous in a certain way, the way that involves making negative judgments about a race. And, one might claim, this virtuous, non-judgmental endogamy is practically impossible under current conditions. So, again, stick with your own.

One problem with this inferential argument is that it depends on psychological facts not in evidence. It's hard to know whether someone is running from something or running to something else; it's hard to know this sometimes even if the someone in question is the one conducting the inquiry. Sometimes we can determine this to a reasonably satisfactory degree; and if one is in fact motivated by distaste for the members of one's own race, that would make the relevant conjugal choice racist and troubling. But when separated from the demand for political loyalty or solidarity (in light of which the inference would be easier: the person in question really has opted out of his or her alleged duties), this argument works best as a request for vigilance, as a recommendation to monitor our attitudes and motivations for signs of racism. Of course, the recommendation should be coupled with the recommendation, to potential critics, that they avoid being judgmental, and jumping to conclusions.

Another approach tries to justify endogamy as a strategic choice, in one of two ways. One argument begins by recognizing the continued influence of colorism, along with the ongoing racialization of relationship capital in the wake of white supremacy. Under these conditions, each member of an historically disfavored race who marries outside the race diminishes the marriage market reasonably available to the other members of the race. What's more, in light of the continued segregation of our marriage markets, the remaining members of the race are not that likely to find someone in another race to make up for the "defector." All of this may be seen to generate some sort of claim on the potential defector, especially among populations that are or have been unevenly split along gender lines, so that, so to speak, supply and demand are already out of joint. Think of African-American women, with African-American men famously at risk for being in the criminal system, unemployed, or otherwise "unmarriageable." Or think of Asian men, who for many years were allowed to immigrate in much larger numbers than Asian women.

This argument, call it the market solidarity argument, joins all the others in failing to support a duty to remain endogamous. If the aim, put crudely, is just to find partners for everyone, then the real solution involves de-racializing relationship capital and liberalizing the marriage markets. Strategic endogamy, or altruistic endogamy, or whatever it would be, is only a provisional solution to the problem of skewed marriage markets, and one that seems unduly restrictive to individuals in search of such notoriously evasive and unpredictable goods as love, or whatever.

We could make the same response to the second argument for strategic endogamy; call this one the argument from risk aversion. Here we rely on pointing out the difficulties that interracial pairs, and the children they might produce, continue to face. These difficulties are real, of course. Hate crimes continue to plague our society, and some white supremacist groups take particular delight in targeting interracial couples; in addition, mixed-race individuals often find themselves multiply alienated, at considerable psychological cost. But if one is concerned about the hostility toward "race-mixing" that makes 40 percent of Alabama voters protest the abolition of an unenforceable anti-miscegenation law, or about the isolation that mixed-race children will face in a social world defined by the one-drop rule, then the real solution, one might say, is to fight the forces of hostility and isolation, not to give in to them. Participants in the mixed-race identity movement make precisely this argument.

Of course, responding to the arguments from markets and risk by demanding that we struggle for justice provides little comfort to the parties affected by the markets and facing the risks. Black women and Asian men (to stick with the examples) who feel spurned inside their segregated conjugal markets, and who don't have much luck when they venture outside, could reasonably protest that they'll derive no immediate benefit from the long-range project of undermining the racialization of relationship capital. And the person who wants to raise safe and healthy children may balk at the suggestion that he or she ignore the present potential for harm that interracial children and families face.

The gap between these long-term solutions and these pressing current needs may take us beyond talk of duties, of acts that one is obliged to perform, and toward the more subtly distinguished ethical categories. Consider the person who declines to pursue an interracial relationship because he knows he wants children and doesn't want to expose them to the special challenges of growing up (clearly) mixed in a race-conscious society. This seems not to be a blameworthy choice, as if the agent has a right to be color-conscious at least in this case. Similarly, consider the person, a member of an historically subordinate racial population, who declines to make herself available for interracial relationships because she knows that doing otherwise would negatively impact others in her race, however remotely. This route to endogamy seems vaguely praiseworthy, even though it fails to generate any obligations. Perhaps here we find a narrow window for supererogation, or acts that are above and beyond the call. We praise people for volunteering at homeless shelters, even though, and perhaps because, we recognize no duty to serve in this capacity. Maybe we would praise someone who remains endogamous not because she hates or otherwise harbors negative attitudes toward other races, and not because she thinks she is under some duty, but because she wants to play a small part in improving conditions for some, perhaps only for one, of the other people with whom she shares a subordinate racial position. As I say: perhaps.

Let's try an argument for color-conscious endogamy from the standpoint of a certain kind of late-modern racialist. From this perspective, one might think not just of the failures of classical racialism, but also of the way that racialized bodies work as signs in a world ever more attuned to signs and images. Specifically, one might think of our obsession with the beauty and desirability of human bodies, and of how this obsession reflects a lingering pro-white bias. Beauty is a commodity and a virtue, the key to being desired and to being valued as a person. To be white, or light, is to have cornered the market on this commodity, and to have gone some way toward establishing one's value. This is not news. There is a venerable tradition of white supremacist writing that ranks the races in terms of beauty, of visual art and journalism that depicts angelic whites and beastlike non- and almost-whites (like Jews and the Irish), and of literature that extols the virtues, aesthetic and ethical, of "the lighter races" (like nearly anything from Jack London). We can still see the effects of this white-oriented somatic aesthetics in the relative dearth of dark-skinned people among our black and brown models, actors, and image culture personalities.

Thinking about the lingering influence of racism and colorism may lead one to worry about the message that the members of historically disfavored races send to each other when they enter into interracial relationships. One might think that seeing black people with white partners, for example, will perpetuate the idea that lighter is better, which may in turn lead blacks to despise their black features, or themselves, as surely as rail-thin models encourage young girls to aspire to impossible thinness. And all of this may move one to argue that blacks have some duty to avoid non-white partners. I'll call this the conjugal expressiveness argument, because it highlights the expressive or habituating force of our choices in the conjugal sphere.

Perhaps to its detriment, the conjugal expressiveness argument depends on some facts of empirical psychology: JJ's relationship with Inga is supposed to affirm, reinforce, or otherwise inspire beliefs about the greater desirability of white women. It isn't obvious that this happens. But even if the facts come out right, it's hard to see how JJ's role in producing this outcome makes him blameworthy. Our culture is saturated with images of beauty and attractiveness. If these images also tend to reinforce pro-white standards of bodily beauty – a pro-white somatic aesthetic, or somaesthetic – then it's hard to see why JJ has to bear such a heavy burden for his small contribution to the cause, especially relative to the contribution made by, say, magazines like *Vogue*. Here as before, strategic endogamy targets the symptoms instead of the disease, in this case, colorist ideologies of bodily beauty. If JJ were a celebrity or a public figure, whose private choices become public knowledge and have public effects, then we might get closer to some sort of obligation. Some people have an outsize impact on public discourse or visual culture, and we may be inclined to hold these people responsible for the images they project, in the same spirit in which we (oddly) expect professional athletes to be role models. (Call this the role model corollary to the expressiveness argument.) But for those of us who stand in more typical relations to the forces of image and knowledge production, it appears once more that the better solution will target the conditions that give JJ's choices their troubling meanings, or that allow people to receive them with those meanings: the conditions that make strategic endogamy useful.

Even worse for this conjugal expressiveness argument, our overall cultural inclination toward a pro-white somaesthetics has weakened considerably. It has for most of its history called forth oppositional responses, especially in the African-American community. I'm thinking of the covers of the NAACP's *Crisis* magazine under the editorship of Du Bois, and of the mildly provocative images of beautiful, swimsuit-clad young women that still appear in *Jet* magazine's "Beauty of the Week" features, in the middle of what is otherwise a general purpose newsweekly (think of *People* crossed with *Time*, with the "community" section of your local paper thrown in for good measure, and focused on African Americans). These images indicate more than that heterosexual men rather than women or gay men controlled the means of production in the black press, or that these men assumed a masculine gaze on behalf of their readership. They do indicate these things, but they also indicate a tradition of resistance to white norms of bodily – in this case, as in most, feminine – beauty. This tradition continued through the 1960s, encouraging activists to insist that "Black is Beautiful," and inspiring contemporary artists like writer Toni Morrison, filmmaker Spike Lee, visual artist and philosopher Adrian Piper, and, of all people, phallocentric rapper Sir Mix-a-Lot (author of the immortal ditty, "Baby Got Back").

One could argue that these cultural strategies of self-affirmation by African Americans and others have done their work, abetted by other, mostly economic, forces, and that the monolithic white standards have loosened their grip. Black women have won the Miss America crown, or tiara, or whatever; an Asian woman (Lucy Liu) joined Charlie's Angels on film, while a black woman (Annie Ilonzeh) joined them in the 2011 TV series reboot; people like Denzel Washington and Sofia Vergara have become sex symbols for people of all backgrounds; and a heavy-set former rapper (Queen Latifah) gets paid to endorse cosmetics. We might also consider the emergence in recent years of a kind of interracial chic. Articles in major newsweeklies, taking their cue from psychological studies, have borrowed facial features from various racial "types" and constructed hybrid human images that are supposed to represent the ideal of human beauty. At the same time, mixed-race models in various shades of brown have become increasingly popular, and we've seen figures like Halle Berry, Mariah Carey, and Tiger Woods (before his extremely public fall from grace) hit the heights of crossover appeal.

I could go on detailing the decline of somaesthetic white supremacy, citing factors both new and old: white people, stars and non-, plumping their lips with collagen or lying in the sun or in tanning booths to darken their skin; the crossover appeal of hip-hop styles; the parallel emergence of a kind of Asian chic. But as you can probably tell from the examples I've chosen, I don't think of these as seamlessly good developments. For one thing, making the objectification of women more racially egalitarian still leaves women struggling to have the full breadth of their personhood appreciated. And for another, the admiration, if that's the word, for Washington, Liu, or Vergara can easily dovetail with age-old racial stereotypes, like the depiction of the black man as brute, or body, or the seductive Asian dragon lady, or the hot-blooded Latina. That is: a more racially egalitarian distribution of aesthetic praise is perfectly compatible with the denial of personhood and rights, especially when male supremacy and racist stereotypes linger. But progress with seams is better than no progress at all, and the widespread recognition of non-white beauty is progress.

There are those seams, though, and they may provide us with some room to use the expressiveness argument to generate an individual right to color-conscious conjugal choice. Perhaps JJ knows specific young people who might be influenced by his choice, young relatives, say, who look up to him, or the elementary school students for whom he acts as a tutor or mentor, and this is why he feels the pull of endogamy. He doesn't want them to think that he prefers white women, or non-black women, because that may encourage them to think of non-black women as objectively preferable. Does he have this right? That is, can he choose racial endogamy for these reasons and remain blameless? Is this a permissible deviation from Dr King's principle? I'm inclined to say no, since it seems that there are less radical measures available. He could, after all, just be open and honest with the children in his life; he could just talk to them and tell them what his choices do and don't mean.

5.2.2 *Racism and criticism*

If we can't support the duty to be racially endogamous, and if we can support rights to that effect only in quite narrow cases, how are we to justify the manifest fact that we are resolutely committed to color-conscious endogamy? Are we just behaving without regard for the ethical status of our acts and choices? I think so, in two ways.

First, as we've noted, there are many indirect causes for conjugal segregation: individuals, acting quite reasonably in their personal spheres of influence, can systematically reproduce this segregation without ever thinking about it. And in the USA we're not used to subjecting the accumulated effects of individual choices to ethical scrutiny. This is in part why we can't have a coherent discussion about, for example, the ecological effects of our profligate use of natural resources. Individual desires, we think, are to be acted on and serviced, preferably for a profit, not criticized; and this extends to the realm of conjugal choice (except, mostly, for the profit part).

We are encouraged to disregard the ethical import of racial endogamy also because we are still, as I promise to quit pointing out soon, just a few years past the decline of *de jure* segregation. Color-conscious conjugal choices, with their direct, attitudinal causes and their indirect institutional causes, are just part of the legacy of white supremacy in this country. Like the residential segregation that contributes to it, endogamy persists quietly, escaping our notice. After all, we're used to it: it seems natural, and it's not the sort of thing that one brings up in polite company anyway.

Racial endogamy continues to seem natural where racial preferences in other spheres seem unnatural or at least in need of explanation – and we are, after all, talking about racial preferences – in part because the conjugal sphere strikes us as essentially private. We, as state or civil society, are loath to interfere with private lives unless there is quite a good reason. In the language of the courts on related subjects, we want compelling reasons to interfere, and ways of intervening that are not too aggressive. And since we seem not to feel any pressing need to integrate the conjugal world, and since any way of doing so would seem deeply, problematically invasive – who are you to tell me whom to marry, we'd say – we just leave it all alone.

As we know from the history of segregation and, for that matter, from the history of all sorts of intolerance and sociopolitical subordination, an appeal to privacy can mask quite unfortunate attitudes and conditions. Our children learn in private, by instruction and example, that men and women are fit for certain social roles, that the inhabitants of these roles should limit themselves to certain configurations of sexual desire and conjugal attachment, and that these configurations intersect with our ways of assigning generic meaning to human bodies and bloodlines. This education guides us on our journeys to and through adult life, and privacy insulates us as adults from having our attitudes challenged and our perspectives broadened. So an appeal to privacy is in fact an appeal to entrenched attitudes and established practices, in this case, to the attitudes and practices of a racially segregated and stratified society.

So where does that leave us ethically? Apparently with nothing systematic to say about interracial relationships. As with any other sphere of life, people make their choices here for many different reasons, under the influence of many different factors. Perhaps we should let them choose whom and what they choose, subject to the normal duties of fair play: dealing honestly with potential partners, refraining from manipulation and coercion, and so on.

Then again, perhaps there are at least two broader conclusions to draw. First: If conjugal choices presuppose direct racist beliefs, then they are unfortunate and ethically problematic. This is the easy part of interpreting Dr King's principle, and it applies even here. Racism involves an inappropriate disregard for the members of a race, and, a bit paradoxically, we are racists when we let the fact of someone's racial identity – or the classical racialist fictions about it – obscure their personality and personhood.

Second, we need more ethical subtlety when we talk about race, particularly when we talk about race in the conjugal sphere. Most of the time, we choose endogamy under the influence of forces that operate, as it were, behind the scenes, escaping notice. "I'm just not attracted to them," we say, perhaps because we've never been around people of other races in settings that conduced to romantic interactions, or because it just never seemed like a live option, because, well, "What would Grandma think?" In this case, our standard modes of ethical theorizing leave us with little to say. We're used to talking about rights and duties, about individual entitlements and obligations to behave, or not, in certain ways. And when we do move beyond individuals, we start in pretty quickly with talk about states, about how political society can constrain individuals and help them pursue their goals. But we need to split the difference between individuals and states and bring ethical scrutiny to bear on the general drift of culture and on the workings of civil society. Desires, preferences, and expectations are the appropriate objects of ethical criticism, but sometimes we have to push past the individual bearers of those mental states and look at the social conditions that routinely produce them.

A society that leaves its colorist biases uncriticized, that says nothing about the racialization of its discourses of beauty, desire, and marriageability, will cultivate in its members racially preferential habits and impulses. A society whose members routinely and unthinkingly act on the basis of these preferential impulses will also routinely segregate people for the purpose of distributing affection, romance, and aesthetic praise. And a society that distributes these goods in these ways, ways that are not just segregated but stratifying, separate and un-equal, will threaten the self-esteem of many of its members, and perpetuate divisions that skew the allocation of other goods. If you're not good enough, or not enough like me, for me to accept you into my family as a partner or in-law, then you may not be good enough or enough like me for me to include you in my sphere of ethical concern. I may not consciously exclude you, but I may allow myself unconscious aversions and resistances that encourage me to withhold concern from you – and from the Them that you belong to and that stands opposed to my Us.

I offer all this not to make the *Bulworth* argument, not to say that we should eradicate racial endogamy altogether. As I said in chapter 3, racial populations may serve as incubators for ethnic communities, whose members may choose to relate more closely to each other than to other groups. Segregation needn't always be problematic, particularly when it is chosen by those it would separate (though it can be worrisome even then); and endogamy may be the consequence, sign, and mechanism of some benign segregation.

The point is just that we should keep watch over the conditions that lead to endogamy, and the consequences that follow from it, and we should recur only sparingly to ethical criticism of individual conjugal choices. If my conjugal choices are explicitly motivated by racist beliefs, then I am unproblematically blameworthy. But if my choices are shaped by my social location, then the function of ethical criticism should be to move me to scrutinize my surroundings, and my relation to them. We should be willing to examine the forces that make us who we are, and that use us to create and maintain social arrangements, particularly when it comes to race.

The issue of color conscious conjugal choice forces us to consider the role of entrenched attitudes and arrangements, and the way social inertia can insulate these stratifying and segregating mechanisms from criticism and change. We have long tried to work directly on these entrenched attitudes, using everything from public service announcements to public school curricula. It's probably fair to say that the results have been spotty, at best. Some people think that contemporary research into the psychology of implicit bias will help us do this work more effectively. But until we get a much clearer sense of which behavioral and perceptual buttons we can push in order to weaken the hold of entrenched prejudices, the existence of these prejudices gives us the beginning of an argument for affirmative action. The thought is that in spheres less intimate than the conjugal, it may be appropriate to use race-conscious policy measures to counteract or block the effects of ingrained prejudices and entrenched asymmetries. Of course, policies like this will implicate the ideal of colorblindness just as much as conjugal color-consciousness. They will, moreover, in their most familiar forms, do so with the mechanisms of state coercion on their side and the distribution of fundamental social goods hanging in the balance. All of this makes the stakes fairly high and extremely clear in the affirmative action debates, which is why I'll take the subject of those debates as as our second representative area of racial controversy.

5.3 Colorblindness and affirmative action

5.3.1 Background and arguments

We talk about affirmative action in many ways, in many contexts. But we can cover most of these variations in usage with a broad definition, like this: A practice or policy counts as affirmative action if (a) it organizes the opportunity structure in some domain in a way that seeks to enhance the position of some group or population, and (b) the beneficiary population has been subject to far-reaching patterns of exclusion and subordination.[3] There are many opportunity-enhancing mechanisms, including legacy admissions to prestigious universities, whereby the children of important alumni and alumnae receive special consideration when applying. But we speak of affirmative action most often in the context of race and gender, the principles of social differentiation that have figured most prominently in broadly unjust social arrangements.

We started talking in this way about opportunity enhancement in 1961, when President Kennedy's executive order called for federal contractors to hire and interact with employees without regard for race, creed, color, or national origin. Since then we've developed a number of ways to enhance opportunities in such areas as education, government contracting, employment, and the distribution of government benefits, like broadcast licenses. We use outreach and hortatory techniques, like targeting underrepresented populations for recruitment efforts. We invest in human capital, with special classes and internships. We set numerical goals, or flexible guidelines that help an institution track its efforts at heightened inclusion. We employ weighting techniques, such as considering a candidate's membership in an historically excluded population as we work through the selection calculus for, say, admission to a university. And, at the legally problematic end of things, we might establish set-asides and quotas, which reserve or fill a set number of slots in the opportunity structure – such as an entering class at a medical school – with members of the target group.

These last methods point in the direction of preferential treatment, a notion that overlaps with affirmative action but that's worth defining separately. Preferential treatment also involves opportunity-enhancing mechanisms, but it incorporates hard guarantees, enhancing the opportunity structure by "rigging" it with quotas. It is important to distinguish these two types of mechanisms because doing so allows us to highlight an area of widespread agreement in an otherwise rancorous public debate. Even though public opinion is sharply divided in ways we'll soon consider further, most parties to the debate agree on three propositions: quotas are problematic, outreach and hortatory measures are important tools in the pursuit of racial justice, and colorblindness is an important ideal. If we use "affirmative action" to talk about outreach and exhortation, and if we use "preferential treatment" to talk about quotas, then the issue becomes much less divisive, and the application of Dr King's rule – other things equal, we shouldn't judge people by the color of their skin – becomes quite clear in a wide array of cases. (I take this as the moral of certain events in the state of Washington, which in 1998 called itself proscribing affirmative action policies with a statewide initiative and referendum, while those who wrote the initiative's language insisted that they did not mean to eliminate policies of outreach and exhortation.)

Of course, circumscribing the topic in this way still leaves a significant area of contention. Between outreach and guidelines on one end and quotas on the other we find the opportunity-enhancing policies that employ race as some sort of weighting mechanism, or "plus" factor, in selecting the recipients of some good. We use this technique most prominently in educational institutions, in admissions policies from preschool to professional school, at the cost of considerable controversy. Here the scope of the colorblind ideal remains unclear, subject to competing interpretations in debates that have become increasingly frequent and strident, and increasingly tilted against affirmative action. Starting in the 1980s, federal court rulings methodically began to limit the applicability of race-based opportunity-enhancement policies, and in the 1990s the voters of California and Washington passed referenda that precluded their states from using such policies.

During the course of these debates we've developed a stock body of arguments that we can sort into two broad classes. Following philosopher Bernard Boxill, let's call them backward-looking and forward-looking.[4] Backward-looking arguments invoke affirmative action as a way of remedying, compensating for, or blocking the continuing effects of some past act, condition, or systemic practice of unjust discrimination; while forward-looking arguments invoke it as a way of bringing into being some valuable future condition, such as greater diversity and inclusion, or the prevention of future discrimination. If we decide that the increasingly diverse USA will be better served in the future by a more diverse set of doctors or teachers, then we might enhance opportunities for underrepresented populations to enter medical school or teaching certificate programs. If, by contrast, we conclude that past discriminatory practices have kept the number of, say, Asian fire-fighters artificially low, we might require the fire department to enhance opportunities for Asian applicants until the numbers come closer to what seems appropriate.

If that's all affirmative action comes to, what could be wrong with it? Three basic kinds of complaints have become popular. One kind asks detailed questions about how to implement the policies that are supposed to accomplish the various backward- and forward-looking goals. If you wish to remedy a diffuse historical harm like employment discrimination under Jim Crow, are you sure you can identify the right people to restore to wholeness? Do policies that help people get into professional schools or acquire broadcast licenses effectively target the truly disadvantaged? And if you're aiming for diversity, what makes you think that race serves as an adequate proxy for diversity of opinion, which is surely all that matters?

Another set of complaints focuses on the untoward side effects of opportunity enhancement plans. Enjoining our institutions to think racially, to be color-conscious, may just entrench the patterns of race-thinking that led to discrimination in the first place. Or the beneficiaries of these plans may find themselves stigmatized, branded by the assumption that they weren't good enough to succeed alone (which may in turn sap them of the will to succeed, leaving them worse off than they would have been without this dubious help). Or, even worse, maybe the beneficiaries really weren't good enough to succeed on their own, and we've simply succeeded in promoting unqualified people over qualified ones. Or, finally, we may be inflicting reverse discrimination on innocent bystanders: those who lose opportunities so that others might gain them are in effect paying the costs of historic harms that they didn't cause, or of social amelioration policies that they didn't endorse.

Just this glimpse of the arguments pro and con should show that the question of affirmative action is exceedingly complex. If we went any further with these arguments, we'd have to reckon with the fact that each has spawned its own satellite debate, and surrounded itself with a wall of scholastic disputation and, sometimes, of empirical detail. The scope of our discussion here prevents us from scaling or tearing down these walls, and even from mapping the discursive terrain that they enclose. But there's a sense in which there's not much need. These arguments unfold in the context of utterly divergent interpretations of the ideal of colorblindness. And here, when it comes to deciding just what colorblindness requires, is where the battle over affirmative action really gets joined. Focusing on a couple of the aforementioned arguments will help to make this point clear.

5.3.2 Suspect classifications

In a fine treatment of the stigma argument, Walter Russell Mead, a white political analyst, begins by announcing that he benefited from a policy of opportunity enhancement. An elite prep school decided that it needed more students from southern states, so it recruited in the south and counted southern origins into the admissions calculus. And all of this helped the young Mead get into a highly selective prep school that would otherwise probably not have considered him. He goes on to argue that if his experience didn't brand him with some mark of inferiority, then it's not clear why race-based affirmative action is supposed to have this effect.[5]

I cite Mead's argument not for his eloquently argued main conclusion, which is that the stigma argument in its usual forms is radically underdeveloped, but for the parallel cases he invites us to consider. What might distinguish the policy that benefited him from an otherwise identical policy that takes a race as its target population? What might make the race-based version of the policy worse? We could follow Mead in asking the same questions about legacy admissions to elite schools.

The answer seems to be that races are somehow problematic populations. To put it in the language that US constitutional law uses to make the point: race is a suspect classification, which we have to be particularly vigilant about using for any purpose. Southern origin isn't that big a deal, as potentially suspect classifications go; there are fewer stereotypes about it, and there's nothing like a history of degradation to overcome, notwithstanding the paranoia of lingering Confederate sympathizers (of which there are plenty), or the prejudices of surviving Yankee chauvinists (of which there are plenty). Race, by contrast, is one of the main stumbling blocks in the way of achieving the promise of the American democratic (and capitalist) experiment. Or, perhaps better, race has been one of the keys to interpreting our democratic ideals, and to satisfying capitalism's hunger for labor and markets.

Here we start to see the peculiar appeal of the argument for colorblindness. We should be colorblind where we are not bound to be, say, region-blind, because color is a suspect classification. But when can we overcome our suspicion of the category and allow ourselves to use it? We saw in the discussion of conjugal choice that there seems to be quite little room in our personal lives for consciously focusing on race, if there is any. We can look a bit more closely – only a bit – at the language I've borrowed from the US constitutional law for help in determining how much room we have in the political sphere to be permissibly color-conscious.

When our courts deal with policies like affirmative action, the color question sometimes takes this form: is there a compelling reason to use this color-conscious policy, and is it tailored narrowly enough to do its work without causing too much collateral damage (or, as we say elsewhere in the law, too many "unnecessary trammels")? But what counts as a compelling interest? For whom? And how much collateral damage – to bystanders, to existing patterns of resource distribution, to existing ideas of power and social relations – is too much? As soon as we foreground these questions, we should come to see that we apply and interpret the ideal of colorblindness in ways that are beholden to our other commitments.

To see these other commitments at work in the attack on affirmative action, let's consider the worry about reverse discrimination. Here's a standard way to generate the worry. Imagine a law school that uses race as one among many factors in evaluating applicants for admission. Imagine further, as is likely to be the case, that if a white person and a black person with identical test scores both apply, the black person is much more likely to be accepted. Let's say that this scenario plays out; that a black applicant gets in while a white applicant with similar scores doesn't. Doesn't the rejected applicant have some justification for feeling like the victim of discrimination? After all, she has been excluded from the class, passed over for the conferral of a benefit, because she had the wrong racial identity.

It is difficult for this worry to arise unless we assume that places in selective schools are awards, or, better, rewards, and that admissions processes are competitions to find individual winners, or tests to measure individual desert. As a cultural matter, we do tend to think this way; Americans are often knee-jerk individualists and uncritical proponents of meritocracy. But we don't always think this way, especially in some of our more reflective moments; and we don't have to think this way. We might think of educational opportunities as social resources, as points of entry into the institutions that society uses to provide for its needs – its doctors, lawyers, and so on. On this approach, the schools become mechanisms that society uses to cultivate the human capital that we'll invest in the collective projects that define social life, like our economy, or our systems of law and health care. In the alternative, we could think of the schools as institutions with their own aims and purposes, and of the admissions process as the point at which individuals are recruited into the institutional project. If we decide that promoting racial diversity is an important or permissible project for a school or for society to have – notice the "if" – then it is not at all obvious, on any of these views, that we should speak of the rejected applicant as being excluded or passed over.

The reverse discrimination worry arises more easily also if we assume that the two applicants are similarly situated. But the probabilistic account of racial identity in chapter 3 highlights the fact that whites and non-whites have different degrees of access to social goods, from favorable terms on mortgage and auto loans to intergenerational transfers of wealth. If, as a society, we are interested in giving everyone a reasonable chance of prospering, it isn't obvious that we shouldn't distribute the social resource of education in ways that compensate for the mal-distribution of these other goods. In addition, the very idea of similarly situated applicants, taken in a certain way, gives short shrift to the array of dimensions along which humans might excel, and reinforces the individual reward model of admission. In the thought experiment I said only that the two applicants had identical test scores. But in a truly multi-factor admission process, test scores are only part of the story. Applicant profiles will include a great deal of information and background, including scores and race. I limited the example to scores because, as I said, that is a standard way of generating the worry about reverse discrimination: opening the door to other factors also opens the door to the possibility that schools have more complicated aims than just allocating awards to individuals who excel in some way – testing, say – that makes for easy interpersonal comparisons. (Comparisons that are too easy, if the critics of testing are right.)

The reverse discrimination complaint may also depend on the assumption that colorblindness is most saliently a rejection of color-consciousness, rather than a response to white supremacy. On this assumption, the policies that historically reserved such goods as citizenship, land, and jobs for whites are morally equivalent to the policies that are supposed to block or correct for the effects of centuries of pro-white preferential treatment. It's all unjust discrimination, and it's all wrong. And using one form of wrongdoing to correct for another is still wrong. As current US Supreme Court Justice John Roberts recently put it in a much-scrutinized decision, "the way to stop discrimination on the basis of race is to stop discriminating on the basis of race."[6] But surely this is too quick. Even if it is appropriate to describe the rejected applicant as having been excluded, it is misleading to pretend that this exclusion is the same thing, ethically, as Jim Crow segregation. Jim Crow presupposes and enacts a kind of social stigma, depriving some people of rights and opportunities on the assumption that those people are inferior. Affirmative action, by contrast, is about assistance, compensation, or inclusion, not denigration; exclusion in this context, again, if that is the right way to describe it, is a side effect of a laudable goal, rather than the key technique in securing a pernicious goal.

It is easy to slip into this assumed ethical equivalence. We've already seen how the cultural inclination toward individualism and away from collective goals leaves us oblivious to the social dimensions of educational opportunities. This same inclination also encourages us to forget the systematic nature of white supremacy, the degree to which it was not simply a matter of individual prejudices and slights but an affair of statecraft, of meticulously crafted distributive schemes, and of methodically expropriated resources. We incline not just toward individualism, but also toward cultural amnesia: we are, by and large, ahistorical, in ways that allow us to forget the systematic social engineering that led to current patterns of inequality as surely as it led to cities built around automobiles, freeways, and suburbs.

None of these considerations are meant to be knockdown arguments in support of affirmative action. I've said little, and will say nothing more, about the problems with details and side effects, and there are similar considerations to raise against the arguments on the other side, as we'll soon see. The point is just that the assault on affirmative action typically presupposes a great deal that remains implicit, and that we should unpack these assumptions about individuality, collective social projects, and history if we want to have a meaningful debate. (Whether we do want this is an important question.)

On the other side, the arguments for affirmative action can also presuppose troubling assumptions about history and social projects. Those who treat opportunity enhancement as a key instrument in, for example, the struggle for African-American advancement often gloss over the political limits and costs of the policy. We're told that affirmative action is an issue for the entire black community and an obvious *sine qua non* of racial justice, when it does rather little for the truly poor and often complicates the development of the interracial coalitions that a multi-faceted justice movement would need.

More to the point, we're never told that affirmative action, with its limits, is an artifact of the way we resolved the mid-twentieth-century struggles for racial justice. Of course, there's a sense in which this so obvious that we don't need to be told. But there is a deeper sense in which it speaks to the historical myopia that we considered above. The civil rights movement as we know it was sandwiched between state efforts to cut off radical opposition to the pro-capital, pro-white status quo. After World War II, the "red Scares" purged US politics of progressive and socialist activists, many of whom, like W. E. B. Du Bois, were also active in international, multi-racial campaigns for racial justice. Then, after the mid-1960s legislative successes, the broad-based political coalition that unevenly drove the movement broke apart, in part thanks to internal problems and external harassment, but in part due to different degrees of ambition. The more conservative wings of the movement wanted little more than to abolish the official exclusions of white supremacy, so that non-whites could participate in liberal electoral politics and capitalist market economics. The more radical wings, by contrast, wanted a thoroughgoing reorientation of US political economy, which included a critique of the international projection of US military and political power. We can see the disjunction between these two wings in the bafflement with which Dr King's usual allies greeted his determination to embrace causes like the sanitation workers' strike that brought him to Memphis in April of 1968, and his vocal opposition to the Vietnam War – which for him was just another manifestation of the racist, capitalist, and militarist commitments that led the USA to oppress the people he called American Negroes.

King was killed in the midst of a public move to the left, as Malcolm X was a bit earlier, after embracing a newly internationalist and multi-racial agenda. (Yes, this means that the Nation of Islam was radical but right-wing, in its way.) Take their deaths as a symbol for the extinguishment of the movement's visionary possibilities, as the radicals either succumbed to harassment, assault, and imprisonment by the government, or, driven by their disenchantment with the slow pace of change and the American public's refusal to embrace it, decamped for other countries or more traditional views. This left King's former allies at the head of the movement, to put the matter a bit allegorically, and most of these people were men with securely middle-class sensibilities and aspirations, happy to throw themselves into the fray of liberal capitalist electoral politics and power-brokering. This is where affirmative action comes in, joining the red Scares as the other bookend to the civil rights movement, the other state attempt to suppress opposition. With affirmative action the state could contain opposition instead of crushing it; it could keep a remnant of the movement in the fold, accommodating opposition that might otherwise become more aggressive. (Using jargon I don't have room to unpack, Omi and Winant call this the move from domination to hegemony, from rule by coercion to rule by consent.)

So this is what the affirmative action debate is about: a piecemeal policy, or, rather, a grab-bag of related policies, none of which attack the roots of racial inequality in the USA. Affirmative action, and by extension the struggle to define colorblindness, is, as we say, a political football: the players toss, kick, and carry it around as they make their way about a field that is defined by other issues and circumscribed by the limits, the historically and coercively established limits, of US political discourse. Once we're on the field, it is important to know the rules and strategies and to play to win. But if philosophy is to live up to its higher ambitions, if it is to be, as Dewey once said, a criticism of the influential beliefs that underlie culture,[7] then we should remember to ask whether we're playing the right game, and if there aren't other fields to occupy.

5.4 Conclusion

Our racial controversies are overdetermined. They have multiple causes and occur at the intersection of multiple axes of political and ideological conflict. Think of lynching, with its muddled and horrific expression of ideas not just about race, but also, and unavoidably, about social control, gender relations, class, and sexuality. Or think about how the late Victorian, postbellum attitudes that led to lynching continue to shape our experience of the relation between race and conjugal choice.

Or, to settle accounts with JJ and his friends, think of racial profiling, and of JJ's claim that it is the same as affirmative action. There is a sense in which JJ is of course being provocative, and glossing over important differences. Profiling concerns what philosophers call negative goods, in this case, the condition of being subject to police surveillance, while affirmative action concerns positive goods like jobs and government contracts. Profiling presupposes and threatens to reinforce some of the stigmas of classical racialism, while affirmative action tries to overcome the persistence and the consequences of these stigmas. But there are other senses in which the two policies, or political-administrative techniques, are the same. Profiling does, after all, involve opportunity enhancement: it enhances a race's opportunities to receive the negative good of police attention. It does so on the assumption, shared by certain ways of arguing for affirmative action, that social identity is a reasonable proxy for some other socially and ethically relevant trait. And it is subject to the same sort of cost-benefit questions as any other race-conscious measure: Are we attending to race in the service of a compelling interest? (If we're concerned with our security, or our lives, then perhaps we are.) And is there a way to serve this interest efficiently, without unnecessarily trammeling the rights, dignity, and individuality of our fellow moral agents? (In the case of criminal profiling, there almost always is a better way, one based on better information about risk factors that we probably already possess.)

More than this, though, profiling resembles affirmative action in that it reveals the way that race expresses and locates other conflicts. I argued above for three claims about the affirmative action debate, and about both sides of the debate: first, that it can reveal a myopic historical sense that ignores much of the history of US racial formation; second, that it often depends on truncated visions of social life that fall far short of imagining a truly common good; and third, that it is an artifact of developments in political economy, as what Howard Winant calls the US racial order shifted to accommodate calls for racial justice. I could make similar claims about the profiling debate.

It is easy to forget the way policing has always been used as a device for controlling racial minorities in the USA, and the way the criminal system has frequently been a way of dealing with undesirable populations. It is more difficult to ignore the way police work frequently depends on a Manichean mentality, with good and evil clearly separated, frequently along old racial lines. It is comforting to turn away from the fact that the profiling controversy is concurrent with a heightened fear of criminal activity, shaped by racial mythologies, fueled by a militarized and criminalized war on drugs, and expressed by the way our political elites scramble away from the accusation of being soft on crime. And it is an open secret – which is to say, everyone knows it, but we try quite hard not to mention it – that our fear of crime comes to a head just when we turn the building of prisons and housing of criminals – we call this corrections – into a profit-seeking growth industry, one that leases its prisoners out as low-wage labor.

I'm not making my way to a conspiracy theory; it's too easy to suggest that someone manipulated this convergence of forces and commanded this outcome. The harder suggestion is that US politics, like politics anywhere, is a jumble of competing forces, economic, ideological, cultural, and more; and that race, as one of these forces, enters into symbiotic relations with the others, expressing them in its own idiom, using them to express itself. This harder suggestion, that race is a way of expressing and locating other political conflicts, is what philosopher David Theo Goldberg has in mind when he describes race as a way of inscribing social conflict on human bodies.[8] This is also why what we've referred to as the merger thesis is so important. On one level it is a virtue ethicist's injunction: monitor your attitudes and ideas, cultivate the habit of thinking about things from multiple perspectives. On another level it is a metaphysical point, about the interpenetration of the many aspects of social reality. But on yet another level, it is a political diagnosis, and injunction; it reminds us that interpenetration has shaped the flow of power in our social world. And it insists that if we really want to understand race, how it works and has worked, then we have to move from discussions like this one – hopefully edified – to discussions of history, sociology, and political economy.

6

From Anchor Babies to Obama: Are We Post-Racial Yet?

Prologue

"Boyd, why are you so down in the mouth?"

"What do you mean?"

"I mean, your bottom lip's poked out so far you look like you're trying to give it a tan."

"You must not have heard about Troy Davis."

"You mean little Troy down the street? Nay-nay's boy? What's he gone and gotten into now?"

"No, I mean the latest casualty of our criminal justice system. A man who was just executed by the State of Georgia for a crime he almost certainly didn't commit."

"Oh. *That* Troy Davis." JJ looked down and went silent for a moment. When he looked up again his original good mood seemed to have reasserted itself. "Well, I hadn't heard. But I am not surprised, it being Georgia and all. And since I am not surprised, I am not disappointed. I don't expect any better from those crackers."

"I'm not surprised either. But I'm still saddened. And angry. And it's not about 'crackers,' as you call them. This wasn't just about race. It was about a law and order politics that railroads people into the electric chair without regard for their guilt or innocence."

"How can you fix your mouth to say some mess like that? Not just about race? How many black and brown brothers are under the watchful eye of the state right now? What percent, I mean? And what percent are we in the country?"

"Brothers *and* sisters, you mean. It's not just the men. And yes, I know the statistics. My point is just that it has more to do with –"

"I don't care *what* it's got more to do with." JJ was in full Sam Jackson mode now. I half expected him to say *Say "what" one more time, I dare ya.* Instead, he continued: "If the police hear about a crime and they got to pick between me and that old Scotsman over there" – with this he gestured at our friend Patrick, who is Irish – "who do you think will get the privilege of riding in the back of the squad car?

If Pedro over there goes to Arizona" – he gestured at Patrick's friend
and lunch companion Pablo – "and makes the mistake of opening his
mouth to talk, how long do you think it will be before they ask him
for his papers and send him back to Meh-hee-coe?"

("My grandparents came here from Ecuador," Pablo protested,
with some puzzlement.

"Do you even speak Spanish?" Patrick asked.)

"Do you hear something?" JJ said. "I thought I heard something.
Nevertheless, you see my point. When it comes to our public safety
officials and our many-hued brotherhood of potential perpetrators,
some hues are guilty until proven innocent. And for poor brothers like
Troy Davis, they probably wouldn't even accept the testimony of God
himself as proof."

"That may be. I just mean that it's not *just* about race. It's about our
culture's indifference to truth, and a punitive politics of scapegoating
and oversimplifications, and –"

"Man, nothing is *just* about race. But in the end it's *all* about race."

"That doesn't make sense."

"Exactly."

6.1 Thinking race philosophically

We have gone to the trouble, my publisher and I, of positioning this
book specifically as a *philosophical* introduction to race. This declara-
tion of idiom seems not to mean much to some. The notoriously fas-
tidious clerks at the Harvard Bookstore decided that the book's first
edition belonged in their sociology section, alongside other non-
philosophical texts like Lou Outlaw's *On Race and Philosophy*. For
whatever it's worth, I take the idiom seriously. To undertake this work
philosophically is to court certain dangers, to take on specific
burdens, and to help oneself to particular conceptual and discursive
resources.

The philosophical resources that inform this book are probably
clear enough. These pages have been littered with references to icons
like John Austin and John Dewey, as well as to contemporary figures
like Anthony Appiah and Linda Alcoff. And those figures have helped
us work through questions in distinctly philosophical areas like metaphysics, ethics, and the philosophy of existence.

There is however a danger implicit in using expressly philosophical
resources to explore distinctly philosophical questions. At least since
the days of Aristophanes, philosophy has been ridiculed for its occa-
sional indifference to the real world. There is some warrant for this
charge. Like participants in any other specialized form of inquiry,
philosophers can mistake what's meant to be a detour – from concrete

problems and conflicts to abstract speculations and debates – for a permanent relocation.

I have tried to face this danger directly. Among the principles that animate this book is the thought that philosophers of race, as of many other subjects, must not lose touch with the concrete ways and contexts in which the world generates the questions they hope to answer. My commitment to this thought has led me to appeal in a variety of ways to statistics, to history, and to the peculiar ways in which racial practices vary with time and place.

Unfortunately, none of these appeals to context have been both sustained and current. The references to current events and trends – the politics of immigration, racial profiling, and so on – have been episodic and hasty. And the discussions that have been more deliberate and sustained – the previous chapter's discussions of affirmative action and conjugal choice – have been rather less topical than I would like. It was important, I think, to discuss those issues, because they quite clearly lay bare the ethical stakes of the contest between colorblindness and color-consciousness. But neither is exactly at the top of the list when it comes to currently pressing racial controversies.

For these reasons, it will be useful to conclude the argument of this book with a more sustained study of some more topical issues. I will focus on unauthorized immigration, and move from there into much shorter discussions of policing and globalization. These are among the most pressing issues for anti-racist activists, and they have the virtue of being both current and historically rooted. I will conclude with some thoughts on the meteoric rise of Barack Obama, whose ascension, whatever else it means, clearly shows that the old rules for race-thinking and racial politics have changed. I propose to do all of this in the way I've conducted the argument for the rest of the book: by focusing most intently on the way these issues register in the place that I know best, the contemporary USA, while remaining alert to the possibility that the lessons learned in the US context might apply to other places as well.

6.2 On post-racialism

The reasons I've given for exploring these additional issues might lead some people to conclusions precisely opposite the ones I've drawn. To replace older issues like affirmative action with newer ones, these people might say, would be to mistake an epochal shift for a change in fashion. On this approach, the older issues have declined in significance not because they are dated but because race itself has declined in significance. The career of Barack Obama shows this: the rules have not changed – they've been abolished.

The dissenter I'm imagining is an advocate for the kind of post-racialism I mentioned in chapter 3. For this person, the end of late-modern racialism is the end of racialism as such. When the black-identified son of a racially mixed-marriage between a black man from Kenya and a white woman from Kansas can become president of a country built on racial slavery and a horror of miscegenation; when, moreover, he can do this in the post-9/11 USA despite bearing (what the President himself described as) a funny, Muslim-sounding name; when things like this happen, the post-racialist concludes, we have put race behind us and embarked on a new phase of human social relations.

One journalist sums up the post-racialist's thought in relation to electoral politics in this way: "In the post racial era personified by Obama . . . Americans start to make race-free judgments about who should lead them."[1] And this willingness to set race aside when it comes to questions of leadership is, for the committed post-racialist, just one example of a wider commitment to colorblindness in all spheres of human relations.

The prospect of post-racialism gives me an additional reason for taking up the topics this chapter will explore. Post-racialism of this sort can seem plausible only if issues like immigration can be rendered as non-racial phenomena. If we think of these as racial problems only out of habit, if what's noteworthy and difficult about them now has nothing interesting to do with race, then perhaps we have put race behind us. And perhaps people who claim otherwise, who claim that race remains deeply relevant to our lives – people like the author of this book – are simply old-fashioned, or pessimistic, or paranoid.

Attending to concrete issues in the sustained way that I propose for this chapter can serve as an important brake on the runaway hopes of post-racial exuberance. Working carefully and critically through specific examples of working racial formation processes will help ward off the charge of obsolescence by showing just *how* race remains relevant. I should say: doing this, doubling down on race-theoretic analysis in the age of post-racialism, will show how race remains relevant, *if and where* it remains relevant.

I do not assume from the outset that post-racialism is foolish, or that race is at the heart of each and every public – or private – contro-versy that we feel compelled to take seriously. I am, however, suspi-cious of the easy assumption that race is *not* involved in these controversies. It takes careful reflection and study to determine just whether and how much some racial project frames and informs our everyday affairs. Unfortunately, one of the functions of some forms of post-racialist discourse is precisely to obscure the way racial projects continue to frame our individual experiences and shared prospects. (I suggested above, in chapter 3, that this is, paradoxically, why post-racialism counts as a racial project.)

I propose, then, to approach the topics for this chapter as windows onto a few contemporary racial projects. To speak of a racial project, you'll recall, is to point to a double-barreled tangle of conflicts. On one side we find a struggle over racial meanings, while on the other we find a struggle over the distribution of some social goods. Think of the US civil rights movement: the North Carolina A&T students who occupied whites-only lunch counters in Greensboro in 1960 (like the many other people in many other places) were making a claim to certain goods, beginning with access to public space and other rights of citizenship. They were also, however, doing this in a particular way, by way of what Evelyn Brooks Higginbotham calls "the politics of respectability." They did this because they were also contesting certain racial meanings. The students dressed in their "Sunday best" in order to shift the public meaning of blackness from "savage" and "brutish" to "civilized" and "respectable." The struggle for civil rights, insofar as it was a racial project (because it was more than that), had both symbolic and material dimensions. This is true also for the racial projects I will consider below.

6.3 On immigration, authorization, and the US–Mexico border

The question of who can and cannot lawfully enter a state's territory has been a vexed political issue ever since modern states came into being. The specifically racial dimensions of this issue make themselves manifest at certain moments in time, in ways that are indexed to these moments. We've already seen that the United States practically began its career as a country by putting race at the heart of the Naturalization Act of 1790. What we didn't stress in that earlier discussion is that on the dominant modern approaches to statecraft, a state needs to specify its criteria for naturalization only if it expects to receive citizenship petitions, presumably from immigrants. The familiar saying is right: the USA has always been a nation of immigrants. What the saying leaves out – in addition to the fact that there were people already here to greet the immigrants – is that our idea of the immigrant has always been racialized, and in ways that explicitly shaped public policy for most of the nation's history.

After this portentous beginning, the nexus of race and immigration came to a head in the United States at the end of the nineteenth century, when policy-makers seeking to cultivate a populace that could function both as a democratic citizenry and as an effective labor force had to wrestle with the question of whom to let in and whom to keep out. They wrestled with this question in a very particular, racially fraught context. It was no longer legal to own Africans and their descendants and to use them for (virtually) whatever purposes their owners chose. At the same time, various domestic and international factors were conspiring to push and pull immigrants to the United States from racially problematic populations in Europe (the not-quite-white Irish, Italians, and so on) and Asia. Finally, the periodic reconsideration of what to do with and to America's indigenous peoples had begun once again, this time taking as its point of departure the thought that these people were close enough to being civilized that a crash course in Western life, undertaken when the savages were young and pliant, could bring them into the modern world. All of this (and other factors, like the beginnings of the modern labor movement) put fears about unruly workers and citizens (or semi-citizens, or subjects) at the forefront of public discourse. There they got bound up with prominent and popular ideas about eugenics – about how to harness and manage human nature scientifically, for the good of society and the advancement of the human race.

All of these factors together – a growing nation's hunger for labor, long-standing anxieties about the fitness of certain kinds of people for labor and for citizenship, an influx of overseas migrants, and the conviction that human populations could be scientifically managed – all of these factors came together to produce a particular kind of racial project. Like all racial projects, this one involved the dialectical interplay between a contest for resources and a struggle over meanings. Questions about who could join the nation's labor force and democratic life, and under what conditions, got read through convictions about what a people is, and of which peoples are fit to contribute to a democracy and an industrial economy. The results were predictable, and well known. The Chinese exclusion act, discussed above; national origin quotas in their original forms; a political culture on the US Pacific coast dominated by worries about The Yellow Peril; and serious proposals for regulating, by force of law, the fertility and birth rates of particular domestic populations.

Fast-forward to the politics of immigration today and much of this will seem familiar. There have been changes. For one thing, the domestic Yellow Peril has become Brown, and threatens us, in one of its forms, not from the mysterious Orient but from the too-close-for-comfort states of Central and South America. For another thing, the emphasis has shifted from regulating naturalization and legal immigration – what I will call "immigration administration" – to discouraging and regulating illegal immigration – what I will call "immigration enforcement," and will focus on going forward. Nevertheless, the shape of the worry remains the same. *They will swarm over us, take our jobs, and swamp "our" way of life with theirs.*

(I referred above to a specifically domestic Yellow Peril because there was, and still is, a version of the idea informing a great deal of thinking about US foreign policy. I am thinking here of late nineteenth- to early twentieth-century worries about Japanese nationalism and the rise of the yellow race. Like the question of how to grow the labor force and the citizenry responsibly, this question of geopolitics – I want to be clear: this *real* question of how to handle the unambiguous increase in the global influence wielded by one state or region – was layered over, infused, and distorted with racial meanings. Once this happens, the world power becomes threatening not just because it will compete with us for resources, but because it represents a different form of life, a civilization with which we will inevitably clash. This form of the yellow peril idea was revived after World War II by the rise of Japan as an economic power, and persists today in worries about China's rise as a superpower.)

The history of US efforts to regulate unauthorized immigration from Central and South America begins just as federal legislation chokes off arrivals from Asia in the beginning of the twentieth century. This history begins in earnest when the US Border Patrol, set up in 1924 to combat prohibition-era smuggling from Mexico, starts paying attention to the Mexican workers who helped satisfy US demands for labor during World War I. The end of the war and the onset of the Great Depression put US citizens desperately in need of jobs, so Mexican laborers were deported en masse. This pattern repeated itself during the Second World War, when the US government's Bracero Program – a guest worker treaty with Mexico – officially paved the way for Mexican immigrants to bolster the US wartime labor force. When the war ended, the demand for extra labor decreased but the supply continued to grow, which led to the mass deportations of the unfortunately named Operation Wetback in 1954.[2]

Unauthorized immigration grew after the end of the Bracero Program, leading to a wave of national panic. Driven by persistent poverty at home and lured by the opportunities beckoning just across the northern border, Mexican citizens constituted the overwhelming majority of a steadily increasing number – a number that tripled between 1965 and 1970 – of migrants seeking unauthorized entry to the USA.[3] The sense of panic created a push for immigration reform, which after some false starts in the 1970s led to the Immigration Reform and Control Act of 1986. This piece of federal legislation united the two dominant lines of thinking about how to approach its subject: more aggressive border enforcement on the one hand, and clearer ways for undocumented immigrants to achieve recognized legal status.

The passage of the IRCA in 1986 provides us with an opportunity to quantify the country's growing interest in unauthorized immigration. Between 1985 and 2002, US government spending on immigration enforcement grew nearly 500 percent – from US$1B to US$4.9B. Most of this increase – $2.1B of it – went to appropriations for border control activities, an increase of 300 percent. Detention, removal, and intelligence work saw an additional $1.4B, for an increase of 751 percent. Additional reforms in the mid-1990s required the detention of "criminal aliens," and increased appropriations for detention and removal by 64 percent (nearly $400M).[4]

Despite these efforts, and despite the passage of the North American Free Trade Agreement (NAFTA) in 1994, unauthorized immigrants entered the USA in even greater numbers. NAFTA proponents had argued that the agreement would create enough jobs in Mexico to absorb more of the country's reserve labor. Unfortunately, population growth, lost jobs in the agricultural sector, and persistent economic malaise kept the number of job seekers high, and led to "a dramatic rise in the number of [Mexican] migrants to the United States."[5] Of the roughly 12 million unauthorized immigrants in the USA in 2009, 59 percent were Mexican nationals, and another 22 percent were from the Caribbean, Central America, and South America.[6]

Like the migrations that inspired it, the US panic over unauthorized Mexican immigration outlasted the late twentieth-century reforms that it helped bring into being. I describe this as a panic because the public outcry and political gravity of the relevant debates seems to be rather disproportional to, and out of touch with, the actual dangers that illegal immigration creates. US media are rife with claims that unauthorized migrants drain public resources, steal jobs from US citizens, and increase crime, despite the fact that the evidence seems not to support these claims.

The panic over immigration has led not just to flawed arguments but also to serious public policy proposals. Some of the proposed policies are expensive, such as the recurring schemes to erect fencing – fortified with state-of-the-art armaments and surveillance equipment – along the US–Mexico border. Others are of dubious legality, such as the Support Our Law Enforcement and Safe Neighborhoods Act, signed into law in the US state of Arizona in 2010. Among the other things it does, this law (Arizona SB 1070) "requires Arizona state and local law enforcement officers to question the immigration status of anyone they stop for possible [criminal activity] . . . if an officer has a 'reasonable suspicion' that an individual is an unauthorized immigrant."[7] All of these proposals have been controversial and divisive.

Along with the policy proposals has come a wave of social activism and mobilization. The number of state and local civil society groups devoted to anti-immigration politics has exploded in recent years, with one estimate putting the increase at 600 percent between 2005 and 2007. In 2007, thirty-five of the most significant of these groups had between 600,000 and 750,000 members altogether, and just ten of the groups operating in 2005 "channeled $4.2 million into anti-immigration lobbying." What's more, fully one quarter of these groups were chapters of the Minutemen Civil Defense Corps, a "volunteer paramilitary group" that patrols the US–Mexico border, and that heightens tensions along the border with the predictable and tragic excesses of vigilantism.[8]

This anti-immigration backlash in governance and civil society has provoked immigrant rights advocates into action. SB 1070 has, like laws in other states targeting unauthorized immigrants, provoked marches, litigation, and boycotts. And one of the recurring themes of this counter-activism has been the charge of racism: that worries about unauthorized immigration from Central and South America are really, at bottom, worries not about immigrants but about particular kinds of people. On this view, campaigns against illegal immigration are really expressions of anti-Latino racism.

6.4 Immigration enforcement as a racial problem

As has typically been the case in this book, I've been using events in the USA to make a point that applies more widely. There are stories to tell about the politics of immigration in other places that closely track the dynamics of the story recounted above. These stories – involving, for example, Somalians in Italy, Turks in Germany, Eritreans in Sweden, Ethiopians in Israel, Zimbabweans in South Africa, Malaysians in Australia, or the Roma in France[9] – would differ in a number of crucial details, beginning with the question of why the immigrants set out for their new homes. But the stories would converge on the same basic plot.

Like Latinos and Latinas in the USA, immigrants in many places find their new neighbors treating them as inassimilable, perpetual foreigners – even if they happen to have been born in their "new" home. Even worse, though it will play nearly no role in what I say from this point on: *citizens* in these places, people whose forebears have been citizens for generations, may be subjected to the same sort of "othering" if they happen to have roots in populations or places that now contribute to the influx of migrants. These perpetual foreigners, whether citizen, legal resident, authorized visitor, or unauthorized migrant, then receive a disproportionate share of the blame for societal ills like crime and economic malaise. And a multi-faceted collection of political operations, from overheated electoral campaigns to expanded surveillance and security apparatuses, comes to focus on removing or otherwise controlling them, and on policing the borders the migrants have crossed.

The key to these stories, and to their similarity, is a shared and easily exportable central mechanism. In each case, a real question of social ethics, public policy, and political right – how to deal with certain immigrant populations – gets swept up in a maelstrom of existential and cultural panic. And this happens because the immigrants, like the nation that they are said to threaten, are imagined in *racial* terms.

In places roiled by the politics of immigration enforcement, the problems of real people – the migrants, the workers who will compete with them, the citizens who will live next to them and try, or not, to communicate with them – get symbolically shifted onto the backs of the easily identifiable and demonized foreigners. The immigrants then come to inhabit mainstream public discourse not as people with problems but as problem people, as inassimilable Others who embody the dangers of social and cultural decline. Many people now think of this process, this way of investing a real person's presence with an excess of cultural and social meaning, as a form of racialization. My aim in this section and the next is to try to make clear why it makes sense to think of it in this way.

If, as I've suggested, race-thinking assigns generic meanings to human bodies and bloodlines (and if "body" can be understood broadly, to include dress, language, and any other aspect of a person's perceptible presence in the world), then it is easy enough to see how racialization works in the politics of immigration enforcement. Take as an example the passage of laws like Arizona's "Safe Neighborhoods" act. In places with laws like this, though elsewhere as well, people who register as immigrants in the field of social perception – people who "look like" Mexicans, or who speak Spanish-accented English, or whatever else – are subject to increased state surveillance. (The law does not directly mandate this, but it is hard to see how its "reasonable suspicion" test can be insulated from garden-variety forms of racial perception.) This link between the body and the likelihood of certain encounters with the state already points to a form of racialization, not just on my account but in the minds of critics who describe this surveillance as a kind of racial profiling.

Proponents of this sort of heightened surveillance argue that it's less about race than about the real threats that certain people represent to civic life, and about the real correspondence between such traits as language use, national and ethnic origin, citizenship status, socioeconomic viability (that is, whether you are a net contributor to or drain on the economy), and criminality. On this approach, the link between the body and certain modes of treatment is adventitious. It just so happens that people who look and sound a certain way tend to do certain things, like raise crime rates and drain the public coffers. And the tendency to do these things creates problems for the wider society, problems that society has to manage. If this is right, then an attempt to deal with these problems may have the shape of a racial project, but it will have neither the problematic motivations nor the unjustifiably disparate impacts of a *racist* project. The motivations will be pure – to deal with a social problem – and the disparate impacts will be justifiable and, for that matter, unavoidable, given the source and nature of the problem.

If this defense of immigrant surveillance goes through – a big "if," as we will see in a moment – it blocks the attempt to trace the politics of immigration enforcement directly to racist intentions. But this just pushes us to a deeper level of race-theoretic analysis. To put the point in the language made available by the idea of post-racialism as a racial project, noted above: the claim that race-neutral motivations lie behind and justify racially disparate impacts might be a sign that a certain kind of racial project is at work, not that race is no longer relevant.

Immigration enforcement is expensive, especially when it is heightened and put at the heart of policing in the way we saw above. It is so expensive, in fact, that its costs seem to outweigh its benefits. More to the point, the threats that seem to require immigration enforcement, such dangers as drained public resources and falling living standards and skyrocketing crime rates, seem either to be overstated or not interestingly related to immigrant status as such. The impact of unauthorized immigration on the US economy and on the wages of US workers seems to be minimal at best – one scholar describes the relation between the costs and benefits of unauthorized immigration as "essentially a wash."[10] Similarly for the much-ballyhooed criminality of unauthorized immigrants: the link here seems to be considerably exaggerated at best, and willfully misleading at worst. Recent work in criminology in fact seems to show that immigration can *reduce* crime.[11]

How can we explain the determination to focus on a problem that doesn't have to be a problem, and to offer solutions that don't target the problem? One answer might appeal to the peculiarities of electoral politics in contemporary post-industrial nation-states, which seem to prize spectacles and scapegoating more highly than intelligent inquiry and productive policy debates. But a more precise appeal to the workings of certain racial projects will help to clarify the exact nature of this political obfuscation.

It is important to be clear about what we're trying to explain. Immigration enforcement plays a role in our national politics that seems to be completely out of proportion to its impact on our national well-being. This asymmetry seems, moreover, to be the sort of thing that a dispassionate review of the relevant evidence would reveal. So how can this asymmetry, and the failure to notice it, persist?

Questions like this are familiar to students of critical race theory, because the dominant forms of modern race-thinking are among the more effective mechanisms for short-circuiting inquiry that humankind has ever produced. On the view I've recommended, race-thinking licenses certain inferences. Different kinds of race-thinking tend to produce inferences with varying degrees of epistemic warrant. Critical race-thinking points us to the social locations that people with certain bodies and bloodlines are likely to occupy, the modes of treatment they're likely to be subject to, and the norms they're likely to feel subject to (irrespective of whether they accept the authority of the norms). This sort of race-thinking can be illuminating and revelatory: a critical racialist account of my racial identity, if it is carefully rendered, will let me know what I'm likely to face in certain settings, and will perhaps prepare me to navigate these settings more productively (or safely, or whatever).

By contrast with critical racialism, classical race-thinking points us to fictitious racial essences that are supposed to underwrite the links between body, bloodline, and social location. This form of race-thinking is obscurantist rather than revelatory, mystifying rather than illuminating. If I understand some phenomenon in the way that classical racialism recommends, I will most likely be turned away from its real causes and miss its real significance. If I want to explain why black people are and have been so influential in US pop culture and athletics, the claim that *blacks are just naturally good at sports and performing* will get in the way of my inquiry rather than advancing it. The *widely held belief* that blacks are good at these things and not at others will surely play a crucial role in my explanation. But to say this is to commit to telling a story about the origins and workings of the belief, not to endorse it.

Philosophers have recently begun describing this sort of obscurantism as an "epistemology of ignorance." This expression comes from Charles Mills, who points out that "officially sanctioned reality is divergent from actual reality" in societies that are racialized in the standard modern ways. If one is to be a conforming member of societies like this, "[o]ne has to learn to see the world wrongly, but with the assurance that this set of mistaken perceptions will be validated. . . ." To accept the ways of seeing and thinking recommended by such societies is to acquiesce to "an epistemology of ignorance, a particular pattern of localized and global cognitive dysfunctions [that] are psychologically and socially functional" – functional in the sense that these dysfunctions do important work for the people who "suffer" from them. The devotees of racial supremacist ideologies – both oppressor and oppressed, master and servant – will construct for themselves "an invented delusional world, a racial fantasyland" populated by "invented Orients, invented Africas, invented Americas . . . inhabited by people who never were – Calibans and Tontos, Man Fridays and Sambos."[12]

Epistemologies of ignorance are crucial aspects of modern racial projects, and are very much at work in the politics of immigration enforcement. Just as Mills suggests (following Edward Said and others), invented immigrants inhabit the worlds depicted by certain contemporary racial ideologies. These ideologies are not explicitly racial in the way that their nineteenth-century predecessors were: they do not depend on explicit claims about the inferiority of various racial types. But like those old racial ideologies, they require that certain peoples and populations be animated by practically unalterable essences, essences that necessarily carry with them certain traits and that do their work in ways that we can know with confidence no matter what the facts actually say. The drama of immigration enforcement can swirl around non-existent problems because, as I said above, immigrants just are problem people. As we'll see more clearly in a moment, The Illegal Immigrant is a racial type, and regulating that type's presence on US soil is a racial project.

6.5 Immigration enforcement as a racial project

It helps to invoke the theory of racial projects at this point because we have clearly made our way into the domain of contests over meaning. Debates over immigration enforcement are clearly about ways of distributing such social goods as citizenship and legal residence. But these issues are also bound up with questions about what race means now, just as the racial project framework suggests.

To say that arguments about immigration policy are entwined with questions of racial meaning isn't to say that contemporary parties to these arguments must think of themselves as taking stances for or against something called the Hispanic race. It is to rather to say things like this: A tradition of political argument stretching back at least to Operation Wetback has made illegal immigrants – or, as many now say, simply "illegals" – into stock characters in US political discourse. The most recent contributions to this tradition have given us a variety of such characters, including "anchor babies" and their mothers. (These are the beneficiaries and executors of what anti-immigration critics call the "drop and leave" strategy, which counsels foreign women to enter the USA, bear children on US soil, and then return to their homelands, thereby giving the family a legal stake in the USA by way of the citizen to whom they've just given birth).[13] The roles that these characters play in our political narratives make sense only if we understand them as racial symbols – as dehumanized figures ("illegals") rather than persons, and as figures defined by the links between bodies, bloodlines, and deeper meaning that constitutes the Hispanic mode of (what we learned in chapter 4 to call) outsider racialization. And, finally: contemporary immigration debates are defined in part by arguments about how, and whether, our continued interest in these characters can be reconciled with our avowed and official commitment to anti-racism.

There is much more to say about this form of outsider racialization, beginning with the links between its connections to other racial projects. For example, the worry about the "drop and leave" strategy – as tenuously based in quantifiable reality as worries about runaway criminality – expresses some of the same anxieties as the racial project that gives us the "welfare mother." Also, the racialization of "illegals" intersects in a variety of ways with the emergence, after 9/11, of the terrorist as a racial symbol.

I will return to some of these links below, but propose to devote the rest of this section to a different connection: one involving the politics of whiteness. In chapter 5 we briefly considered Ron Sundstrom's discussion of "the browning of America." This is the idea that demographic shifts in the US population – mainly racial intermarriage and increased immigration from South and Central America – will turn what was once an overwhelmingly and proudly white nation into a "majority-minority" country. The idea that the US population will soon have more non-whites than whites strikes some as an occasion for rejoicing, on the theory that this shift will both reflect and require a more advanced orientation to racial politics than we have so far been able to achieve. But for others the browning of America is a threat and a problem.

Just as in the late nineteenth and early twentieth centuries, the politics of immigration seizes the popular imagination in part by raising questions about national identity in the destination community. The politics of US immigration enforcement emerges from and advances a racial project not just in its treatment of *Latinidadé* (of Mexican-ness, or Bolivian-ness, or whatever), but also in the meanings it assigns to US identities. This is why English-only campaigns emerge in states with large and growing populations of Latino and Latina immigrants. For some, the USA is an essentially *English-speaking* nation. On this view, some people who reside here might happen to speak other languages, but giving official sanction to those languages in schools, on official paperwork, and so on would mean giving up one of the things that makes us who we are.

The argument about language generalizes quickly into other spheres. We eat hot dogs, not tamales. We celebrate Thanksgiving, not Cinco de Mayo. We are Protestant, not Catholic. And so on across the entire range of defining cultural practices – all of which may lose their centrality in our civic life if we let too many people with other ways of living experiment with those other ways in our space. (As I keep saying, this pattern shows up in other places. I think immediately of the difficulty that Margaret Thatcher's UK had with the idea of [Jamaican-descended] black Britons.)

As described so far, this resistance to cultural difference needn't have anything to do with race. All cultures must figure out how to accommodate change and difference without putting themselves out of business. Race enters the picture when we consider what holds together the range of practices that are thought to define US national identity. Once upon a time one could have argued directly that the USA (or Australia, or South Africa, or the UK) is a white nation, and that it naturally follows that white people's practices are the ones that matter. But we tend to frown on arguments like that now.

Appeals to history seem poised to do some of the work that we used to assign directly to race. *These foods and holidays and so on define our way of life*, we say, *because they always have.* But the "always" in this formulation is hyperbolic. "Our way" started at some point in time, and it started just then because someone decided that the generic past ended at that moment and "our" history began. People in the USA usually locate this moment in 1620, when the Pilgrims landed at Plymouth Rock, or in 1607, when the Jamestown settlement began its ill-fated career. But why do we pick these moments? And how do we decide that novelty was possible in these moments but not later? Why can't something happen now to redefine our sense of peoplehood and political community the way those long-ago events once did?

There are no good answers to these questions, not of the sort that philosophers sometimes want. There are no airtight, logically necessary, assent-compelling justifications for accepting some practice rather than another into "our" way of life. There are just arguments about how to understand ourselves as products of history, and about whose experiences and perspectives count in our histories. This is why the pre-history of the USA (at least in its canned varieties) begins not when the Spanish arrive, or when the Iroquois Confederacy emerges, but with the onset of colonization by the English: because the experiences of some people count as "our" history, while the experiences of others do not. The appeal to history presupposes answers to the very question – about the boundaries of our political and cultural communities – that it was supposed to settle.

Put differently, arguments about political and cultural identity are themselves part of the history that we use the arguments to define. That is to say, part of what makes a people into a people is the way it tells the story of who and what it is. All of which leads me to the point that I have probably, hopefully, telegraphed by now: the most familiar arguments and ideas about what the USA is – about what America is, as proponents of those arguments would put it – descend from traditions that were forged in the fires of classical racialism. In those traditions America just was a white nation, and the willingness of many Americans to say so even as they extolled the virtues of liberty and democracy helped make it the kind of place it actually was (which was *not* a white nation, protestations to the contrary notwithstanding). And *it is still that kind of place, at least in its behavior if not usually in its explicit avowals.* It is still that kind of place even though much of it is unevenly, half-heartedly trying to figure out how to be something else.

I am not suggesting that all anti-immigrant mobilization and sentiment is a direct expression of old-style racism. Some of it surely is, and even more of it can be traced to the influence of white supremacists and their fellow-travelers in think tanks and NGOs.[14] Once we grant this, though, there is still something more, and more elusive, to say about the rest of it. We know well enough what to say about old-fashioned racism, so I'll spend no more time on it here. I'll focus instead on the harder and more philosophically interesting case: the reconstructed nativism that refuses outright racist reasoning but still obsesses over the overstated dangers of unauthorized immigration.

If there is something more to say about reconstructed nativism, perhaps it is this: anti-immigrant activism is an American tradition, defined, like any other tradition, by proprietary rituals and conventions and rhetoric. And this tradition is constituted in part by ritual genuflections to the whiteness of America and to the dangers of immigrants. As with many rituals, these genuflections persist despite the loss of their original motivations to the mists of time. (Why does that particular gesture count as the expression-of-respect-for-a-superior that we call a salute? Why do men wear neckties?) What's key for a race theoretic analysis of reconstructed nativism in immigration politics, though, is the content of the ritual. It consists in linking certain forms of physical appearance and lines of ancestry to the prerequisites for citizenship. It consists, I might say, in taking certain bodies and bloodlines *as* prerequisites for cultural and political belonging. (It consists, I should say further, on doing this under certain conditions, such as when the economy sours.)

With more space I would supplement these gestures at cultural traditions and rituals with a more precise theoretical vocabulary, relying perhaps on the phenomenology of habit or on the psychology of implicit bias. While recent work in and near race theory has used both approaches to good advantage, I've gone on too long already to follow suit. Suffice it to say for now that the workings of these rituals, habits, and biases show that a certain kind of racial project is at the heart of the politics of immigration enforcement in the USA. This project combines a scheme for distributing a social good – authorized entry to and residence in the country – with a template for reinterpreting the meaning of race. The racial meanings at stake clearly have to do with what it is to be a Latino or Latina. But they also have to do with what it is to be white. Reconstructed nativism in immigration enforcement is, among other things, a way of dealing with the declining significance of whiteness in what will soon be a majority-minority nation. It is a way of committing to the existence, or worrying about the imminent disappearance, of a world that we would once have described with statements like *America is a white nation*, while also accepting that one can no longer make statements like that.

6.6 Immigration, securitization, globalization

I said above that reconstructed nativism is, *among other things*, a way of dealing with the declining significance of whiteness. Some of the other things it is also appeared above. It is part of a tradition of political argument and representation. It is a habit of thought that our culture learned over many generations. And it is a genre of rhetoric and expression that helps itself to stock images of various racial types, and that borrows from and interacts with other genres relying on other racial types.

One of the things that I didn't say above must surely be said before I bring this discussion to a close. The resurgence of nativism in the politics of immigration enforcement has a great deal to do with the questions and arguments that we find in other areas of political controversy and policy debate. Immigration enforcement in particular is bound up with the dynamics of securitization and globalization. And it is difficult to understand either of these dynamics fully without considering the degree to which they are also entwined with certain racial projects. I've left myself rather too little room to do much more than gesture at the racial dimensions of these other subjects. But a gesture, as swift and unsatisfying as it must be, is better than nothing.

6.6.1 Globalization

The relevance of globalization to immigration may be obvious. People, products, money, and information flow across national boundaries much more easily today than ever before. The migratory flows that inspire programs of immigration enforcement are among the forces that define globalization today. And the web of conditions that help define globalization further – the ease with which migrants can remit funds to family members in their homeland, the proliferation of techniques for communicating across great distances, the simmering military conflicts receiving sustenance from transnational networks of illicit trade and pushing formerly settled peoples to seek refuge in other lands – all of these contribute to the problem of unauthorized immigration.

The connections between globalization and racial formation processes should be only a little less obvious. The first thing to say is that globalization is not new, though its current pace and mechanisms are. One might argue that European modernity's signature racial projects were also the first indications of its global potential and aspirations. The globe-spanning quests for land, resources, and labor; the transoceanic and transcontinental trade in slave labor; the connections between both of these and the global trade in spices and other commodities – all of these effectively shrank the world in just the way we claim for contemporary globalizing processes, hundreds of years *avant la lettre*.

These early, globe-spanning racial projects not only shrank the world but also tilted it, creating injustices and inequalities that continue in many ways to shape the contemporary world order. It is no accident that the richest countries in today's world are, by and large, the colonial powers of high modernity, or that the poorest countries are by and large the former colonies. From the long expropriation of the indigenous Americans and Australians, through the scramble for Africa and for influence in South America, to the end of the twentieth-century wars in Southern Africa and Southeast Asia: the world we now know, with its familiar asymmetries of wealth, influence, and prestige, was built on foundations laid (in part) by modernity's explicitly racial projects.

Modernity's classical racialist projects bequeathed its racial asymmetries to us in a variety of ways, two of which are particularly relevant right now. Most obviously, it explicitly distributed vital resources along racial lines, and left them there. This may be self-explanatory, but in case it isn't: who owns the controlling shares in South Africa's diamond mines – still? Where did Firestone get the rubber that it used to become the corporation we know today? How much of its wealth has it shared with the descendants of the workers on its rubber plantations?

Somewhat less obviously, it offered us a vision of the world that can reconcile us to conditions that we might otherwise find unjust. I am once again thinking of the habits, biases, and expectations that implicitly shape our paths through the world. Many of us don't think as carefully as we might about the conditions under which failed states fail and poor nations struggle because *we've never known them to be self-sufficient*. The fact that independent and viable political arrangements predated our colonial maps rarely affects the discussion, because those polities exist outside the "racial fantasyland" of modern myth. In this fantasyland, Haiti struggles not because it was from the moment of its independence saddled with a crushing debt to France – negotiated to compensate for the "property," the human property, liberated by the independence struggle; and not because the United States has at multiple points since intervened, routinely and forcibly, to keep the island nation from managing its own relationship to the global economy. This invented Haiti doesn't even struggle because of its internal problems, which it, like any nation, has in abundant supply. It struggles because Haitians are problem people, whose internal problems and self-inflicted wounds are sufficient to explain any difficulty they have.

Interestingly, this connection between past racial projects and the current world order somehow rarely makes its way into accounts of global ethics and global justice. More to the point, the connection between past racial projects, the expectations and habits they bred, and what the current world deems worthy of the name "injustice" rarely makes its way into those accounts. Instead we focus on development and modernization, both of which sound natural and inevitable, provided that we're not dealing with problem people; and both of which sidestep the question of *under*-development, which is what historian and activist Walter Rodney called the process whereby European powers systematically diverted Africa from the path of "development."

6.6.2 Securitization

I use "securitization" in a way that I've learned from some of the literature on immigration, where it refers to the decision to treat a policy question as a matter for policing and surveillance and, when necessary, apprehension and incarceration. These are all possibilities for any policy backed by the coercive power of the state. But a standing possibility needn't be put at the heart of a policy regime. To put these things at the heart of immigration politics – to focus on enforcement rather than on administrative measures like the issuance of visas and establishment of workable guest worker arrangements – is to securitize the question of authorized entry to the country.

Having imported the term from that literature, I'll use it in a still broader way to refer to the US tendency to treat as many policy questions as possible as questions of policing and imprisonment. We live in a securitized society, one that criminalizes and literally penalizes – subjects to the authority of the penal system – all manner of social problems. From the homeless and the drug addicted to parole violators and *asylum seekers*, we arrest and lock up first, and we ask questions later, if we do so at all.

As with the discussion of immigration enforcement, some numbers will help make the point. The United States is far and away the world's leader in incarceration rates. At the end of 2011 we had over two million people in prisons and jails, which is a staggering *five hundred percent* increase over the comparable figure from thirty years ago. This gives us more incarcerated persons per capita than any other country in the world – more, prison reform advocates often point out, than Russia, or Myanmar, or what used to be Libya, or China. And in terms of sheer size, our prison population in 2008 was larger than the thirty-six largest European inmate populations *combined*.[15]

Like the panic over immigration, the securitization of the USA seems not to have much of a relationship to what one might think of as the relevant facts. The stunning growth in the prison population did not follow a sudden and dramatic increase in crime rates. Nor has it had a discernible impact on the rates of crime or of repeat offenses. Even worse, there is a great deal of hard, systematically gathered evidence that a variety of alternatives to incarceration would be both more effective generally and more cost-effective.

As in the discussion of immigration, one has to wonder: how can a regime of public policy and political rhetoric survive when it refuses to accept the authority of the facts? It is of course the case that politics distorts public deliberation quite generally, in all sorts of areas. But we can start toward an account of the specific distortions in this area by attending to the arguments of certain advocates for prison reform and abolition. (To call for prison abolition is not to claim that criminals needn't be punished. We'll return to this.)

Angela Davis and many others have inserted the idea of "the prison-industrial complex" into public consciousness.[16] I've avoided that language and referred instead to securitization just to avoid provocations that I can't defend while I hurry toward a conclusion. But the analytical framework that this language encapsulates gets a great many things right. What it most importantly gets right is its insistence on *industry*.

Private prisons have become a major player in the US economy, and have used their influence to push policies based on detention. Sometimes they do this directly, through lobbying and financial contributions to supportive legislators. But other times they do it indirectly, by creating a vast and impressive array of hammers, and then suggesting to lawmakers and others – to downtrodden post-industrial communities, for example, looking for an economic engine to replace the closed factory or mine, or to border communities worried about criminals streaming into their towns – that many more problems look like nails than one might think.

On the picture advanced by prison abolitionists, the securitization of US society results in part from the success of a particular business model, the model formulated and sold by the corrections industry. The business model is only part of the story, though, because we have to talk also about the conditions that made society receptive to the model. These conditions have a great deal to do with race.

As with the politics of immigration enforcement, securitization advances with the help of certain racialized traditions of argument, habits of thought, and genres of rhetoric and expression. The surge in the US prison population began after we declared a war on drugs in the 1980s (the moment, not coincidentally, of Reagan's call for states rights, and of the turn to immigration enforcement). We waged this war primarily in, and on, poor black communities, both because of preexisting biases in the processing of criminal defendants (persuasively and massively demonstrated in a variety of studies) and because of biases and other racial asymmetries built into the conduct of the "war."

Some of these asymmetries are well known, while some are more obscure. Anyone who knows anything about race and the law knows that convictions involving the form of cocaine (crack) that blacks tend to prefer require much higher sentences than those involving the form whites prefer (powder). Such a person would also have some sense of the dire statistics in this area:

> If current trends continue, 1 of every 3 African-American males born today can expect to go to prison in his lifetime, as can 1 of every 6 Latino males, compared to 1 in 17 White males. For women, the overall figures are considerably lower, but the racial/ethnic disparities are similar: 1 of every 18 African-American females, 1 of every 45 Hispanic females, and 1 of every 111 White females can expect to spend time in prison.[17]

Fewer people know about the racially disparate impact of laws that increase criminal penalties for offenses committed close to schools: drug transactions in densely developed urban areas, which are disproportionately black, are more likely to trigger these penalties. And fewer people still know about the cumulative damage that mass incarceration does to communities of color, from long-term electoral disenfranchisement to family dissolution and severely delimited opportunities for gainful employment.[18]

As we discussed in chapter 3, critical racialism refuses the orientation to this sort of information that classical race-thinking recommends. The classical response – *all this just proves that black and brown people are dangerous and pathological* – has to give way to a deeper question. *What links these people to these social conditions, now that we know better than to rely on racial essences?*

Once we accept the continued and well-documented effects of implicit bias on the reproduction of social hierarchies, we have to take seriously the thought that many prison abolitionists most want to press. The current securitized, prison-obsessed system for identifying and dealing with anti-social behavior – which is what they want to abolish – has been built using a template borrowed from older systems of explicitly racialized social control. (Here they insist, in ways I don't have time for, on the zeal with which the corrections industry turns inmates into forced and underpaid laborers; on the equanimity with which we accept the permanent disenfranchisement of a disproportionately minority population, and more.)

Not everyone who defends the current corrections system is an old-fashioned racist. Vanishingly few are. But many of those who assent to the workings of this system either don't know or don't want to know how closely the structures of our new, allegedly post-racial world align with the blueprints provided by the old racisms. If, as we claim, we find racism objectionable, and if, as we've learned from Jorge Garcia to say, racism is a form of disregard, then we should surely object to our placid acceptance of the current criminal justice system, our indifference to its racially disparate impacts, and our willful ignorance of the real causes and meanings of these disparities.

6.7 Conclusion: Race-ing the Obamas

I've been trying to locate some contemporary phenomena within what Foucault calls a "polyhedron of intelligibility." He uses this unlovely phrase – it sounds better in French – to describe a mode of explanation that locates social phenomena in networks of other phenomena. In this spirit he explains, "the more one analyzes the process of. . . penal practice down to its smallest details, the more one is led to relate them to such practices as schooling, military discipline, etc." He goes on: "the internal analysis of processes goes hand in hand with a multiplication of analytical 'salients.'"[19]

I've been trying to multiply the "analytical salients" for practices like immigration enforcement, policing, and globalization. The point has not been that these phenomena are always and only about race. It has been that race is *relevant*: that insisting on the salience of race to these phenomena will reveal things about them, and connections between them, that we might otherwise miss. Other factors are of course relevant, and I have tried to mention some of these along the way. For example, we can't understand immigration without understanding securitization, and we can't understand that without understanding something about the political economy of the corrections industry.

My point is just that we can't fully understand the correction industry's ability to establish itself in the way it has without thinking about race. A country built on race-related modes of terroristic and fascistic social control – as well as on much else, like ideals of freedom and equality – will be susceptible to a politics of "law and order" that implicitly promises to put certain people back in their places. Or so I've tried, rather indirectly, to suggest.

It seemed important to insist on the relevance of race because we are so often, these days, invited to think that it is irrelevant. Race-talk is passé, we're told: *nous avons changez tout cela* – we've changed all that. And the clearest evidence of this is that a black man is now the most powerful man in the world (if one thinks that's what the US president is).

The ascension of Barack and Michelle Obama has been a complex and momentous phenomenon, and it does surely point to the degree to which a great many things have changed for the better. But Mr Obama's campaign and election, like Mrs Obama's career as the first black "First Lady," is yet another phenomenon that one can't fully understand without reading it as a continuation of US racial history, rather than as a repudiation or transcendence of it. For example: Mr Obama's famous "race speech" in Philadelphia was widely regarded as a triumph, but he delivered it only because he had to distance himself from the pastor of his church, whose views on racial justice were too radical – too black – to be reconciled with a viable run at the Oval Office.

Similarly, it is difficult to understand the behavior of the Obamas' opponents and critics without recourse to a level of racial analysis. What else can explain the peculiar resonance of the claim that Mr Obama was not born in the USA, that he is, in essence, an illegal immigrant? Or the assumption that he is a Muslim? Or the willingness to bring up this "fact" about him as if it disqualified him from the presidency? What else can explain the obsessive focus on Mrs Obama's body, on the muscularity of her arms and the size of her derriere?

I should say, in the Foucauldian spirit described above: how else can we explain these things *without* relying on some kind of free-floating irrationality or ill-will? Other first ladies had bodies too. Why subject Mrs Obama to this fetishistic appraisal? Perhaps because we have traditions (genres, habits) of treating blacks as essentially bound up with their bodies, especially when the blacks are women and the bodies have certain shapes. Mr Obama has a US-issued birth certificate, just like every other president since the advent of modern administrative techniques. So why doubt the veracity of his claim to citizenship? Perhaps because he doesn't look American, and his name doesn't sound American: because our habits tell us that Americans, real Americans, *look* a certain way.

To the Obamas' credit, they have managed this maelstrom of racial meaning more adroitly than anyone had any right to expect. But that they have had to manage it is evidence that race does still matter. If this book has done its work, its readers should be able to reflect more productively on whether race matters, and when, and how much.

Further Reading

Books inevitably leave things out, some more than others. Introductory books are particularly prone to omission, especially when they aspire to breadth as well as depth, and when they cover interdisciplinary subjects or subjects that have yet to generate a dominant method or vocabulary. All of this means, of course, that there's a great deal more to say on all of the issues that we've encountered in the foregoing pages. The endnote references already point to many of the texts that I'd recommend for further study – in fact, I've mentioned several of them precisely for the purpose of making such a recommendation. Still, I'll mention a few more useful texts below, to supplement the ones cited in the notes.

Judicious selectivity also comes in handy when introducing a highly contextual topic. This is particularly the case when the relevant contexts are geographical and cultural, as they are with race-thinking. There is room for abstract analysis, of course, and I've done what I can on that score. But, as I've repeatedly said, race theory requires that one remain mindful of the details of concrete social practices, institutions, and arrangements. Since this book has focused mostly on US race-thinking, I'll also mention below some texts that explore racial formation processes in other places. Two warnings are in order. First, I'll identify these other places in terms of continental and national boundaries, but never fear: none of the texts deny the international, transnational, and global possibilities of modern racial projects, and many explore social phenomena that realize these possibilities. And second, the world is a big place, with too many different peoples in it for me to compile a list that comes close to capturing all the modes of racialization, everywhere. Think of what follows as a beginning, based on texts that I've found particularly useful.

Linda Martín Alcoff, *Visible Identities: Race, Gender, and the Self* (New York: Oxford University Press, 2006). This is an essential collection by one of the central figures in the establishment of philosophical race theory as a viable field. Alcoff manages to develop an intersectional ontology of social identity that takes fluidity and historicity seriously *without* diminishing the political and existential stakes of identity talk and practice.

Gloria Anzaldua, *Borderlands/La Frontera: The New Mestiza*, 2nd edn (San Francisco: Aunt Lute Books, 1987). Anzaldua's eclectic master-piece is one of the founding texts of third-wave feminism, and opens the door to a growing and still lively body of work in feminist epistemology, among many other things.

K. Anthony Appiah, *In My Father's House* (New York: Oxford University Press, 1992). Appiah elegantly combines analytic philosophy, literary criticism, and the essay form to explore the metaphysics of race, the politics of racial identity, the ethics of racism, the possibility of African philosophy, and much more besides. Like Alcoff's, this is a classic text.

Les Back and John Solomos, *Theories of Race and Racism: A Reader* (New York: Routledge, 2000). If you need one book to introduce you to the primary texts of critical race theory, this is it. Back and Solomos have brought together 41 important theorists of race and racism, from founding figures like Du Bois and Fanon to contemporary writers like bell hooks, Stuart Hall, and Chandra Mohanty. The editors are sociologists, and they include the indispensable race theorists from their discipline – Du Bois, Ruth Benedict, John Rex, Robert Park, and so on. But they also include philosophers like Appiah and Goldberg. For a similar anthology assembled from the standpoint of philosophy, consider Leonard Harris, ed., *Racism* (Amherst, NY: Humanity-Prometheus Books, 1999).

Scott Bennett, *White Politics and Black Australians* (St Leonards, Australia: Allen and Unwin, 1999). Moderately detailed but accessible introduction to the treatment of indigenous peoples under Australian law and politics. Especially good if paired with a nice general history, like Stuart Macintyre's inestimable *A Concise History of Australia* (New York: Cambridge University Press, 1999), which also does well on racial dynamics.

Robert Bernasconi and Sybol Cook, eds, *Race and Racism in Continental Philosophy* (Bloomington: Indiana University Press, 2003). A valuable compendium of commentaries on race-thinking in canonical figures in continental thought, from Arendt to Sartre. Also includes some of the figures we have to take up when our sense of the canon comes to track more closely the actual content – and in some cases, the history – of philosophical inquiry. Which is to say that this text also includes fine pieces on Douglass, Du Bois, Richard Wright, and Suzanne Cesaire.

Bernard Boxill, ed., *Race and Racism* (New York: Oxford University Press, 2001). Usefully gathers in one place some of the important (mostly analytic) early pieces in the field, though with a couple of clunkers thrown in for good measure. This anthology is worth the price of admission just for reprinting classic essays by Ned Block (on racial arguments from heritability), Marilyn Frye ("White Woman Feminist") and Richard Wasserstrom (analyzing discrimination), along with newer pieces (cable TV execs have empowered us to speak now of "new classics") by Robert Gooding-Williams and Anthony Appiah.

Chris J. Cuomo and Kim Q. Hall, eds, *Whiteness: Feminist Philosophical Reflections* (Boulder, CO: Rowman and Littlefield, 1999); Ruth Roach Pierson and Nupur Chaudhuri, eds, *Nation, Empire, Colony: Historicizing Gender and Race* (Bloomington: Indiana University Press, 1998). In Cuomo and Hall's collection, feminist philosophers reflect on the connections between whiteness, identity, gender, and sexuality, usually using their own lives as the "data." The pieces in the Pierson and Chaudhuri anthology make less personal connections, with essays examining the experiences of Jews in nineteenth-century Austria, Korean women under Japanese domination, indigenous and settler women under dominant Australian notions of chasteness and femininity, and more.

Yen Le Espiritu, *Asian American Panethnicity: Bridging Institutions and Identities* (Philadelphia: Temple University Press, 1993). This is another classic text, best known for demonstrating the way formerly distinct peoples – from Korea, the Philippines, Japan, and elsewhere – can come together under the pressures of racialized social structures to create new identities.

Joshua Glasgow, *A Theory of Race* (New York: Routledge, 2009). This is one of the first book-length arguments produced by the generation of analytic race theorists inspired by Appiah's musings in metaphysics and the philosophy of language. Glasgow's careful study nicely prepares the way for the later work that he and others would do in experimental philosophy and philosophical psychology.

David Theo Goldberg, *The Threat of Race* (Malden, MA: Blackwell, 2009). Continuing the incisive and challenging line of inquiry that Goldberg undertook in *Racist Culture*, this book explores in detail the connections between race, philosophical anthropology, politics, and geographic imaginaries. With its reflections on subjects like "racial Palestinianization" and neo-liberal politics, this is a valuable restraint on the apolitical abstraction that we philosophers sometimes give too long a leash in our work.

Juan Gonzalez, *Harvest of Empire: A History of Latinos in America* (New York: Viking, 2000). In this exemplary historical narrative and analysis, journalist Juan Gonzalez tracks the emergence of the Latino/a population from Spanish and Portuguese colonization to NAFTA and beyond (with US military adventures in the various Latin American states in between, and ongoing). Race is not the subject here, but it is never far from consideration. Any attempt to understand the racialization of Latino and Latina peoples has to begin with the information that Gonzalez makes so readily accessible.

Jorge Gracia, *Race or Ethnicity? On Black and Latino Identity* (Ithaca: Cornell University Press, 2007). True to its title, this collection examines the links and gaps between racial and ethnic identity categories. Its main virtue may be that it explicitly engages questions of public policy while resisting the black–white binary that frames so much race theory (and, as I have already confessed and tried to atone for, much of this book).

Stuart Hall, "New Ethnicities," in *Stuart Hall: Critical Dialogues in Cultural Studies*, eds, David Morley and Kuan-Hsing Chen (New York: Routledge, 1996). The central figure in British Cultural Studies provides a clear, thoughtful statement of the contemporary challenges of identity. One of the best short pieces I've ever read, from the standpoint of balancing accessibility and theoretical sophistication, while making the existential and political stakes of the discussion clear. For something much less accessible but equally important, see Stuart Hall, "Race, Articulation, and Societies Structured in Dominance," in *Black British Cultural Studies: A Reader*, eds, Houston Baker, Manthia Diawara, and Ruth Lindeborg (Chicago: University of Chicago Press, 1996), pp. 16–60.

Anthony Marx, *Making Race and Nation: A Comparison of the United States, South Africa, and Brazil* (New York: Cambridge University Press, 1998). Marx presents a highly detailed analysis of the racial trajectories of the three named countries, debunking the myth of Brazil's racial "democracy" while also identifying the factors that cause the three paths to diverge and converge where they do.

Thomas McCarthy, *Race, Empire, and the Idea of Human Development* (New York: Cambridge University Press, 2009). This is a short but deep study of the way racialism, imperialism, and philosophical modernism conspired in the making of the modern West, undertaken from the perspective of contemporary critical theory.

Howard McGary, *Race and Social Justice* (Malden, MA: Blackwell, 1999). This collection gathers several important essays by one of the pioneers and pioneering institution-builders in race theory and Africana Philosophy. Like Boxill's *Blacks and Social Justice*, mentioned earlier in chapter 5, McGary's measured studies of the questions that in some ways launched the field – affirmative action, reparations, alienation, and so on – provides a valuable introduction to the forms of philosophical race theory that emerge from analytic social philosophy and Africana thought. This book provides the model for valuable later work like Anna Stubblefield's *Ethics Along the Color Line* (Ithaca: Cornell University Press, 2005).

Falguni Sheth, *Toward a Political Philosophy of Race* (Albany: SUNY Press, 2009). This important text provides the first in-depth philosophical exploration in English of the racialization of Muslims, Asian Indians, Arabs, and immigrants. It also attempts to bridge the strangely distinct approaches that philosophers of race and postcolonial and poststructuralist theorists take to similar issues.

Shannon Sullivan, *Revealing Whiteness: The Unconscious Habits of Racial Privilege* (Bloomington: Indiana University Press, 2006). This is one of the key texts in the recent flowering of work on race in American Philosophy. Blending Dewey and Du Bois with psychoanalytic theory and feminist thought, Sullivan provides valuable resources for thinking through the meanings of whiteness in a recognizably American idiom.

Peter Ratcliffe, ed., *"Race," Ethnicity, and Nation* (London: University College London Press, 1994). A collection of sociological papers exploring the role of race, ethnicity, and nation in social conflicts, and considering the demands this places on researchers. Includes essays on racial and ethnic conflict in Israel, Poland, the former Soviet Union, Nigeria, South Africa, Australia, the USA, Sri Lanka, and India. (Reprinted in the USA as *The Politics of Social Science Research: "Race," Ethnicity and Social Change* (New York: Palgrave, 2001).)

Richard Siddle, *Race, Resistance, and the Ainu of Japan* (New York: Routledge, 1996). Siddle carefully applies racialization theory to the experience of the people of Hokkaido under Japanese rule, effectively debunking the myth of Japanese homogeneity and racial egalitarianism. George Hicks performs a similar service, with less theoretical precision and more ethnographic detail, in *Japan's Hidden Apartheid: The Korean Minority and the Japanese* (Brookfield, VT: Ashgate, 1997).

Cornel West, "A Genealogy of Modern Racism," *Prophesy Deliverance!* (Philadelphia: Westminster Press, 1982). West provides an impressive model for the kind of sweeping historical narrative that I've occasionally attempted in this book. Here we start to see how Western discourses of rationality and beauty, as articulated by our most prominent philosophers, connect to the emergence of modern racism. If the tie to the philosophers piques your interest, consider Julie Ward and Tommy Lott's *Philosophers on Race* (Malden, MA: Blackwell, 2002), with essays on race-thinking in the work of Plato, Aristotle, Hobbes, Sartre, De Beauvoir, Nietzsche, and Dewey.

Howard Winant, *The World is a Ghetto* (New York: Basic Books, 2001). Giving himself more room to maneuver than in any of his previous books, Winant provides a brilliant book-length exposition of the racial formation approach to modernity that I attempted earlier in this book. A detailed, passionate, and thorough study of the role race has played, and continues to play, in creating global patterns of advantage and disadvantage. Ronald Takaki's *Iron Cages* (New York: Oxford University Press, 2000) is only slightly less ambitious; it tracks the development of US racialism alongside US conceptions and practices of republican self-government, capitalist striving, and imperial domination.

Notes

Preface to Second Edition

1 See Michael Hirsh, "The Big Lie Grows," *Informing the 99 Percent* (blog), December 23, 2011, accessed December 23, 2011 at http://informingthe 99percent.blogspot.com/; Karen Petrou, "How Freddie Mac Forgot About $244 Billion," *Federal Financial Analytics* (blog), December 16, 2011, accessed on December 23, 2011 at http://www.fedfin.com/index.php?option= com_content&task=view&id=797&Itemid=30.

1 What Race-Thinking Is

1 Michael Root, "How We Divide the World," *Proceedings of the Biennial Meeting of the Philosophy of Science Association*, Philosophy of Science Association, 1998.
2 See Audrey Smedley, *Race in North America* (Boulder, CO: Westview, 1993).
3 J. L. Austin, "A Plea for Excuses," in *Philosophical Papers*, 2nd edn (New York: Oxford University Press, 1970), p. 185.
4 J. L. Shulman and J. Glasgow (2010), "Is Race-Thinking Biological or Social, and Does It Matter for Racism? An Exploratory Study," *Journal of Social Philosophy*, 41, 244–59; L. Faucher and E. Machery (2009), "Racism: Against Jorge Garcia's Moral and Psychological Monism," *Philosophy of the Social Sciences*, 39(1), 41–62. For a general and readable discussion of experimental philosophy, see K. Anthony Appiah, *Experiments in Ethics* (Cambridge, MA: Harvard University Press, 2010).
5 Charles Mills, *The Racial Contract* (Ithaca, NY: Cornell University Press, 1997).
6 Dinesh D'Souza, "Is Racism a Western Idea?" *The American Scholar*, Fall 1995, 517; Frank Dikötter, *The Discourse of Race in Modern China* (Stanford, CA: Stanford University Press, 1992).
7 Maria Michela Sassi, *The Science of Man in Ancient Greece* (Chicago: University of Chicago Press, 2001), pp. 20–1, 120–39. The question of race-thinking in the pre-modern world has become something of a growth industry in recent years. Among the important products of this work are Benjamin Isaac's *The Invention of Racism in Classical Antiquity* (Princeton

University Press, 2004) and a special issue of the *Journal of Medieval and Early Modern Studies* on race in the middle ages (Volume 31, Number 1, Winter 2001).

8 See Thomas Holt, *The Problem of Race in the Twenty-First Century* (Cambridge, MA: Harvard University Press, 2000), pp. 30, 59.

9 Michael Omi and Howard Winant, *Racial Formation in the United States*, 2nd edn (New York: Routledge, 1994), p. 55.

2 Three Challenges to Race-Thinking

1 American Civil Rights Coalition home page: http://www.acrc1.org/Reasons.htm.

2 J. L. A. Garcia, "The Heart of Racism," in *Race and Racism*, ed. Bernard Boxill (New York: Oxford University Press, 2001), pp. 257–96. See also Tommie Shelby (2002), "Is Racism in the Heart?" *Journal of Social Philosophy*, 33, 411–20; and L. Faucher and E. Machery (2009), "Racism: Against Jorge Garcia's Moral and Psychological Monism," *Philosophy of the Social Sciences*, 39(1), 41–62.

3 My sense of these stages derives from Michael Banton, *Racial Theories* (New York: Cambridge University Press, 1987); Matthew Jacobson, *Whiteness of a Different Color* (Cambridge, MA: Harvard University Press, 1998); Neil MacMaster, *Racism in Europe: 1870–2000* (New York: Palgrave, 2001); and Thomas Gossett, *Race*, 2nd edn (New York: Oxford University Press, 1997).

4 Smedley, *Race in North America*, p. 39.

5 Eric Voegelin, *The History of the Race Idea* (Baton Rouge: Louisiana State University Press, 1998), p. 82; François Bernier, "A New Division of the Earth," in *The Idea of Race*, eds Robert Bernasconi and Tommy Lott (Indianapolis: Hackett, 2000), pp. 1–4.

6 Johann Blumenbach, "On the Natural Variety of Humankind," in *The Idea of Race*, Lott and Bernasconi, p. 27.

7 Walter Scheidt, cited in Emmanuel Eze, "The Color of Reason: The Idea of 'Race' in Kant's Anthropology," in *Postcolonial African Philosophy*, ed. Emmanuel Eze (Oxford: Blackwell Publishers, 1997), pp. 103–40, 129.

8 *Notes on the State of Virginia*, in *Writings*, Thomas Jefferson (New York: Library of America, 1984), pp. 268–9.

9 Eduardo Mendieta, "Plantations, Ghettos, Prisons: US Racial Geographies," *Philosophy and Geography*, 7.1 (2004), 43–59.

10 For the account of the Tuskegee Experiment given by the US government's Center for Disease Control, see http://www.cdc.gov/tuskegee/timeline.htm (accessed December 15, 2011).

11 Ian Haney-Lopez, *White By Law* (New York: NYU Press, 1996), p. 90.

12 John H. Relethford, *The Human Species* (Mountain View, CA: Mayfield, 2000), p. 12.

13 Ibid., see p. 105.

14 Charles Murray and Richard Herrnstein, *The Bell Curve* (New York: The Free Press, 1994); Jesse Bering, "Getting a Little Racy: On Beauty, Evolution, and the Science of Interracial Sex," *Bering in Mind* (Scientific American blog), May 13, 2011, accessed at http://blogs.scientificamerican.com/bering-in-mind/2011/05/31/getting-a-little-racy-on-black-beauty-evolution-and-the-science-of-interracial-sex/ on 18 December 2011.

15 Relethford, *The Human Species*, p. 106.

16 Robert McKee, *Sociology and the Race Problem* (Chicago: University of Illinois Press, 1993), pp. 131–2.

17 "Wanderings Over, a Son Is Laid to Rest," Susan Sachs, *New York Times* (Print Media Edition: Late Edition – East Coast) February 18, 1999, p. 5.

18 "Racial and Ethnic Classifications Used in Census 2000 and Beyond," Office of Management and Budget, 2000; "Overview of Race and Hispanic Origin," US Department of Commerce, Economics and Statistics Administration, US CENSUS BUREAU, issued March 2011.

19 Benedict Anderson, *Imagined Communities: Reflections on the Origin and Spread of Nationalism* (New York: Verso, 1991).

20 Dorothy Roberts, *Killing the Black Body: Race, Reproduction, and the Meaning of Liberty* (New York: Vintage Books, 1997).

21 Immanuel Wallerstein, "Social Conflict in Post-Independence Black Africa: The Concepts of Race and Status-Group Reconsidered," in *Race, Nation, Class: Ambiguous Identities*, eds Etienne Balibar and Immanuel Wallerstein (London: Verso, 1991), pp. 187–203, 199.

22 Stuart Hall, "Race, Articulation and Societies Structured In Dominance," in *Black British Cultural Studies: A Reader*, eds Houston Baker, Manthia Diawara, and Ruth Lindeborg (Chicago: University of Chicago Press, 1996), pp.16–60, 55.

23 "Caste Discrimination: A Global Concern," *Human Rights Watch Reports* 13:3 (August 2001) 2, 59; "The Durban Review Conference and Caste-Based Discrimination," HRW-IDSN (International Dalit Solidarity Network) position paper (2009), 1, downloaded on 18 December 2011 from http://www.idsn.org/international-advocacy/un/durban-review-conf/.

24 "The Durban Review Conference," 2.

25 See Nira Yuval-Davis, "Intersectionality, Citizenship and Contemporary Politics of Belonging," *Critical Review of International Social and Political Philosophy (CRISPP)* 10.4 (2007): 561–74. Patricia Hill Collins, "It's all in the Family: Intersections of Gender, Race, and Nation," *Hypatia: A Journal of Feminist Philosophy*, 13.3 (1998), 62–82.

26 Gloria T. Hull, Patricia Bell Scott, and Barbara Smith, eds, *All the Women Are White, All the Blacks Are Men, but Some of Us Are Brave: Black Women's Studies* (Old Westbury, NY: The Feminist Press, 1982).

27 K. Anthony Appiah, "Race, Culture, Identity: Misunderstood Connections," in *Color Conscious*, K. Anthony Appiah and Amy Gutmann (Princeton, NJ: Princeton University Press, 1996), pp. 30–105, 103.

3 What Races Are: The Metaphysics of Critical Race Theory

1 Lee Baker, *From Savage to Negro* (Berkeley: University of California Press, 1998), p. 209.
2 Sundiata K. Cha-Jua, "The New Nadir: The Contemporary Black Racial Formation," *The Black Scholar*, 40:1 (2010), 38–58, 44.
3 Adolph Reed, "The 2004 Election in Perspective: The Myth of Cultural Divide and the Triumph of Neoliberal Ideology", *American Quarterly*, 57: 1 (2005), 1–15, 6.
4 Census Brief, "Coming to America: A Profile of the Nation's Foreign Born," CENBR/00–2, August 2000; Yesenia D. Acosta and G. Patricia de la Cruz, 'The Foreign Born From Latin America and the Caribbean: 2010 (US Census Bureau – American Community Survey Brief ACSBR/10–15, issued September 2011).
5 Louise Bennett, "Colonization in Reverse," in *Selected Poems*, ed. Mervyn Morris (Kingston, Jamaica: Sangsters, 1982); Cited in David Hart, "Louise Bennett," in *Africa and the Americas*, eds Richard Juang and Noelle Morrissette (Santa Barbara, CA: ABC-CLIO, 2008) 157.
6 Angelo Ancheta, *Race, Rights, and the Asian American Experience* (New Brunswick, NJ: Rutgers University Press, 1998), p. 11.
7 Omi and Winant, *Racial Formation*, p. 133.
8 From DeNavas-Walt, Carmen, Bernadette D. Proctor, and Jessica Smith, US Census Bureau, Current Population Reports, P60–233, *Income, Poverty, and Health Insurance Coverage in the United States: 2006*, US Government Printing Office, Washington, DC, 2007; DeNavas-Walt, Carmen, Berna-dette D. Proctor, and Jessica C. Smith, US Census Bureau, Current Popula-tion Reports, P60–239, *Income, Poverty, and Health Insurance Coverage in the United States: 2010*, US Government Printing Office, Washington, DC, 2011.; "American Indians by the Numbers," *InfoPlease*, http://www.info please.com/spot/aihmcensus1.html, accessed on December 22, 2011; DeNavas-Walt, Carmen and Robert Cleveland, US Census Bureau, Current Population Reports, P60–218, *Money Income in the United States: 2001*, US Government Printing Office, Washington, DC, 2002.
9 Randall Kennedy, *Race, Crime, and the Law* (New York: Pantheon, 1997), p. 11; Kati Haycock, "Closing the Achievement Gap," *Educational Leader-ship* 58, 6 (2001); Melvin Oliver and Thomas Shapiro, *Black Wealth/White Wealth* (New York: Routledge, 1997), pp. 24–5.
10 David Leonhart, "Wide Racial Disparities Found in Costs of Mortgages," *New York Times*, May 1, 2002, A19; Randolph Schmid, "Minorities" Health Care Found to be Inferior, *Seattle Post-Intelligencer*, March 21, 2002, A4; Ian Ayres, "Fair Driving," 104 *Harvard Law Review*, 817 (1991); see also Manning Marable, in *States of Confinement*, ed. Joy James (New York: St Martin's Press, 2000), pp. 53–9.
11 Z. Qian and D. T. Lichter (2011), "Changing Patterns of Interracial Mar-riage in a Multiracial Society," *Journal of Marriage and Family*, 73, 1065–84, 1067; Rose Kreider, "Intermarriage: Profiles of the Most Common

Interracial Combinations Using 1990 Census Data," Paper presented at the Southern Demographic Association Annual Meeting in October 2000.

12 Qian and Lichter, 1072.

13 Sue Chow, "The Significance of Race," *Sociological Inquiry*, 70:1 (Winter 2000).

14 Lawrence Blum, "Racialized Groups: The Sociohistorical Consensus," *The Monist*, 93: 2 (2010), 298–320; Ron Mallon, "Race: Normative, Not Metaphysical or Semantic," *Ethics*, 116:3 (2006), 525–51.

15 Ann Morning, "Man's Most Dangerous Myth Endures," unpublished ms (2001); compare Ann Morning, "Toward a Sociology of Racial Conceptualization for the 21st Century," *Social Forces*, 87:3 (2009), 1167–92; Naomi Zack, *Thinking About Race* (Albany, NY: Wadsworth, 1998).

16 Ian Hacking, *The Social Construction of What?* (Cambridge, MA: Harvard University Press, 1999), 22.

17 David Roediger, *Towards the Abolition of Whiteness* (New York: Verso, 1994), p. 11, quoting Terry Eagleton.

18 David Theo Goldberg, *Racist Culture* (Cambridge, MA: Blackwell, 1993), p. 88.

19 Omi and Winant, *Racial Formation*, 55.

20 Jacobson, *Whiteness of a Different Color*, p. ix.

21 Molefi Kete Asante, "The African American as African," *Diogenes*, 45 (Winter 1998), 39–51, emphasis added; Molefi Asante, *Kemet, Afrocentricity, and Knowledge* (Trenton, NJ: Africa World Press, 1990), p. 35.

22 Phillip Kitcher, "Race, Ethnicity, Biology, Culture," in *Racism*, ed. Leonard Harris (Amherst, NY: Humanity Books – Prometheus, 1999), p. 107.

23 Jonathan Marks, "Scientific Racism, History of," *Encyclopedia of Race and Racism*, ed. John Hartwell Moore. Vol. 3. Detroit: Macmillan Reference USA, 2008. 1–16. *Gale Virtual Reference Library*. Web. 24 Dec. 2011.

24 See Nancy Etcoff, *The Survival of the Prettiest* (New York: Doubleday, 1999); Geoffrey Cowley and Karen Springen, "The Biology of Beauty," *Newsweek*, 127, no. 23 (June 3, 1996), 60–7.

25 Harris, *Racism*, p. 106.

26 Lucius Outlaw, *On Race and Philosophy* (New York: Routledge, 1996), p. 5.

27 Robert Gooding-Williams, "Race, Multiculturalism, and Democracy," in *Race and Racism*, Boxill, pp. 422–47.

28 Paula Moya, "Postmodernism, 'Realism,' and the Politics of Identity," in *Reclaiming Identity*, eds Paula Moya and Michael Hames-Garcia (University of California Press, 2000), p. 83.

29 Noel Ignatiev and John Garvey, *Race Traitor* (New York: Routledge, 1996).

4 Existence, Experience, Elisions

1 See Linda Alcoff, "Who's Afraid of Identity Politics?" in *Reclaiming Identity*, Moya and Hames-Garcia, pp. 312–44.

2 Lewis Gordon, *Existentia Africana* (New York: Routledge, 2000).

3 W. E. B. Du Bois, *The Souls of Black Folk*, in *Writings* (Library of America, 1986), pp. 364–5.

4 See bell hooks, "Representing Whiteness in the Black Imagination," in *Black on White*, ed. David Roediger (New York: Schocken Books, 1998).

5 Du Bois, *Souls*, p. 365.

6 Linda Alcoff, "What Should White People Do?" *Hypatia*, Summer 1998, v13 n3 p. 6 (21).

7 María Elena Cepeda, "Shakira As The Idealized, Transnational Citizen: A Case Study Of Colombianidad In Transition," *Latino Studies* 2003(1), 211–32.

8 Ancheta, p. 162.

9 Paul C. Taylor, "Malcolm's Conk and Danto's Colors," in *African American Literary Theory*, ed. Winston Napier (New York: New York University Press, 2000).

10 "The Lived Experience of the Black," in *Race*, ed. Robert Bernasconi (Malden, MA: Blackwell, 2001), pp. 184–6.

11 See Paul Gilroy, *Against Race* (Cambridge, MA: Harvard University Press, 2000), p. 217.

12 Ralph Ellison, *Invisible Man* (New York: Vintage Books, 1989), pp. 3–4.

13 Walker Percy, *The Moviegoer* (New York: Bard Book–Avon, 1982), p. 17.

14 Richard Dyer, *White* (New York: Verso, 1997); Richard Rodriguez, *Brown: The Last Discovery of America* (New York: Penguin, 2003).

5 The Color Question

1 Cf. Charles W. Mills (1994), "Do Black Men Have a Moral Duty to Marry Black Women?" *Journal of Social Philosophy*, 25 (s1), 131–53.

2 Ronald R. Sundstrom, *The Browning of America and the Evasion of Social Justice* (Albany: SUNY Press, 2008).

3 See Christopher Edley, Jr, *Not All Black and White* (New York: Hill and Wang, 1996), p. 15.

4 Bernard Boxill, *Blacks and Social Justice* (Lanham, MA: Rowman and Littlefield, 1992), p. 148.

5 Walter Russell Mead, "The Bogus Man," *Gentleman's Quarterly*, 65:11 (1995), 106.

6 PARENTS INVOLVED IN COMMUNITY SCHOOLS v. SEATTLE SCHOOL DISTRICT NO. 1 551 US 701 (2007).

7 John Dewey, "Context and Thought," in *The Collected Works of John Dewey: Later Works, 1925–1953*, vol. 6 (1931; Carbondale, IL: Southern Illinois University, 1985), pp. 3–22, 19.

8 David Theo Goldberg, *Racist Culture* (Cambridge, MA: Blackwell, 1993).

6 From Anchor Babies to Obama: Are We Post-Racial Yet?

1 Daniel Schorr, "Postracial Politics," *New Leader*, Jan/Feb. 2008, Vol. 91 Issue 1, 3–4.

2 Andrew Becker, "Immigration Timeline," multi-page companion website for *Mexico: Crimes at the Border*, part of the *Frontline/*World series by WGBH

Educational Foundation, aired on May 27, 2008; http://www.pbs.org/frontlineworld/stories/mexico704/history/timeline.html#; accessed on December 28, 2011.

3 Becker, "Illegal Immigration Deemed Out of Control," p. 3.

4 "Immigration Enforcement Spending Since IRCA," *Immigration Fact Sheet*, 10, Migration Policy Institute (November 2005), 1–2.

5 John Audley, "Introduction," in *NAFTA's Promise and Reality*, John Audley, Demetrios Papdemetriou, Sandra Polaski, Scott Vaughan (Carnegie Endowment for International Peace, 2004), pp. 5–10.

6 Gordon Hanson, *The Economics and Policy of Illegal Immigration in the United States* (Washington, DC: Migration Policy Institute, 2009), p. 5.

7 Muzaffar Chishti and Claire Bergeron, "New Arizona Law Engulfs Immigration Debate," *Migration Information Source* (online), Migration Policy Institute (May 17, 2010), par. 5; http://www.migrationinformation.org/USfocus/print.cfm?ID=782, accessed December 30, 2011.

8 Solana Larsen, "The Anti-Immigration Movement: From Shovels to Suits," *NACLA Report on Latin America*, https://nacla.org/article/anti-immigration-movement-shovels-suits, accessed December 28, 2011.

9 See Allan Pred, *Even in Sweden: Racisms, Racialized Spaces, and the Popular Geographical Imagination* (Berkeley: University of California Press, 2000), pp. 42–3; Anthony Faiola, "Italy's Crackdown on Gypsies Reflects Rising Anti-Immigrant Tide in Europe," *The Washington Post*, Tuesday, October 12, 2010, http://www.washingtonpost.com/wp-dyn/content/article/2010/10/12; Weber, Leanne, "It Sounds Like They Shouldn't Be Here": Immigration Checks On The Streets Of Sydney," *Policing and Society*, 21.4 (2011), 456–67. *Academic Search Complete*. Web. January 3, 2012.

10 Hanson, *Economics and Policy*, p. 10.

11 Martinez Jr, Ramiro, "Economic Conditions And Racial/Ethnic Variations In Violence," *Criminology and Public Policy*, 9:4 (2010), 707–13. *Academic Search Complete*. Web. January 3, 2012.

12 Charles Mills, *The Racial Contract* (Ithaca: Cornell University Press, 1997), pp.18–19.

13 Julie Hollar, "Time to 'Drop and Leave' Loaded Language: From 'Illegals' to 'Anchor Babies,' media warp immigration debate," *Extra! Online* (March 2011), accessed January 4, 2011 at http://www.fair.org/index.php?page=4258.

14 Larsen, par. 2.; "Selling the Anti-Immigration Story," *Extra! Online* (June 2011), accessed January 4, 2011 at http://www.fair.org/index.php?page=4309.

15 "Facts About Prisons and Prisoners," The Sentencing Project (January 2012), downloaded on January 5, 2012 from http://www.sentencingproject.org/template/page.cfm?id=156; "Incarceration," The Sentencing Project, http://www.sentencingproject.org/template/page.cfm?id=107, accessed December 27, 2011; Jennifer Warren, "One in 100: Behind Bars in America 2008," The Pew Center on the States (February 2008), downloaded on December 27, 2011 from http://www.pewcenteronthestates.org/initiatives_detail.aspx?initiativeID=56212#2008.

16 See Angela Davis, *Are Prisons Obsolete?* (New York: Seven Stories Press, 2003); Angela Davis and Eduardo Mendieta, *Abolition Democracy* (New York: Seven Stories Press, 2005). Michelle Alexander's *The New Jim Crow* has given systemic critiques of the corrections industry the kind of mainstream visibility that typically eludes radical thinkers like Davis. But as Alexander herself notes at the beginning of her book, people she once ignored began talking about these issues long before she ever took them seriously. To see this observation turned into an incisive and provocative political argument, see Gregg Thomas, "Why Some Like *The New Jim Crow* So Much," http://www.voxunion.com/why-some-like-the-new-jim-crow-so-much/, accessed December 12, 2011.

17 Marc Mauer, "Addressing Racial Disparities in Incarceration," *The Prison Journal*, Supplement to volume 91:3 (2011), 87S–101S, 88S.

18 Mauer, "Addressing Racial Disparities" 95S, 96S.

19 Michel Foucault, "Questions of Method," in *The Foucault Effect: Studies in Governmentality*, eds Graham Burchell, Colin Gordon, and Peter Miller (University of Chicago Press, 1991), 73–86, 77.

Index